THE WISEGUY COOKBOOK

THE
WISEGUY
COOKBOOK

MY FAVORITE RECIPES
FROM MY LIFE AS A GOODFELLA
TO COOKING ON THE RUN

HENRY HILL
and PRISCILLA DAVIS

FOREWORD BY NICK PILEGGI

 NEW AMERICAN LIBRARY

New American Library
Published by New American Library, a division of
Penguin Group (USA) Inc., 375 Hudson Street,
New York, New York 10014, USA
Penguin Group (Canada), 90 Eglinton Avenue East, Suite 700, Toronto,
Ontario M4P 2Y3, Canada (a division of Pearson Penguin Canada Inc.)
Penguin Books Ltd., 80 Strand, London WC2R 0RL, England
Penguin Ireland, 25 St. Stephen's Green, Dublin 2,
Ireland (a division of Penguin Books Ltd.)
Penguin Group (Australia), 250 Camberwell Road, Camberwell, Victoria 3124,
Australia (a division of Pearson Australia Group Pty. Ltd.)
Penguin Books India Pvt. Ltd., 11 Community Centre, Panchsheel Park,
New Delhi - 110 017, India
Penguin Group (NZ), cnr Airborne and Rosedale Roads, Albany,
Auckland 1310, New Zealand (a division of Pearson New Zealand Ltd.)
Penguin Books (South Africa) (Pty.) Ltd., 24 Sturdee Avenue,
Rosebank, Johannesburg 2196, South Africa

Penguin Books Ltd., Registered Offices:
80 Strand, London WC2R 0RL, England

First published by New American Library, a division of Penguin Group (USA) Inc.

First Printing, October 2002
10

NEW AMERICAN LIBRARY and logo are trademarks of Penguin Group (USA) Inc.

LIBRARY OF CONGRESS CATALOGING-IN-PUBLICATION DATA:

Hill, Henry, 1943–
    The wiseguy cookbook : my favorite recipes from my life as a goodfella to cooking on
the run / Henry Hill ; foreword by Nick Pileggi.
        p.   cm.
    Includes index.
    ISBN 0-451-20706-8
    1. Cookery, Italian.   2. Cookery, American.   I. Title.

TX723 .H55   2002
641.5945—dc21   2002141572

Set in Goudy
Designed by Patrice Sheridan

Printed in the United States of America

This book is dedicated to

Kelly and Julian,

and to Peter—
whose unwavering support made this project happen—

with our deepest love and gratitude.

ACKNOWLEDGMENTS

··

We would like to thank the following:

Nick Pileggi, Peter Doyle for helping us put together the concept, Joel Gotler and Jerry Kalajian (for "bringin' home the carrots"), Alan Nevins, Marie Timell, Dan Slater, Hillary Schupf, Bryon Schreckengost, Alec Doyle, Rabbi Mark and Harriet, Elaine Breslow, Steve and Denise Oleesky, John Brenner, my sister Lulu (Lucille) and Ray's Elbow Room Restaurant, my sister Marie, my niece Bonnie, my sister Stella, and even my brother Joe, Donald Brown, Tommy Bosco, Contemporary Caterers, Joe Palozzi, Scott from the FBI, Bob Pick, Karen, Michael and Gayle, Debby Cromwell, Nancy Vialpando, Amy Newlin-Davis, Mr. and Mrs. Walter Davis, the Berfield family, David and Denise Ellenstein, Quinn Harmon and Jim Kelly, Eric Meza, Sue Leedom, Fran Ferrucci and Mr. Mike, Susan Angelo, Stephanie Nino Pick, Marty and Rebecca Nakell, Ruth Silverman, Andrew Reisini, Diane Gray, Jamie Stolz, and all the food testers for their patience, palates, and wonderful input on the recipes.

CONTENTS

■■

Foreword

▪▪

Henry Hill was obsessed with two things—being a gangster and being a cook. They infused everything in his life. When he was in hiding because his former compatriots were planning to kill him, he repeatedly endangered his life for dinner.

For instance, while hiding from both the Mob and his Federal marshals in Cincinnati, Henry went out on a food binge because he suspected that the Feds were planning to send him to the Deep South where he heard there were no decent Italian restaurants or suppliers.

At the end of the weekend, when the marshals finally caught up with him, they were furious. They said they knew of at least two hit men who were touring Cincinnati's better Italian restaurants looking for him. Henry was immediately whisked off to Kentucky, but along the way Henry convinced the marshals to stop their armored car so he could pick up a few cans of San Marzano tomato sauce and a hefty chunk of imported Parmesan cheese. It didn't hurt that he promised his bodyguards a feast as soon as they found a safe motel with a kitchen.

In fact, it was probably Henry's obsession with food and cooking that sped up the end of his life of crime. Had he just gone about his business like a normal racket guy—peddling his dope or making usurious loans—and not tried to include a large Sunday dinner for his family and associates, he might have had more time to spend on the street before getting caught.

Danny Mann, the Nassau County narcotics detective who initiated the Henry Hill investigation, was certain that Henry had to be preparing for an Appalachian-style banquet for his colleagues after tailing him all day Saturday from butcher to grocer to fish monger to baker to cheese shop. Mann, who is partial to bologna sandwiches on Wonder bread, had never seen anyone buy so much food and therefore chose to make the Sunday raid on Hill's Rockville Centre, New York, house, assuming he'd bag Hill's crime bosses and most of the crew.

When he pulled off the raid, Mann was astounded to find that Henry's food buying and preparation was not for a Mob confab, but for a typically chaotic Sunday dinner for Hill, his wife, kids, brother, assorted relatives, friends, and ditsy drug courier.

Nevertheless, Mann got a terrific arrest and Henry Hill started a new life in the Federal Witness Protection Program testifying against his old life on the streets.

Henry not only loves eating and cooking food, he loves talking about cuisine. While interviewing him for the book *Wiseguy*, hours of our time were spent talking about the great meals he had eaten and cooked. He talked about helping his Sicilian mother make her own dough for pasta, how he started out breaking the eggs into the mound of flour, revelling in the exotic smell of the mixture as his mother taught him to blend the ingredients properly and go on to knead the dough.

It was in his mother's kitchen that Henry learned to razor slice garlic before dropping it into the frying pan so it practically melted into the oil. Henry was very proud of the fact that his mother's garlic slicing technique was so well received by his Mob pals that it was enthusiastically taken up by his entire crew doing time in the Italian Mob suites at Lewisburg Penitentiary in Pennsylvania.

In fact in those days, Henry recalled, prison was never hard time for wiseguys. They usually had their own wing, their own pots and pans and stoves, and an endless supply of fresh produce, lobster, veal, steak, and wine, brought in by cooperative corrections officers.

"Prison was very expensive back then," Henry says. "It cost between fifteen hundred to two thousand dollars a month just in bribe money and that's not counting the cost of the food."

It was still "easy time," especially for certified wiseguys doing reasonably short bits of eighteen to thirty-six months. They usually lived in a dormitory setting with their own Mob crew and quickly got into the routine of coffee, cards, and dinner.

"They had the same routine they had on the outside except it was even better in the joint, because at the end of the day they didn't have to go home."

According to Henry, going home was the worst part of a wiseguy's day. Or, more specifically, having to go home to the wife. All day long a wiseguy could be out on the street terrifying everyone in sight, having tycoons throw money at them, having union officials slip him hard-to-get membership books, having his shoes shined and car waxed, until he got home and was subjected to the endless grousing and lack of respect.

Henry always felt that the Justice Department would have been far more successful in its battles against organized crime if it had sentenced the convicted hoods to house arrest—with their wives.

"A guy could do eighteen months in Allenwood standing on his head, but eighteen months at home with Angelina, who scaled in at about two-twenty in spandex, had four-inch nails, and a mustache, was enough to make Al Capone do honest work," Henry says.

But the only reason Italian Mob guys could get away from their wives and escape their homes was that they were gastronomically independent.

"Being able to cook means you can take care of yourself," Henry says. "I know guys—let me be honest, most of them are cops—who can't boil water. What good are they? They walk around proud because they can't boil water. Can't make their own coffee. They can't fry an egg. What's to be proud about that?"

Italian kids grow up in the kitchen, Hill says. There is no shyness in the most macho of Italian men about the delicacy of their taste, or their dexterity at dropping a six-quart aluminum pot of boiling ziti into a colander without spilling a drop on a silk tie.

As far as Henry is concerned, when he was on the street, it was a rare wiseguy who did not know his way around a stove. Most of them grew up in their mother's kitchen, just like Henry. They were pulling the strings off fresh stringbeans and prepping artichokes before they could read.

"There isn't a wiseguy worth his button who hasn't helped his mother or wife drape fresh fettuccini across the backs of chairs to dry," Henry says.

Years ago, while still being debriefed by the FBI and testifying in a dozen Mob trials, Henry Hill used to say that if he lived long enough on the lam, he would someday write a cookbook.

The FBI agents, marshals, and prosecutors all laughed. I laughed, too. He fooled us all.

—Nicholas Pileggi

Introduction

▪▪

In 1980 my life as a Goodfella came to an end, and I entered the Federal Witness Protection Program. My wiseguy days were over—I traded my Brioni and Armani suits for T-shirts and jeans. I became a normal citizen. I became Joe Shmoe.

It gets worse. My love affair with good food would now be tested. Cooking is my salvation, my therapy, and for what it's worth, my art. Whipping up a good sauce can make me feel better than any shrink. Even in prison, while other guys were dreaming of white sands, sparkling blue waters, and bikini-clad babes, I would have traded them for Lobster Fra Diavolo with a side of linguine and a chilled bottle of Verdicchio.

In the '80s I went from my boss Paulie's great table at Rao's to the end of the line at Burger King, God help me. The Feds let me keep my pots and pans and one gallon of imported olive oil. They took everything else I owned, except my appetite and love of good food and cooking.

The Mob is all about the food. Eating is just as important as making a score or bribing a cop. When's the last time you saw a thin mobster presiding over a sit-down at a bare table? How you dice and slice vegetables was given as much thought as whacking members of other crews.

Wiseguys are strong, but they're not slim. Think about it—a wiseguy's day centers around food. He eats everywhere he goes. He gets up and starts with a meeting over breakfast, then he has espresso and huddles with someone else. Then he goes to his office, which happens to be a restaurant, where he hangs out until he either goes to a club for more meetings and dinner or home to a big meal with his family. Everywhere food awaits.

The first recipe I ever collected aired on the radio after the Appalachian raid in 1957. I was thirteen. I remember hearing the special bulletin on the radio that was always on in the kitchen. The Feds raided the meeting of all the Mob heads in the U.S. The Goodfellas ran for their lives into the woods. Instead of giving chase and putting the top guys in jail, the agents ended up nibbling on what was left at the table: radicchio and good prosciutto. (That's when the government finally figured out there was a Mafia—the quality prosciutto, a dead giveaway.) The next meeting of the Mob bigwigs was in Sicily a few years later. People said they learned their lesson, it was too dangerous to meet like that in the U.S. Me, all I was thinking about was the food on those tables!

And I concluded that being a good cook was just as important as being a Goodfella in good standing.

I remember Paul Castellano getting hit on his way into Sparks Steakhouse. Throughout Mob history, whenever the godfathers were killed, food was involved—they were either going into a restaurant, eating there, leaving, buying vegetables. Where else could you catch a wiseguy "with his pants down"? Either on the shitter or having a meal. As far as I was concerned, if he was eating good Italian food, at least he died happy.

Once I entered the Witness Protection Program in '80, over the next twenty years and in most of the places the Feds stashed me, eating good Italian food was nothing more than a memory. Try buying arugula in Omaha, Nebraska, or good Italian sausage in Butte, Montana. So I learned to fake it—improvise, substitute ingredients to make flavors close to what I remembered in Brooklyn. Hey, I already knew something about improvising—try looking for real pecorino-siciliano cheese at 2 A.M. in Flatbush with the Feds on your trail (it turned out cheap Romano with white pepper worked just fine). But being in the Program I learned a lot more about cooking Italian in different parts of America, and a whole lot about cooking fast when your "safe house" is suddenly not so safe.

In this book I will share some stories from my life and cooking secrets from my early years in Brooklyn, my twenty-five years in the Mob, what I learned from the four restaurants I've owned, plus my twenty years on the run. These include recipes I learned from my mom and family, glommed from members of the Mob, their wives, restaurant owners, and those I came up with myself. They're pretty much presented in the order I learned them. But if you want to find a recipe quickly, there are handy indexes at the end of the book. I hope you find it entertaining—to read, and to cook.

Buon Appetito!

SECTION ONE:

BROOKLYN
AND THE
MOB

ITALIAN FOOD, A QUICK HISTORY

First, a little about Italian cooking and a little history.

Italians are as proud of their food as the French. Some even claim Italians taught the French the basics of cooking when the Roman Empire conquered them—but try telling that to a Frenchman.

In Italy, there are lots of ideas about what makes for good cooking, and everyone thinks their way is best. Two Italians can get in a fight over what's real Italian food faster than you can boil pasta water, and they'll both be right.

All you have to do is look at a map to see why. Italy is about seven hundred miles long; the geography covers a huge range—from mountains that are covered with snow to pastures and farmlands perfect for cows and wheat, down to drier hills where cows don't do well but goats and olive trees thrive. And all around are the beautiful seas.

Long before the days of shipping by train, truck or FedEx, people made their meals from what animals they could raise, what crops would grow in their backyard, what fish they could catch. I mean, if you can't raise cows for milk, you aren't going to be using a lot of cream sauces in your cooking. But if you're like the people in Florence, in the north, then you'll use butter even in a tomato sauce—almost a crime to someone from the south.

My mother was Sicilian. The food I grew up eating and learned to cook was from Sicily, one of those islands at the foot of the Italian "boot" that look like maybe it was kicked off. Some mainland Italians scoff at Sicilian food—they call it "peasant" food. They're right. There were and still are lots of "peasants" in Sicily. The food has to be cheap, fill you up, and hopefully taste good. A lot of dishes can be made very fast if you want, or cooked all day if you're an at-home mom or out of a job.

The Southern Italians' diet is very different from ours. They eat a lot of fish and vegetables. You can't get fish every day in all parts of Sicily, even though it's surrounded by water, but it's grabbed whenever it shows up. Meat is even harder to come by. Italian Americans eat a lot more meat than Sicilians because it's available. Southern Italians eat pasta every day, but they sauce it very lightly. Their idea of a good balance of sauce to pasta usually makes Americans think the dish doesn't have enough "stuff."

The best Sicilian food is very simple, usually made from a small number of ingredients. I think that's part of what makes it so good. Sicilians learned to appreciate what they could get and make the flavors stand out rather than lose them by adding too many different things. I still follow that idea—if a dish has more than a dozen ingredients, I get suspicious. What are they hiding? A tomato should taste like a tomato, a steak like a steak. (Chicken may be different—more about that later.)

Sicily and the other islands near it are different from the rest of Italy. They're right on the early Arabian trade route to the Mediterranean, and Sicily was a major stopping off place for water and provisions. It was also overrun by many other groups: Franks, Goths, Arabs, Greeks. In fact, a lot of Greeks settled in Sicily, and there's still a large population there today. The musician Buddy Greco is Greek, from Sicily. All these different groups influenced the cooking. Some of those guys' ideas got mixed in with the Sicilians'. The result is some recipes contain ingredients and spices you wouldn't think of as Italian—like couscous, which they got from the Arabs, and saffron from Spain and North Africa.

So Sicilian is its own kind of Italian cooking. Besides that, I learned to cook Sicilian by way of Brooklyn—which makes it very different from pure Sicilian. To me, there is nothing static about cooking, no recipe is set in stone, except maybe when it comes to baked goods. My mother picked up non-Sicilian ideas in the neighborhood and they became part of her food. And then I got ideas from the Goodfellas, some of whom were from other parts of Italy. And in the Program we were moved so many different places, I didn't even know if the kitchen would have a real stove or just a couple of burners or a microwave. So I learned some new ways to keep Italian food on the table while also learning something about the food of the region where I was living.

CHILDHOOD

When I was young, my dad moved my family from Second Avenue on the Lower East Side of Manhattan, to East New York in Brooklyn. Brooklyn was the suburbs back then. People moved their families out there to escape the lousy living conditions in Manhattan.

My dad never owned a car or knew how to drive. He was an electrician who helped build the subway into Brooklyn. When they'd built it as far as they were planning to, he went just past the end of the line and bought us a house. It was an Archie Bunker house he got for fifty-six hundred dollars. He'd take the subway he built to work in Manhattan every day.

My cousins from back on Second Avenue thought my house was in the country. There were still dirt roads. There was a real dairy with cows down the street, and right next door were stables for horses for the local businesses. I can remember horse-drawn carts—the milk cart, the junk man who collected rags one day and newspapers another. I saw horses die in the street from overwork. People even had goats, like in Sicily. There were delis that made their own mozzarella and *ricotta salata* cheeses and olive oil, there were sausage makers, there were Italian bakeries every few blocks. There was an area called the Old Mill at the end of Brooklyn where Paulie and his four brothers lived. Paulie would become my boss for many years.

A lot of people moved out to Brooklyn because it was safer, but even there they'd find bodies every day: the Old Mill, Canarsie, and Howard Beach were big dumping grounds for Murder Inc. No one really cared what we did then. J. Edgar Hoover and the government didn't give a rat's ass about crime in Italian neighborhoods until Italians started getting power in the unions or started whacking people who were important to them. Until then, it was, "Let the guineas kill each other off—what does it matter to us?"

And we were killing each other. The Black Hand organization of extortionists was made of Italians. They were taking from other Italians, their own people. And they were just one group—there were extortionists all over the place. When the Mafia started, it wasn't the romantic version of Italians protecting Italians against other groups. The Mafia started when you had to protect your mother and your cousins from another Italian family down the street. You had to be vicious to survive.

My grandfather was a member of the Black Hand. I remember going with my mom to visit him in a church basement where people were gambling. He wore a big black hat and smoked crummy cigars called "guinea stinkers." We didn't see him much because my mom hated her stepmom. When my mom first came to New York, she had to work in a sweat shop, and the fat stepmom insisted she hand over her paychecks as soon as she got them. She wasn't even allowed to open them. And for that, she'd give her back twenty-five cents.

Except for the stepmom, my mother was very proud of her Sicilian roots and kept close to her relatives. All the uncles, aunts, cousins, and half sisters were welcome at our house. The fact that my father was Irish made no difference—ours was a Sicilian household, including the kitchen, where my mom cooked only Sicilian food. And for me, that's where it all began.

Chapter One

The Basics

∎∎∎

MOM'S KITCHEN

My earliest memories in my mother's kitchen are of me holding her apron strings, and getting a little extra attention, which was hard to come by in a family with eight children. My mom was a good-hearted woman who provided us all with three square meals a day, and those meals were a labor of love.

When I started going to school, I would race to be the first one home, because then I could do the shopping for her. By going to the markets for supper, I knew I would make her happy and have her affection for one minute more. The smells and sounds in the kitchen, the excitement of pleasing my mom—that was all that mattered to me then. And I did please her—I was a great little shopper! And as a by-product, guess what? I learned how to cook!

Sometimes she would say to me, "Henry boy, go to the chicken market; get me some fresh chickens." Yes, we had a chicken market, a kosher market where I even saw them cut their throats. Poor little chickens—but they sure tasted good!

Sometimes she would send me into the garden behind our house. It was a true Italian garden—two dozen tomato plants, zucchinis, eggplant, scallions. She had a big herb garden with every kind of herb we needed—basil, parsley, mint, sage, rosemary. My mom could grow anything. We had a fig tree with figs the size of your fist. My father had encouraged a part of a neighbor's grapevine into our yard and wound it around the branches of our peach tree, so we had beautiful purple grapes growing next to the peaches. But best of all were the lilac trees, my mother's favorite. Lilacs in Brooklyn smell oh so sweet.

Without even trying, I absorbed my mom's basic recipes and cooking lore that I still use today. Of course, there are some things I don't do much—things that take a lot of time, like making the fresh bread she always had on the table. Somehow even with eight children Mom found time for slow-cooked sauces and homemade bread. With all us kids around, I think the cooking kept her sane.

Thirty, forty years ago in Brooklyn, we ate differently than we do now. Today people are much more health conscious. In a restaurant now, you order ravioli, you get four little raviolis in a pool of some kind of fancy sauce. Four raviolis that would maybe fill your cavities. In Brooklyn my mom made fourteen, fifteen raviolis per person. And that was just one dish in a meal.

There was always a big platter of antipasto to start—it was a work of art she and my sisters made, enough for a whole dinner in itself. On Sundays, my aunt Nina would bring her special *caponatina* for the antipasto. Then we'd have pasta, like raviolis, followed by meat dishes like my mom's gravy, which had meatballs and sausage, roast pork, stuffed veal, and chicken cacciatore, along with whatever vegetable was in season—asparagus, spinach, zucchini. There was always homemade bread and then desserts and espresso. Aunt Nina brought desserts—a dozen Italian pastries "just to have around." We'd have cheesecake, cannolis, spumoni. There was red wine for the grown-ups and cream soda for the kids—except on Sundays, when we each got half a glass of wine mixed in our soda. My sisters would never finish theirs, so I would "help 'em out." I got buzzed almost every Sunday at eight or nine years old—and learned a habit that got me in all kinds of trouble later.

ABOUT THE RECIPES

Remember that not all of these are "on the run" recipes. Meaning, there are a number that take more than an hour to make. As one of my favorite chefs, Emeril Lagasse, says, "Not everything gets made in fourteen minutes and delivered." Cooking time was not a big concern for my mom—her job was to be home raising all of us. Some things took her ten minutes to make, others many hours. It didn't matter—she was gonna be there anyway.

As I've said, how my mom cooked is basically how I cook. So her kitchen ideas aren't just in this section—they show up throughout the book. I've used her recipes in all my restaurants, and on the run. Even if I can't get the real ingredients, I'll make a version of one of her dishes. It reminds me of home.

■■■

Basic Tomato Sauce

Makes 3 cups

of sauce

(enough sauce

for 4–6 people).

A simple tomato sauce is the basis of all Southern Italian cooking, even though tomatoes are not native to Italy. (Can you believe it? They were brought over from the Americas.)

I love this sauce. It is light, sweet, and delightful. You can use it with any and everything—tossed with pasta, as a base for Lobster Fra Diavolo or Chicken Cacciatore, you name it. And because you skim it (remove the acid), it's guaranteed to be heartburn free. When I cook, it often starts with getting this sauce going (if there's none left in the refrigerator), and then the rest of the meal can happen.

I don't usually like onions in my sauce, but some people always add them. When I did a stint in prison, Vinnie Aloi, the head of his family, used to make us sauce and he used tons of onions. I didn't like it, but believe me, I ate every bite.

Remember this is a "basic" recipe. You can add a little of this, a little of that. I don't know if I've ever made sauce the same way twice. I'll add a bit of red wine one day, some tomato paste the next, more basil, etc. It's like making love—you do it a little different every time, but the end result will always put a smile on your face.

    6–8 cloves of garlic, minced or thinly sliced (about 2 tablespoons; see garlic note, page 19)
    ¼ cup olive oil
    ½ cup chopped brown or white onions or shallots (optional; see onion note, page 18)
    2 28-ounce cans peeled plum tomatoes with basil, drained, reserving juice (see canned tomatoes note, page 16)
    12 large basil leaves, torn in large pieces, or 1 tablespoon dried
    ¼ cup finely chopped fresh Italian parsley, or 2 teaspoons to 1 tablespoon dried parsley (see parsley note, page 15)
    ½ teaspoon each salt and pepper

In a large skillet or medium-large wide pot, cook garlic briefly in olive oil over medium-low heat. Do not brown, or it will get bitter. If using optional onions, cook them 3–5 minutes in olive oil, then add garlic and cook 1 minute. Add the juice from the canned tomatoes to stop the garlic cooking. Crush tomatoes with your hands or chop well on a cutting board and add to the pan. Add basil, parsley, and ¼ tea-

HENRY'S NOTES AND TIPS

Stirring the sauce mixes the acid into it. It's okay to stir briefly *right after* you skim, to keep it from scorching. You can tell the acid's coming out by the foamy stuff and little pools of oil that form on the top—that's what you skim off. My mom would put one of the empty tomato cans next to the stove to catch the skimmed-off part—something I still do today.

Though a lot of people disagree, I never add sugar to sauce—never! If I had to use lower quality canned tomatoes, I add half a small carrot, peeled and finely grated for sweetening. Add the carrot early enough in the process so it gets completely soft.

If you crush the tomatoes with your hands, watch they don't squirt you. Or your clothes.

My mom taught me a way to slice garlic so thin it liquefies in the pan: with a razor. Do this at your own risk.

spoon each of the salt and pepper. Bring to a boil, stir thoroughly once, then reduce heat to a low simmer. As the acid from the tomatoes flows to the top, skim it off every 10–15 minutes. Sauce is ready in half an hour, but cook up to 1 hour if you want it thicker. Check for seasoning and add the rest of the salt and pepper, if desired.

PARSLEY (AND OTHER FRESH HERBS)

When I say parsley, I mean Italian parsley, not curly. I never use curly parsley to cook, only as a garnish. Italian parsley has fatter leaves which are dark green. It looks kind of like fresh cilantro; don't get them confused!

My mom always used to say eating parsley is so good for you it's like taking vitamins. Just recently scientists found out that it and many other herbs are as good for you as fresh fruits and vegetables, sometimes better!

If you can't find fresh Italian parsley, use dried parsley. Use 2 teaspoons to 1 tablespoon of dried instead of the ¼ cup fresh, and add the dried stuff halfway through or its flavor will get cooked away.

To clean fresh parsley (and any number of other herbs), rinse with water, shake off excess, then pinch the leaves off the stems (unless the recipe says to use whole stalks, like when you're making a soup or stock, in which case you toss in the whole thing).

You don't have to be a fanatic about getting rid of all the stems. The top part of most herbs is pretty tender and sweet like the leaves. I chop the leaves very fine on a cutting board until they start to give off their odor before adding to a dish. Grinding in a mortar and pestle is a great way to get the most flavor from fresh herbs.

If you're using dried herbs, crumble in your fingers a bit to start releasing the flavor.

CANNED TOMATOES

For best results with canned tomatoes, use Progresso or another good quality brand. If you can't find canned tomatoes with basil, add a bit more fresh or dried basil. If you can afford it, canned San Marzano tomatoes or La Valle from Italy are the best, but we're talking major bucks to buy them. Be careful about San Marzanos—an American company is calling their domestic tomatoes San Marzano, but they're from here—they're not the same! I think you can use all kinds of tomatoes for sauce, you just have to compensate if they're not as sweet straight out of the can.

If you want to use fresh tomatoes, see page 200 for uncooked fresh tomato sauce, and one for cooked fresh tomatoes on page 294.

BASIL

Basil is the king of Italian herbs. I love to catch a whiff of it in a bag of groceries on my way home from the market. Put it in a glass of water on the counter and it fills the kitchen with its strong sweet smell. It can be used a zillion ways: the whole leaves tucked among the fresh tomatoes and *bufala mozzarella* in an *insalata caprese*, sliced in ribbons and scattered over a salad or antipasto platter. There's hardly a pasta sauce I make without it, plus any number of chicken or vegetable dishes.

There are a bunch of kinds of basil: purple, holy, globe, fever. I use what's called sweet basil or Italian basil, which has medium to large green leaves and long stems. Use the leaves and throw away the stems and any buds. If you want just large pieces, tear it with your hands —a knife can bruise it easily. For slivers, either stack it or roll up individual leaves and use a very sharp knife to cut crosswise in thin strips.

Fresh basil doesn't last very long. It turns almost black after a few days in the fridge, no matter how you wrap it. You can freeze the fresh leaves wrapped in plastic. It won't look pretty but it works. Use more of the frozen leaves than you would fresh because they won't have as much flavor as the fresh.

Today you can get fresh Italian basil almost anywhere in the U.S., but if for some reason you can't find it (or afford it), substitute about 1 tablespoon of the dried in place of ½ cup loosely packed leaves of fresh. Like any dried herb, crumble it in your hand as you add it to a dish to release its flavor.

Don't use dried basil if it's not going to get cooked. Dried herbs need heat to integrate them into a dish.

OLIVE OILS

Some people swear by extra virgin olive oil. For me, if you're gonna cook with it, it'll lose its special flavor. So I say don't waste your money—buy regular olive oil to cook with. When it's uncooked it does make a little difference to use extra virgin, so I buy extra virgin olive oil for salads or for adding a touch to a dish just before serving.

There are so many kinds of olive oil I can't even begin to go into it. All the raving about the super expensive stuff—I don't know, maybe I don't have the palate to tell the difference. There are some that have a real strong olive taste, so you'd only use it for that strong olive flavor. I hate to tell you, but I think my countrymen are having a field day charging an arm and a leg for stuff that shouldn't cost that much. Italians know a racket when they see one. But then, maybe your taste buds are more refined and you can tell the kind-of-good stuff from the super-duper-good stuff. Hey, if you want to spend extra bucks for a really special extra virgin olive oil to sprinkle on a salad, who am I to say no?

ONIONS

▪▪

When I list onions or shallots as ingredients in a recipe, I mean peeled and trimmed ones. In case you're confused, peeling means taking off the outer dark skin, and trimming means lopping off the root-like bottoms and any funky-looking tops.

The basic kinds of onions are brown or yellow (Spanish fall into this category) and sweet or white (Maui, Vidalia, Bermuda, Walla Walla). You can find brown onions anywhere, and they're fine to cook with. I like to use sweet onions because they're less acidic, which makes them easier on the stomach and they help sweeten a dish. Red or purple onions are good raw in salads or on sandwiches and add a nice color. If you cook a red onion, its color will bleed off and into the dish.

Shallots have a strong onion flavor but are mellower than onions. They don't have the same "edge" or "bite" as onions. You can use them in place of onions, but they cost 3–4 times as much. I use them sometimes when I need only a small amount of onion in dishes like Veal Marsala. It'd be kind of a waste to use them in a tomato sauce— their nice flavor would get overwhelmed. Plus, if you need more than ¼ cup, you'd be peeling for days.

To buy onions or shallots, look for firm bulbs and those without sprouts at the top. Onions with sprouts and/or soft spots are over the hill. Kept in a dark slightly cool place, brown onions last for weeks, and shallots kept in the vegetable bin of a refrigerator will last for months. White onions should be stored like brown onions, but they have a much shorter shelf life and need to be used within a week.

GARLIC

When I mention garlic or garlic cloves in a recipe, I mean peeled. If it shouldn't be peeled the recipe will say so.

There are a lot of theories on the easiest way to peel garlic. Some people say refrigerating it makes it easier, others say put it in a bowl of warm water to loosen the skin.

I think the easiest way is to place the clove on a cutting board on its side, place a large knife on it and hit the knife once with a little force, or "smash" the clove. If you don't hit it too hard, the garlic won't completely break apart, but the skin will be broken and you can then trim the tough end with the knife and the rest of the skin peels off easily in your hands. If you know you're going to be mincing the garlic anyway, you can hit it even harder and it'll break away from its skin easily.

Using whole cloves is a little harder. I use a paring knife. Cut off the tough end and then peel the skin back from that end with the knife.

Some people are fanatical about taking out the green vein that you sometimes see in the middle of a clove of garlic. This is actually the beginning of a new garlic plant—it's growing! The bigger veins can be a little bitter, so if they're large I take them out. Otherwise, I don't bother.

When buying garlic, look for heads that are fat and firm. They shouldn't look brownish or dried out. I also avoid the ones that have green shoots poking out—they're sure to have large green veins inside.

Storing garlic—again there are a number of theories. I go through it so fast it doesn't have a chance to go bad, so I just keep it in a small basket on a kitchen counter. But if you want it to last longer, you can keep it in a cool dark place. There are also garlic holders. Or you can refrigerate it in a plastic bag. This works fine as long as you don't wrap it too tightly, which could make it too damp and make it go bad faster.

Beef Stock

Making stocks is easier than you think. They take time to cook down, but the prep work isn't difficult. The flavor in homemade stock makes a big difference in a soup like Beef and Vegetable Soup (see page 186), so it's worth the time.

4 pounds beef bones for soup
2 stalks celery, coarsely chopped (1 cup)
3 unpeeled carrots, coarsely chopped (1½–2 cups)
2 medium unpeeled onions, trimmed and quartered (1 pound)
3 large or 4 medium tomatoes, halved (1 pound)
6 large unpeeled garlic cloves
4 quarts water
10 peppercorns
2–3 small sprigs fresh thyme or ½ teaspoon dried
1 bay leaf
8 stalks fresh Italian parsley or 1 teaspoon dried
1 whole clove

Preheat oven to 500°F. Toss bones, celery, carrots, onions, tomatoes and garlic together and spread out in a single layer in a large baking pan (such as 9 × 13-inch). Roast in oven until browned, about 20–30 minutes, tossing once or twice.

Put the roasted mixture in a large stock pot. Add 2 cups of the water to roasting pan and heat on stove top, over medium-high heat, scraping up any bits that are stuck to the pan. (The pan will probably cover two burners.) Add mixture to stock pot, along with the remaining (14 cups)

HENRY'S

NOTES

AND TIPS

For a stronger stock, simmer up to six hours. Add water to keep bones covered. Even though you add water, you will probably end up with less stock, about two and a half quarts. I don't add salt to stock because it will get salted when you use it in a soup or other dish.

water and all remaining ingredients. Stir to combine well. Bring mixture to a boil, reduce heat to a simmer, and skim off any foam or fat that rises to the surface. Simmer 3 hours, skimming occasionally.

Strain stock through a sieve into a large bowl and cool to room temperature. Cover and refrigerate until a layer of fat hardens on the surface, about 2 hours. Remove fat. Refrigerated stock lasts for 4–5 days or frozen for one month.

■■■

Makes about

3 quarts.

Chicken Stock

4 pounds chicken bones and parts (backs and necks are good)
4 quarts water
1 large or 2 medium unpeeled brown onions, trimmed and
    quartered (1 pound)
2–3 medium carrots, scrubbed, cut in large chunks (2 cups)
2 large stalks celery, scrubbed, cut in large pieces (1½–2 cups)
1 bay leaf
4–6 cloves garlic, separated, unpeeled
10 whole black peppercorns
8 stalks fresh Italian parsley or 1 teaspoon dried
2 small sprigs fresh thyme or ½ teaspoon dried

Rinse chicken parts well and place in large pot. Add water and all remaining ingredients except salt. Bring to a boil and skim off any foam or fat that rises to the surface. Reduce heat to a simmer and cook partially covered, skimming every half hour, for 2–3 hours. Strain through

You can add other vegetables for flavoring—parsnips, leeks, tomatoes, mushrooms. It's up to you. And if you want a darker, richer stock, start by roasting the chicken bones, vegetables, and garlic in a roasting pan in the oven at 500°F for about half an hour, turning occasionally. Follow steps described in roasting beef bones in Beef Stock recipe, above.

HENRY'S

NOTES

AND TIPS

a sieve into a large bowl and cool to room temperature. Cover and refrigerate until a layer of fat hardens on the surface (about 2 hours). Remove fat. Refrigerated stock lasts for 4 days, or you can freeze it up to a month.

Makes about

5 cups.

◼◼

Cheater's Chicken Stock

This is for when you want a stronger chicken flavor than you get from canned broth but don't have the time to make the real deal. Make sure you use low-sodium canned broth, or the stock will be very salty.

6 cups canned low-sodium chicken broth
1–2 pounds chicken wings, backs, and necks, or any parts you have hanging around the freezer (except livers)
1 large or 2 medium unpeeled brown onions, trimmed and quartered (1 pound)
A few black peppercorns
1 bay leaf

Bring all ingredients to a boil in a large pot, skim off any foam that rises, and lower heat to simmer. Cook, skimming off fat if necessary, 15–30 minutes. Strain stock through a sieve into a large bowl. Cool to room temperature. If you are in a hurry, you can skim off some of the fat by removing the clear liquid top layer that accumulates at room temperature. If you have more time, cover and refrigerate until a layer of fat hardens on the surface (at least 2 hours). Remove fat. Refrigerated stock lasts for 4 days, or you can freeze it for a month.

HENRY'S NOTES AND TIPS	If you don't have chicken pieces around, adding the ingredients above and cooking the canned broth down will strengthen the flavor.
	Regular canned broth doesn't work in this recipe—it already has a ton of salt and boiling it down just makes it worse.

CANNED CHICKEN BROTH

I use low-salt canned chicken broth when I cook. If you have trouble finding it and use regular canned broth, taste the dish before adding any salt called for in the recipe.

So many times on the run I ended up using the canned, I don't think it's a big deal if you use canned or fresh chicken broth. But I don't like to use American bouillon cubes—they're even saltier than regular canned broth! I've heard European bouillon cubes are a lot more like real chicken broth and not oversalty, so they may be okay to use. Dissolve 1 cube in a cup of hot water to make 1 cup of broth.

Roasted Sweet Peppers

Serves 4–6 as part of antipasto.

It's a breeze to roast sweet bell peppers and their slightly smoky flavor is fabulous. They were always a part of my mom's antipasto, tossed with a little olive oil and spices or served just plain. They're also delicious in vegetable lasagne and will perk up a pasta sauce that needs a little something.

You can roast any quantity of peppers, from one to a hundred. My mom would roast eight to twelve for the antipasto, but then we were feeding a lot of folks.

3 red or other sweet bell peppers

For marinade (if using):

¼ cup extra virgin olive oil
1–2 garlic cloves, minced
Dash salt and pepper

I mostly use red peppers. Green peppers have a very different flavor and are nowhere near as sweet. Nowadays you can get beautiful yellow, orange, even purple ones. They're all fine to use, if you can afford them.

If you have no time, use jarred, roasted red peppers—they'll do in a pinch, but they're expensive and not as flavorful. Use pimientos for a touch of color and a little red-pepper flavor, but not as a full substitute for freshly roasted ones. For some reason they don't taste the same— maybe they add something to the jar.

Preheat broiler, if you have one, or oven to broil setting or highest temperature you can. Wash whole peppers and place on a cookie sheet or broiler pan lined with aluminum foil and place in broiler or oven. Roast peppers, turning with tongs or large spoons as they blacken until all sides are dark. Place in a bowl and cover with foil from cookie sheet, sealing on all sides. Let sit for 15–20 minutes (longer is okay). Discard tops, peel off skins, and remove seeds and veins. Save any liquid the peppers give off. Tear peppers lengthwise into wide strips. They're ready to use in a dish or to be served as is.

To marinate: Toss pepper strips with olive oil, garlic, and salt and pepper. Let sit for at least 1 hour at room temperature or refrigerated before serving.

Makes 1½ cups

of crumbs.

Toasted Bread Crumbs with Cheese

Toasted bread crumbs or toasted bread crumbs with cheese are used as part of a stuffing or on top of or layered into a pasta. It's good to make a batch of plain crumbs and keep them in the refrigerator—they'll last about two weeks.

⅓–½ loaf stale white Italian or French baguette, at least 2 days old
1 teaspoon dried parsley

½ teaspoon each dried basil, onion powder, and garlic powder
⅛ teaspoon each salt and pepper
2 tablespoons grated Parmesan or Romano cheese (any type)

Preheat oven to 375°F.

Finely grate baguette either with a hand grater, or cut into ½- to 1-inch chunks and grate in food processor about 3–4 minutes. You should have 1½ cups fine bread crumbs. Spread on a baking sheet, lined with foil if you want, and toast 3–4 minutes in oven. Toss crumbs to expose any that aren't browning and toast an additional 2–4 minutes. Cool to room temperature. If using immediately, add remaining ingredients and mix well. If not, refrigerate plain and add the optional spices and cheese later. Crumbs last up to two weeks.

Of course you can use packaged bread crumbs, plain or seasoned. On the run, I used the premade. This is for when you have leftover bread and the time.

If you want very consistent size crumbs, you can sift them through a strainer, discarding what doesn't go through.

HENRY'S NOTES AND TIPS

Mom's Antipasto

Antipasto means "before the meal," not before the pasta (*pasto* means meal). It's a first course consisting of pretty much whatever small dishes you choose. You can serve one dish or twenty. My mom and sisters often prepared a huge antipasto platter as the centerpiece, beautifully displayed and garnished with basil, parsley, chicory, and radicchio.

On the platter they always had sliced fennel—my sisters ate it like celery—pepperoncini, black and green olives, roasted peppers, various cold cuts and cheeses, tomatoes drizzled lightly with olive oil, vinegar, salt, and pepper. They'd often have other side dishes around—some hot, some cold, some homemade, some purchased. Below I've listed a number of things you can serve as antipasto, either arranged on a large platter or in separate dishes.

Brined black olives
Green olives
Fennel bulb strips
Carrot sticks
Celery sticks
Scallions
Tomato slices
Cucumber slices
Red onion slices
Radishes
Radicchio leaves
Chicory
Basil
Escarole
Hard-boiled eggs
Salami—Genoa, capocollo,
    etc.
Mortadella
Provolone
Ricotta salata
Marinated artichoke hearts
    (see recipe on page 274)
Roasted sweet red peppers
    (see recipe on page 23)

Prosciutto
Mozzarella (fresh or aged)
Sardines
Sundried tomatoes
Fresh slices of cantaloupe
    wrapped in prosciutto
Grilled eggplant (see recipe
    on page 27)
Ceci e pimienti salad (see
    recipe on page 30)
Caponatina (see recipe on
    page 32)
Marinated mushrooms (see
    recipe on page 30)
Rolled anchovies stuffed with
    capers
Marinated cherry peppers
Pepperoncini
Extra virgin olive oil
Red wine vinegar
Salt and black pepper
Curly parsley sprigs (for
    garnish)

Be careful what antipasto ingredients you put next to each other on a plate. Some of the marinades and sauces won't go well with each other. For example, I wouldn't put cantaloupe wrapped in prosciutto next to pepperoncini or marinated cherry peppers—the vinegars from the peppers will ruin the flavor of the cantaloupe. You can always put an antipasto ingredient in a separate dish if you're not sure about the mix of flavors.

Arrange chosen ingredients on a large platter, if using, or individual plates. Drizzle lightly with extra virgin olive oil, a sprinkling of red wine vinegar, and salt and pepper to taste. Decorate with parsley sprigs.

■■■

Serves 4

as an appetizer

or side dish,

6–8 as part of

an antipasto.

Grilled Eggplant

This is a delicious appetizer or vegetable side dish. It's best on the grill for that real smoky flavor, but you can also cook it under the broiler or even on top of the stove.

1 large eggplant or 2 small (1 pound)
2 tablespoons + ¼ teaspoon salt
2–4 tablespoons olive oil
4 cloves of garlic, minced (1 tablespoon)
¼ teaspoon each salt and pepper
¼ cup diced pimientos for garnish (optional)

Cut off ends of eggplant and cut lengthwise in slices about ¼- to ½-inch thick. (It's not necessary to peel the eggplant, but do so if you want.) To cut the eggplant's bitterness, dissolve 2 tablespoons salt in a large bowl of water and soak the eggplant slices in it for 1 hour, weighted with a plate or pan so they're all submerged. (See page 28 for other ways to prepare eggplant.) Remove from water and pat slices dry with paper towels.

Heat grill or broiler if using. Place eggplant slices on a plate and brush one side with olive oil; sprinkle with half the garlic and salt and pepper; turn over slices and repeat. If grilling, place slices in a grill pan and cook 1–2 minutes on one side, turn and cook an additional 1 minute on the second side. Believe me, it won't take longer than that for them to be done. If broiling, place on a foil-lined cookie sheet and broil the same time as for grilling.

If cooking on a stovetop, do not brush eggplant with oil. Instead, heat 2 tablespoons oil in a skillet over high heat until hot but not smoking (it will "ripple"). Sprinkle one side of eggplant with half the garlic and salt and pepper; turn over and repeat. Cook in skillet 2 minutes on first side and an additional minute on second side.

For all methods, serve warm or at room temperature.

EGGPLANT

My mother had a different way to prepare eggplant for cooking. She had a set of "eggplant towels" that she'd lay out on the counters, tables, wherever she could. Then she'd salt one side of the eggplant slices, put them on the towels, salt the second side, and cover them with more towels. She'd weight the slices down with plates and let them sit for 30 minutes to 1 hour before she'd cook them. This makes the crunchiest eggplant slices.

A fresh eggplant has a taut skin and will sound a little hollow when you tap it. I look for ones with no bruises and an even shape, so the slices will be close to the same size. If you can't find the shape you want and have lots of ends left over, make a small amount of caponatina, or just peel, cube, and add them to a pasta sauce.

ITALIAN COLD CUTS

There are lots of Italian cured meats and cheeses you can use for antipasto or on sandwiches. Here's a list of a few.

Cheeses
Asiago—buy it aged less than six months for a milder flavor. The
    older cheese is good grated and/or cooked.
Pecorinos—any cheese from sheep's milk is a kind of pecorino. Even
    the younger pecorinos, which are suitable for slicing, have a sharp

taste, so use them in antipasto or on sandwiches if you like a strong-flavored cheese. But the most common pecorino is called pecorino-Romano, which is a hard cheese aged up to a year and a half and used in place of or with Parmesan.

Provolone—terrific as part of an antipasto and on sandwiches. The older cheese tastes much stronger and is good on pizza or in pasta. Caciocavallo is a smoky version of provolone that's good in antipasto.

Fresh mozzarella—get *bufala mozzarella* if you can—it has the best flavor. But fresh mozzarella made from cow's milk is very good too. This is not the same as the aged mozzarella used on pizza and in lasagne.

Gorgonzola—a creamy, blue cheese with a strong flavor.

Ricotta salata—a hard, salty version of the smooth, mild-flavored ricotta, it's delicious crumbled on a pasta or salad. Put a small amount cubed or crumbled on an antipasto platter.

Fontina—a smooth cheese with a mild, nutty flavor. You can use this almost anywhere—sliced with antipasto or on sandwiches, grated on pizza or in pasta, even as a topping to a veal cutlet.

Meats

Prosciutto—salted and dried ham, cut so thin you can almost see through it, it's fabulous in many dishes, sliced as part of an antipasto, wrapped around sweet cantaloupe slices, in sandwiches or as part of roast veal stuffing, diced or slivered in pasta sauces, on top of Clams Casino or pizza. The most famous kind is from Parma, but many others are very good—the less expensive ones are fine to cook with.

Salamis—there are a lot of kinds of salami, flavored with any number of herbs and spices. Use them according to your taste. A few examples: Italian dry salami has a very strong flavor. Genoa is milder. Salami cotta is even milder. Salami sardo has hot red peppers in it. Then there's strongly spiced pepperoni (when spelled with one "p" it means peppers) which is so often used on pizza.

Bresaola—cured beef, it has a delicate flavor and is lovely as part of antipasto.

Coppa—thin slices of dried cured sausage, very good on sandwiches and antipasto platters.

Mortadella—really a cooked sausage, it's like bologna with bits of fat in it. Use it the way you'd use any kind of bologna.

Serves 8–10

as part of

an antipasto.

Garbanzo Bean Salad

(Ceci e Pimienti)

Two 15-ounce cans garbanzo beans, well drained
One 4-ounce jar pimientos
½ cup extra virgin olive oil
½ medium red onion, coarsely chopped (½ cup)
2 tablespoons lemon juice
1 tablespoon red wine vinegar
¼ teaspoon each salt and pepper

Combine all ingredients in a bowl and mix well. Allow to rest at room temperature about half an hour before serving, or refrigerate longer to allow flavors to blend. This lasts refrigerated 10–12 days.

Serves 4.

Marinated Mushrooms

This appetizer is so simple you won't believe how good it is. It's excellent as part of an antipasto and also good as a side dish with steak or chicken. I like to make it with baby white mushrooms that are perfectly bite-size.

8 ounces white mushrooms
4 large garlic cloves, minced (1 tablespoon)
½ cup extra virgin olive oil
2 tablespoons lemon juice
2 tablespoons white, rice, or red wine vinegar—or a mix
½ cup chopped fresh Italian parsley
Salt and pepper to taste

Brush mushrooms clean with paper towels or mushroom brush, or rinse quickly and dry. Cut off any tough stems and, depending on their size, cut in bite-size chunks or leave whole. Combine garlic, olive oil, lemon juice, vinegar(s), and parsley in a bowl. Add mushrooms and toss. Season with salt and pepper to taste. Cover and refrigerate for at least half an hour and up to 6 hours (how much time you got?). If you marinate them longer, retoss every couple of hours (or place in a jar and shake the jar gently a few times to remix ingredients). Bring to room temperature before serving.

CLEANING MUSHROOMS

No matter what kind of mushroom you're using, they have to be cleaned and trimmed. My first thought: washing mushrooms is a felony! That's because they're like a sponge and can get soggy very fast. But who knows what kind of organic stuff they're grown in—I don't want to eat that stuff any more than you do. So I usually rinse them briefly and dry them off right after. To clean them without rinsing, use a mushroom brush or rub them with paper towels to remove excess dirt.

For white or cremini mushrooms, I usually cut off the very ends of mushroom stems and then slice them vertically. If you don't want any stems, either pull out the whole stem (like when making stuffed mushrooms) or slice them off flush with the bottom of the cap. Discard or save to add to any number of dishes—they're a great addition to soups or pasta sauces, or tossed in frittatas.

Don't substitute dried parsley here for the fresh. If you can't get the fresh, leave it out. It'll still taste very good.

Use whichever vinegar you like—I put a dash of the red wine vinegar and the rest plain white but I've also used Japanese rice vinegar. It has a nice clean taste.

Makes about

3 cups.

Aunt Nina's Caponatina

Caponatina (also called *caponata*) can include a number of other ingredients: peppers, raisins, garlic. I like the simplicity of this one, and the recipe is close to the canned Progresso eggplant appetizer my mom kept around for emergencies. On the run, I've had nothing for dinner but some of the Progresso stuff and a couple of pieces of toast and been perfectly happy.

  2 tablespoons salt
  2 medium eggplants (about 1 pound each)
  ½ cup olive oil
  1 medium onion, chopped fine (about 1 cup)
  3 stalks celery, thinly sliced (about 1½ cups)
  ½ cup dry white wine
  2 tablespoons sugar
  2–3 tablespoons red wine vinegar
  ¾ cup tomato purée
  ¼ cup chopped pitted black olives
  ½ cup capers

HENRY'S

NOTES

AND TIPS

Add extra vinegar if you want it more tart.

Refrigerated, this will last up to two weeks. If it's not gobbled up sooner.

½ teaspoon salt (to taste)
¼ teaspoon black pepper (to taste)

Fill a large bowl two-thirds full of water, add salt, and stir to dissolve. Peel and slice eggplant into ½-inch slices. Place slices in the bowl and let soak for 1–2 hours (weight them with a pan or plate so they stay underwater). Drain off the liquid and pat dry with paper towels. (See page 28 for other ways to prepare eggplant.) Cut slices into ½-inch cubes.

Heat ¼ cup of olive oil in a large skillet over medium-high heat. Fry eggplant 1–2 minutes, stirring constantly, and drain on paper towels. Add remaining ¼ cup olive oil to pan, reheat, and add onion and celery. Cook, stirring occasionally over low to medium heat until soft, approximately 10 minutes. Add wine and cook until wine has almost evaporated. Return eggplant to pan.

Dissolve sugar in the red wine vinegar and pour over eggplant. Add tomato purée, olives, and capers; stir and add salt and pepper to taste. Simmer over low heat 5 minutes, until well blended. Cool to room temperature and serve.

■■■

Serves 8–10

generously.

Sunday Gravy (Meat Sauce)

This is the sauce on the stove every Sunday morning in most Italian-American homes in Brooklyn. It wasn't Sunday if the sauce wasn't on the stove. Ask one hundred Italian women how to make gravy, and you'll get one hundred different recipes, and they'll all be good.

6 cups Basic Tomato Sauce (see page 13)
2 tablespoons olive oil
4 hot sausages or 2 hot and 2 mild (about ½ pound)
1 recipe Milly's Meatballs (recipe follows on page 38)
2 pounds cooked pasta of your choice (see page 37 for how to
  cook)

To get rid of some of the fat in the sausages, boil them in a half cup of water in the skillet for a few minutes. Then remove the water, add olive oil to the pan, and brown them over medium-low heat.

Begin preparing Basic Tomato Sauce. While it is simmering, heat the olive oil in a large saucepan. Poke holes in the sausages with a fork and put in the pan. Cook on low to medium heat, turning occasionally, until lightly brown, about 8–10 minutes. You don't have to cook them all the way through because they'll cook more in the sauce. Drain on paper towels. Cut in half and add to tomato sauce. While sauce simmers, prepare meatballs.

When meatballs are browned, spoon them carefully into the sauce. Continue simmering until meatballs are cooked through, about 10–15 minutes. Adjust seasoning. Serve family style over pasta in a large bowl. Have plenty of bread on hand to sop up the sauce.

Pasta

Ninety-nine percent of the time, I use dried pasta, whatever the shape. Once in a great while, it's nice to have fresh pasta, but for me it's not the norm. Fresh pasta is so fragile, most of the time I don't want to work with it. So I eat it in a restaurant once in a while—let them do all the work to make it!

There are hundreds of shapes of pasta. There's long, short, flat, round, stuffed, with holes, ridged, curved, curlicued—almost any shape you can think of, they've created it. Why so many? I think it's simple—boredom! Many Italians eat pasta every day—you'd get tired of the same old shape. Plus they can't help it—you give an Italian an idea, he'll give you ten variations before you can blink.

For a cook, what's important is to know which kinds you can get in most grocery stores and what kind of sauce you should use with them.

Most pastas are fine for any tomato-based sauce. There's a theory that long shapes are best for olive oil–based sauces. The way I see it, a heavier pasta should be used with a heavier sauce. For example, I'd never use a thin light pasta like angel hair (capellini) with a heavy sauce—it would get overwhelmed by the sauce. I also use things with curves and holes like fusilli, gemelli, penne, perciatelli for sauces that have a lot of small bits of meat or vegetables or fish—the shape of the pasta helps catch the bits in it. Tiny pastas like orzo or acini de pepe are best in soup, like you'd use rice.

TYPES OF PASTA

Here's a list of basic pastas you can get in most grocery stores, and believe me, you can get a lot more than you could twenty years ago.

Acini de pepe—tiny, even smaller than rice, usually used in soups.

Orzo—similar to acini de pepe but larger—looks like rice. Good in soup but also good as part of a stuffing.

Capellini—or angel hair—very fine, suitable for light sauces like Aglio e Olio. Capellini won't fill you up, so it's great as a side pasta.

Spaghetti—I know you know this kind.

Spaghettini—thin spaghetti, halfway between capellini and spaghetti.

Bucatini—long pasta with a hollow down the middle, good with chopped meat sauces. Perciatelli is basically a smaller version of bucatini.

Cannelloni—means "large reeds"—a large round pasta, usually stuffed.

Conchiglie or cavatelli—shells of different sizes—great for catching small bits of meat or vegetables in a sauce. The large ones are usually stuffed.

Farfalle—butterflies or bowties—I love this pasta with almost anything.

Fettuccine—small ribbons, known for fettucine alfredo, a very rich butter, cream, and cheese sauce.

Fusilli—twisted spaghetti—good for meat or seafood sauces.

Gemelli—"twins," doubled twisted pasta—same as fusilli but heavier, great for meat sauces or any sauce with bits of meat, fish, or vegetables.

Linguine—means "small tongues"—a long, smooth pasta, a thinner version of fettucine if you want flat, smooth pasta but less bulk.

Manicotti—means "small muffs"—these are usually stuffed like cannelloni.

Mostaccioli—means "small mustaches"—very much like penne.

Orecchiette—"little ears"—these look like tiny tiny saucers and are great sauce catchers. They can be a little tricky to cook—with some brands, the outer edges are thinner and cook a little faster than the center, so they'll be overdone by the time the center is cooked through. Look for orecchiette that has a more even thickness from center to edge—this is one time it's worth it to spend a few more pennies if you need to.

Pappardelle—"wide strips"—cook with a smooth sauce.

Penne—"quill pens"—use almost anywhere you want—one of my favorites.

Radiatore—means "radiators"—a strange shape, great for meat sauces.

Rigatoni—means "large grooves"—smaller than cannelloni or manicotti, excellent for heavy sauces.

Ravioli—small stuffed squares of pasta. I'm not a big fan of stuffed pastas; I prefer the bare stuff. My mother sometimes used to buy prestuffed ravioli from the local baker for a party. They were such a big deal to make, she almost never did—she had a few other things to do.

Ziti—like penne, they're small tubes, with their ends cut straight. Can be baked or served with a good meaty sauce.

HOW TO COOK PASTA

There are a lot of variations on how to cook pasta. Here's my version:

For one pound of pasta:

Bring to a boil a large pot of water (at least 3–4 quarts). Add 1–2 tablespoons salt and stir till dissolved. When water is at a full boil, add pasta and stir immediately to keep off bottom. (As they say, stir, stir, stir!)

Once the pasta is boiling again, stir occasionally until cooked al dente, which depends on the pasta—between 5 and 11 minutes (read the pasta box to know the general time, then subtract 2 minutes for first time to check for doneness).

Cook pasta to al dente (which means "to the teeth," or in Americanese, so you can bite through it with no hard bits—still chewy, not soft). Remember, pasta will be hot and continue cooking when off the flame. Drain immediately, reserving 1 cup or more of pasta water if needed. (The easiest way to reserve pasta water is to dip out the amount you want to save before draining the pasta.)

I don't like to add oil to the water when cooking pasta—I think it screws up the cooking process. If you're worried that the pasta will stick together, return it to the pot and toss it well with a little olive oil after draining.

My mom always rinsed drained pasta. I never do. She liked it to be "separated" from the sauce, I like that the pasta still has a little "glue" from the starch it gives off that binds it to the sauce.

Milly's Meatballs (Brooklyn, 1950)

1½ pounds ground beef + ½ pound ground pork or 1 pound ground
    beef + ¾ pound ground veal + ¼ pound ground pork (see Notes,
    below)
2 eggs
1 tablespoon minced fresh parsley
1 tablespoon minced fresh basil
¼ cup chopped white or brown onions or shallots
3 cloves of garlic, chopped fine
¼ cup grated fresh Romano or Parmesan cheese
½ cup dried, seasoned bread crumbs
½ teaspoon each salt and pepper (to taste)
2 tablespoons chopped canned tomatoes, tomato sauce, or Basic
    Tomato Sauce (optional)
3 tablespoons olive oil (or more if needed)

Combine ground meats in a large bowl and mix together well with
your hands. Add in eggs one at a time, mixing after each addition. Add
in all other ingredients except tomatoes or sauce and olive oil, and combine to form a mixture that is soft but still sticks together. If meatballs
are too hard or dry, add chopped tomatoes or sauce.

Heat olive oil in frying pan. Place a small bowl of water and a plate
near meatball mixture. While oil is heating, roll approximately 3 table-

**HENRY'S
NOTES
AND TIPS**

My mother used three-quarters of a pound of ground veal in her
meatballs. Ground veal is hard to find and expensive, but it makes a
lovely flavored, tender meatball. If you can't afford three-quarter pound
you can put in a quarter or half pound, whatever. Just keep the balance
of one egg to one pound ground meat.

If you're going to use them in cooked sauce, cook meatballs about
three-quarters of the way through—they'll finish cooking in the sauce.
(See Sunday-Gravy (Meat Sauce) recipe on page 33.)

spoons of meatball mixture at a time into walnut-size balls in palm of your hand, adding a small amount of water if they don't roll well. Place each completed ball on the plate. Continue forming until all meatballs are done (you can place them on top of each other like a tower). Test the oil temperature—a drop of water should sizzle when it hits the oil. Fry meatballs in batches, turning until browned on all sides and cooked through. Drain on paper towels. Can be served plain, as main dish in any tomato sauce, on an Italian roll with Parmesan, provolone, or mozzarella as a sandwich, or sliced and put on pizza.

Variations:

1. Add ½ cup golden raisins. This is from Tommy DiSimone's father. This makes a sweet meatball.

2. Add ¼ cup chopped pine nuts. Toast them lightly if you want, but keep in mind they'll also get cooked when the meatballs do.

FRESH OR DRIED BREAD CRUMBS

When I was growing up, we always had leftover ends from loaves of bread around. To use them up, my mom would put them in the meatballs instead of bread crumbs. She'd soak them in milk to soften, and then push them through a strainer to make the mixture she'd add to meatballs.

If you're using dried bread crumbs, you can soak them in milk to soften, and then strain them before adding to the mixture. That way you won't have any hard bits when you bite into the meatballs. You may need more bread crumbs to make up for the soaked milk.

I usually make the meatball mixture half an hour before I cook them, in which case the bread crumbs get soft just from being in the mixture and you don't have to presoak them.

▪▪▪

Escarole and Beans

This is what they call a Southern Italian peasant dish. It's a way to take a slightly bitter green like escarole or broccoli rabe, and make it into something you can't stop eating. In Brooklyn it was usually a side dish, but for Neapolitans it can be the whole meal.

If you have trouble finding cannellini beans, they are also called white kidney beans. If you can't find them either, substitute any white bean, like Great Northern or small white beans.

2 bunches escarole
Two 15-ounce cans cannellini beans
2 tablespoons olive oil
2–4 cloves of garlic, minced
¼–½ teaspoon black pepper (to taste)
⅛ teaspoon salt
Grated Parmesan cheese to serve

Discard tough outer leaves of escarole. Trim bottom of leaves. Wash escarole thoroughly, dry, and cut into about 2-inch pieces (it's easiest to stack and cut).

Drain beans, reserving ½ to 1 cup of their liquid. Heat oil in a large skillet over medium heat and add beans, garlic, and ¼ teaspoon black pepper. Cook, stirring occasionally, until bubbling, about 5 minutes. Add a little of reserved bean liquid if mixture appears dry. Add escarole and stir well. Cover and cook until escarole is wilted, stirring once or twice, about 3–5 minutes. Season with salt and additional pepper. Serve with grated Parmesan on the side.

HENRY'S NOTES AND TIPS	A lettuce spinner is a quick way to dry escarole. Or you can pat them between paper towels.

ESCAROLE

Escarole is a great green. It's part of the chicory family, but it looks more like regular lettuce. It's good raw and mixed with other greens, but it's best either quickly sautéed or cooked well with beans or in a soup. It tastes like a bitter lettuce when raw and a smooth spinach when cooked. If you have a recipe that asks for escarole, you can't substitute anything else.

Escarole is in tons of grocery stores and you just don't know it—it's either next to the lettuces or mixed in with things like mustard and collard greens. A lot of grocers don't know what to make of it or where it belongs, so poke around—you'll be surprised how many places have it. And it's not expensive.

Preparing escarole is simple. You treat it like you would any lettuce—just rinse well and dry. Like romaine, you might want to trim off the thicker ends before using it. Store as you would any head of lettuce.

TAKING IT EASY

Nobody rushed. We'd eat for three hours easy. A meal wasn't just about eating—we never ate in front of the TV or bolted our food down in five minutes. It was a social event, a gathering. When you finish an Italian meal, you should feel full not only of food, but satisfied from the event, people, stories, feelings. My mom would stay in the kitchen cooking, and bring out the different courses as the meal progressed. Besides us ten, there were always other people, aunts and uncles, friends—we often had sixteen people sit down for dinner. My mom cooked for an army.

Holiday meals were even more lavish. The Italian tradition is to have fish on Christmas Eve. The general rule is you have seven different types of fish, but we always had lots more. We had shrimp, scallops, flounder, eel, scungilli (conch), calamari, lobster, clams, mussels, baccalà (salt cod) and octopus (polpo). And some types would be prepared more than just one way. My mom would make fried and stuffed shrimp; we ate clams raw, baked, and in linguine with clam sauce. On Christmas Day we had lasagne, antipasti, *braciole*, meatballs, and sausage, followed by turkey or ham.

Serves 8–10.

■■■

Baccalà Salad

One of my favorite things about Christmas Eve is this salad. When I was a kid I wished for more than one Christmas Eve a year just so we could have it. Well, I wanted more Christmas presents too.

2 pounds salt cod
1 cup olive oil
3 large cloves of garlic, minced (1 tablespoon)
1 cup lemon juice
1½ cups black olives, sliced
½ cup green olives, sliced
3 tablespoons capers
1 red pepper, seeded and diced
¼–½ teaspoon each salt and black pepper (to taste)
¼ cup chopped fresh parsley

Place cod in a bowl and cover with water. Soak cod, cover, and refrigerate up to 3 days, changing water every 6 hours the first day and every 12 hours on subsequent days. After about 18 hours, break off a piece of cod and taste it. The cod is ready to use when it doesn't taste salty.

HENRY'S NOTES AND TIPS

How long you have to soak the salt cod varies a lot depending on what's been done to it. Some is ready to eat in twenty-four hours or less, some needs the full three days. Your fishmonger may have an estimate.

Fill a large pot with water and bring to a boil. Add cod and boil 5–6 minutes, just until it can be flaked with a fork. Don't overcook, or it will be dry. Drain fish and cool. Check for bones and break into bite-size pieces. Place in a large mixing bowl.

Heat oil in a skillet over medium heat. Add garlic and cook, stirring, 2 minutes (do not brown garlic). Add oil, cooked garlic, and lemon juice to cod and mix well. Add both kinds of olives, capers, and red pepper and toss mixture. Taste and season with salt and pepper. Place in a serving bowl or on a platter and garnish with chopped parsley.

Serves 6–8.

Braciole

My brother Joe started working for a butcher when he was a young teenager. Then a couple of my sisters got jobs there as cashiers. Let me tell you, it's very handy to have family work for the butcher.

There are a number of ways to make *Braciole* depending on what part of Italy you're from. This is my mom's version, courtesy of my brother Joe, who still makes it—delicious!

1½ pounds beef top or bottom round, sliced ½" thick
½ cup olive oil
1 medium brown or white onion, diced (1 cup)
3–4 cloves of garlic, minced (1 tablespoon)
½ cup chopped fresh parsley + additional for garnish
12–15 basil leaves, chopped
15 ounces whole-milk or part-skim ricotta cheese
1 teaspoon each salt and pepper
4 ounces shredded locatelli or Parmesan cheese
4 ounces shredded Romano cheese
8 ounces shredded mozzarella cheese
One recipe Basic Tomato Sauce, page 13
1 pound pasta, cooked and drained (optional; see page 37 for how to cook)

When tieing the *braciole*, make more loops rather than less to make sure it won't fall apart as it cooks.

Flatten beef to about ¼-inch-thick slices (see page 57 or have your butcher do it). You want the meat slices to end up about 5 × 8 inches so cut to size if they are too large.

Heat 2 tablespoons oil in a medium-size skillet over medium heat. Add onion and cook 3 minutes, stirring. Add garlic, parsley, and basil and continue cooking until onion is tender, about 3 more minutes. Cool mixture.

Mix ricotta in a bowl with ¼ teaspoon each salt and pepper. Toss locatelli or Parmesan and Romano cheese with ¼ teaspoon each salt and pepper in a separate bowl.

Lightly salt and pepper *braciole* pieces on both sides. Lay out each *braciole* and spread ricotta ¼ inch thick in a layer on one side. Cover ricotta with a thin layer of onion/garlic mixture, followed by thin layers of locatelli/Romano mixture and the mozzarella, leaving a ¼-inch margin around the edge of the *braciole*. Tie with heavy thread or butcher's string, making a loop every 2 inches.

Heat remaining oil in a large skillet that will accommodate all the *braciole*. Brown *braciole* well on all sides, turning carefully. The slices need to get brown but not crisp.

Heat Basic Tomato Sauce in a large pot. Slip *braciole* into tomato sauce and simmer over very low heat for 2–3 hours, until beef is fork tender, checking occasionally to make sure sauce is not sticking to bottom and skimming off any fat that rises to the top. Be careful when stirring toward the end so as not to break up the *braciole*.

Remove *braciole* from sauce to a cutting board. Cut string and discard. Carefully slice beef in thick slices and arrange on a platter. Top with some tomato sauce and garnish with chopped parsley. Serve with optional pasta tossed with some of the remaining tomato sauce and good warm bread.

THANKSGIVING

Our version of Thanksgiving started with stuffed artichokes, then Italian dishes with all the trimmings, manicotti, a side dish of eggplant parmigiana. And after that? A full American-style turkey dinner, complete with stuffing, potatoes, pies. As if anybody could eat any more, around 8 at night people would start making turkey sandwiches. If I hadn't been so active, I'd weigh two hundred pounds.

■■■

Serves 8.

Holiday Stuffed Artichokes

My mom would start any number of holiday meals with these lovely artichokes. We'd have one artichoke each, which may sound like a lot, but the artichokes we had in Brooklyn were about two-thirds the size of the giants you can get today. If you're using the big ones, you can make four artichokes for eight people and cut them in half to serve.

CHOOSING ARTICHOKES

■■

Whatever size you're buying, look for artichokes that have leaves closed around it, not opened like a flower. If you bend a fresh leaf, it will snap off, an older one will bend or be flexible. Also, rubbing a fresh 'choke will make it squeak, which means it has moisture inside its leaves. A bright green 'choke is sure to be fresh, but don't worry if there are a few brown patches on the outside leaves—these are from frost and won't affect the taste (you won't eat the outermost leaves anyway).

Artichokes last wrapped in a plastic bag in the refrigerator for at least a week.

Adding raisins or salami makes different tasting artichokes, but I like both versions. They're also fine without either.

There are two methods for cooking these: one on top of the stove, one partly on the stove and partly in the oven. My mother did hers on top of the stove, but I picked up the second way somewhere in the neighborhood, and I think it's easier 'cause you trim them when they're partly cooked.

2 cups seasoned bread crumbs
2 cups grated Parmesan cheese
1 cup olive oil + additional for drizzling
8 medium artichokes (about 3½ inches wide) or 4 large (about
    5 inches wide)
16 garlic cloves, minced (½ tablespoon per artichoke)
1½ cups raisins (optional)
3 ounces hard salami, cut in small pieces (optional)
Salt and pepper to taste
2–4 cups chicken broth

Combine bread crumbs, Parmesan, and ½ cup olive oil in a bowl. Set aside.

Cut off the stem of each artichoke so it sits upright. With scissors, horizontally cut off the tip of each leaf. Push open the leaves and center of the artichoke. Remove the 'choke part in the middle with a spoon or small knife—a grapefruit spoon works well for this.

Stuff two chopped garlic cloves, a few raisins, and/or salami if using in the middle and between the leaves of each artichoke. Spoon the bread crumb/cheese mixture between the leaves and in the middle opening until full. Season artichoke with salt and fresh ground pepper.

Place the artichokes in a covered pan large enough to hold them standing upright. Pour chicken broth in pan. Broth should come about halfway up the side of the pan. If you don't have enough broth, add water. Drizzle olive oil liberally over the top of each artichoke.

Cover and simmer one hour over medium to low heat. Every 15 minutes baste the artichokes with the broth mixture. Keep moisture level consistent by adding more broth or water. The artichokes are done when leaves can pull away easily and are very tender.

Serve in small bowls with some of the broth from the pot drizzled over each artichoke.

To bake in oven:

Follow beginning steps for preparing artichokes through trimming the tops of the leaves. Heat ½ cup of water in a large pot to boiling. Place as many artichokes in the pan as will fit next to each other, bottom side up. Cover pan and steam artichokes for 10 minutes, adding more water if necessary. Remove artichokes and let them drain on a plate or cutting board, still bottom side up. When cool enough to handle, reverse them and spoon out the center. The leaves should already be spread from resting upside down. If not, push apart gently (don't push too hard or the partly cooked leaves will break off).

Stuff two chopped garlic cloves, a few raisins, and/or salami if using in the middle and between the leaves of each artichoke. Spoon the bread crumb/cheese mixture between the leaves and in the middle opening until full. Season artichoke with salt and fresh ground pepper.

Preheat oven to 375°F. Place artichokes in a baking dish large enough to hold them in a single layer. Pour in 1 cup of chicken broth and drizzle olive oil liberally over tops of artichokes. Cover dish with foil and bake about 45 minutes, basting every 15 minutes and adding more chicken broth if pan gets dry. The artichokes are done when leaves can pull away easily and are very tender.

For both methods:

Serve artichokes in small bowls with some of the broth from the pot or baking dish drizzled over each artichoke. Place empty bowls on the table for the discarded leaves.

Manicotti

The original manicotti was homemade rolled crepes stuffed with a variety of meats, vegetables, and cheeses. But my mom and Fat Larry in the pizzeria both used the fat pasta tubes that were already made. My mom often put sausage in hers, Fat Larry used salami. Or you can make them without meat at all for a delicious vegetarian dish.

8 ounces dried manicotti tubes
2 cups Basic Tomato Sauce (see page 13)

For the filling:

1 egg, beaten
15-ounce container ricotta cheese (about 2 cups)
8 ounces shredded mozzarella cheese (about 2 cups)
1 cup freshly grated Parmesan or Romano cheese
¼ cup chopped fresh Italian parsley + additional for garnish, or
    1 tablespoon dried
¼ teaspoon each salt and pepper
4 ounces mild Italian sausage or 2 ounces hard salami
1–2 tablespoons olive oil if using sausage

Cook manicotti noodles until barely al dente (about 6 minutes) and drain well. (See page 37 for pasta cooking directions.)
Preheat oven to 375°F.

HENRY'S NOTES AND TIPS

You use less salami than sausage (if you're cooking with it) in this recipe because its taste is very strong.

To make the filling:

Combine egg, ricotta, 1½ cups mozzarella, ¾ cup Parmesan or Romano, parsley, and salt and pepper in a large bowl.

If using sausage, heat olive oil in a skillet over medium heat. Remove sausage from its casing and crumble meat. Cook in skillet, stirring, until lightly browned. Drain on paper towels. Add to ricotta mixture.

If using salami, dice in ¼- to ½-inch pieces and add to ricotta mixture.

In a small bowl, mix together remaining ½ cup mozzarella and ¼ cup Parmesan or Romano.

To assemble manicotti:

Coat the bottom of a 9 × 12-inch baking pan with a thin layer of tomato sauce. Gently fill the manicotti tubes with ricotta mixture and place side by side in pan. Top manicotti with remaining tomato sauce and sprinkle with remaining mozzarella/parmesan or romano mixture. Cover pan with aluminum foil. Bake 40 minutes and serve.

Eggplant Parmigiana

In our family, eggplant parmigiana was either an appetizer or a side dish to have with a meat course. But it makes sense as a main course—the eggplant is so dense and flavorful it's almost like meat.

1–2 eggplants, approximately 3 pounds, cut into ½" slices
2 eggs
1 cup flour
Salt and pepper
1 cup olive oil (or more)
2 cups Basic Tomato Sauce (see recipe on page 13)
2 ounces mozzarella cheese, grated (optional)
1 cup grated fresh Parmesan or Romano cheese
2 tablespoons fresh Italian parsley, chopped leaves
10–12 fresh basil leaves, cut or torn in large pieces + additional for garnish

Serves 4 people

as a

main course,

6–8

as an appetizer

or side dish.

Make sure the oil is very hot so the eggplant won't absorb a lot of it. Also make sure there is plenty of oil in the pan—add more and reheat if necessary.

You can peel the eggplant or not according to what you like. My mother always peeled hers, but I found out later a lot of people don't. I like the color of the dish when the skin is left on.

You don't have to do more than one layer of eggplant slices. I think it works well as an appetizer when it's just one layer.

In a pinch (but only if you really have to), you can substitute canned or jarred tomato sauce with seasoning for the Basic Tomato Sauce.

To cut the eggplant's bitterness, place the slices in a bowl of salted water and let sit for an hour, weighted with a plate so they stay submerged. Drain off the liquid and dry slightly, but not completely, with paper towels—that way, the flour will stick great, and the slices will cook up crunchy as a cucumber. (See note on page 28 for other ways to prepare eggplant.) While eggplant soaks, prepare the rest of the ingredients.

Beat the eggs in a shallow bowl. Set aside.

Mix the flour with salt and pepper and put on a plate.

Heat the oil in a large sauté pan until very hot but not smoking. Dredge both sides of the eggplant slices first in the flour and then the egg. Slip the slices into the hot oil and sauté for 2–3 minutes or until golden on both sides. Do this in batches if slices won't all fit in the pan without crowding. Drain well on paper towels.

Preheat the oven to 400°F. Lightly oil a 9 × 12 baking pan. Line the pan with a layer of eggplant slices. Spread a layer of tomato sauce on the slices, dot with half the mozzarella (if using) and sprinkle well with Parmesan or Romano, 1 tablespoon of the parsley and a few of the basil leaves. Top with another round of eggplant, tomato sauce, cheeses, parsley, and basil. Bake 30–35 minutes. After the first 15 or 20 minutes, press down on the eggplants and spoon out excess liquid on the bottom of the pan. Serve garnished with more basil leaves.

DISHES YOU DON'T SEE TOO MUCH ANYMORE

We had dishes people would probably think are strange today. On special occasions, my father would bring home a whole lamb's head from the butcher—split in two, right down the middle. It still looked like a sweet little lamb. Or we'd have eels, which kept wriggling even when they'd been cooking for twenty minutes. We had tripe every Saturday. And my mom used to make snails—*babbalucci*. She'd buy a whole bushelful and cook them in tomato sauce. You'd pick them out of their shells with a toothpick—delicious! The night before, she'd soak them in a pot of water to clean, and sometimes they'd sneak out, even if the pot had a lid. I'd come in the kitchen in the morning and find them crawling up the walls.

Octopus (Polpo) Salad

Serves 4–6

as a side salad

or appetizer.

Don't be frightened of eating octopus. Yes, it looks weird, but I guarantee you'll fall in love with the taste.

3 pounds octopus, cleaned
1 tablespoon salt
2–4 tablespoons extra virgin olive oil
1 large stalk celery, trimmed and diced or sliced thin (¾ cup)
¼ cup diced red onion
1 tablespoon drained capers
1 tablespoon black kalamata olives, sliced
¼ cup chopped fresh parsley leaves
3 tablespoons lemon juice (to taste)
½–1 teaspoon each salt and pepper (to taste)

Bring a large pot of water to a boil, add 1 tablespoon salt and drop in the octopus. Cook at a simmer for 45 minutes to 1 hour, until tender

You can get octopus at Hispanic markets. It's usually cleaned already—all you have to do is cook and slice it. If it isn't already, ask them to clean it for you.

If you like things spicy, add half a teaspoon crushed red pepper flakes.

(check after 45 minutes). Drain and cool. When cool, peel or rub off any of its outer purplish skin that is loose. Rinse well, redrain, and slice in pieces—cutting head and tentacles into bite-size slices (½ to 1 inch in size).

Combine the remaining ingredients in a large bowl with the octopus. Chill thoroughly and serve cool.

Serves 8–10

generously.

Honeycomb Tripe with Parmesan Cheese

Saturday mornings, my mom and sisters used to go through this whole long process to make tripe. They had to soak it, scrub it, blanch it—what a chore! Nowadays, all that is done before it gets to the supermarket.

If you have trouble finding tripe, look for a market with Hispanic ingredients. It's used for *menudo*. Or ask your grocery store butcher to order it.

2 pounds ready-to-cook honeycomb tripe (beef tripe)
⅓ cup vegetable oil
1 large onion, peeled and diced

HENRY'S

NOTES

AND TIPS

This can be cooked several days in advance and refrigerated. It just tastes better with time.

1 stalk of celery, chopped
1 carrot, peeled and chopped
1 small fennel bulb, chopped
1 tablespoon chopped fresh parsley
2 medium garlic cloves, minced
1 cup dry white wine
One 28-ounce can Italian plum tomatoes with juice, diced or
    crushed
½–1 teaspoon crushed dried red pepper or chopped hot red chili
    pepper (to taste)
½ teaspoon black pepper
½–1 teaspoon salt (to taste)
1 cup beef broth (if needed)
¾ cup grated Parmesan (fresh if possible)

Rinse and wash tripe well in cold water. Drain and cut into strips approximately ½ inch wide and 3 inches long.

Heat oil in a large pot on medium. Add onion, stir and cook until translucent (about 3–4 minutes). Add the celery, carrot, and fennel, stir to coat them well, and cook 1 minute.

Add the parsley and garlic, cook 1 minute, stirring once or twice, then add the tripe and stir to coat well. Cook 5 minutes, stirring occasionally. Add wine and stir. Bring to brisk simmer, then add the tomatoes with their juice, red pepper, black pepper, and salt. Stir all ingredients well and bring to slow boil. Reduce to a fast simmer.

Cover pot and cook for about 4 hours until the tripe is tender when tasted. Keep heat at a slow but steady simmer. Check the liquid in the pot from time to time; if needed, add some beef broth. If the tripe is thin and watery, cook for the last hour or so with the lid half off.

When tripe is done, transfer to a large bowl and sprinkle with Parmesan. Serve at once, with lots of fresh Italian bread.

■■■

Babbalucci (Snails) in Tomato Sauce

This recipe is for small live snails, which you may be able to find in a Hispanic market. If not, you can use the larger ones they sell in cans as French escargots. You can also get the canned ones with shells. The live snails sold in markets these days are usually already cleaned, but ask to make sure.

1 pound live small snails, or a 7-ounce can
¼ cup olive oil
½ medium brown or white onion, peeled and diced (½ cup)
4 cloves of garlic, minced (1 tablespoon)
½–1 teaspoon red pepper flakes (to taste)
One 28-ounce can plum tomatoes, drained (reserving juice) and
  chopped coarsley
½–1 cup dry red wine
½–¾ cup chopped fresh Italian parsley or 3 teaspoons dried
½–1 teaspoon each salt and black pepper (to taste)

If using live snails, rinse cleaned snails very well in cold water. Set aside in a pot with a secure lid while you make the tomato sauce.

In a large skillet, heat the olive oil over medium-high heat. Add the onion and cook, stirring, 5 minutes, until onion begins to become translucent. Lower heat to medium, add garlic and red pepper flakes, and cook, stirring, about 1–2 minutes (do not brown garlic). Add chopped tomatoes and raise heat to high. Sauté, stirring constantly, for 3 or 4 minutes, until tomatoes begin to thicken. Lower heat to medium and add live snails, reserved tomato juice, wine, parsley, and salt and pepper. Cook 5 minutes, stirring occasionally.

If using canned snails, cook only 3 minutes. Adjust seasonings and serve in bowls. If you wish to serve canned snails in shells, put some tomato sauce in each bowl, put each cooked snail in a shell and place on top of sauce in bowls, topping with a little additional tomato sauce. Serve with toothpicks to pluck snails from their shells.

POP

My pop never set foot in the kitchen. He sat in the dining room with his gallon of Gallo, analyzing electric wiring blueprints like other people read comics. He was an amazing guy—he was a lead electrician at the World Trade Center. He called the wiseguys "bums." He hated it when he realized I was hanging out with them. He wanted me to have a real job, some day a good union job like him. Who knows if I had the smarts to do what he did—I never found out. Before I was even old enough to hold a job I was hooked into the Goodfella world. I had already found my calling—and there was always a kitchen involved.

Chapter Two

In the Mob

▪▪

THE PIZZERIA

I went straight from Mom's kitchen to another—the Presto Pizzeria. When I was about twelve years old, the wiseguys opened up a cab stand and pizzeria right across the street from my house. In no time I was working for them—parking their Caddies, running errands, and dicing and slicing for Fat Larry Bilello, who worked in the pizzeria and was also a baker.

The only job I'd ever had till then was being an altar boy—I'd get five dollars for weddings and three dollars for funerals (no respect for the dead). I loved working for the wiseguys. It meant I got to hang around them, which is what I really wanted. And being in the pizzeria was a natural for me. I already knew how to assist in the kitchen from home, and even though I was doing jobs at the cab stand, I always wanted more to do. I could never sit still; they said I had "ants in my pants."

Fat Larry was a little strange. He went to state prison for twenty-five years for killing a cop (and was the cook for Murder Inc. inside). Eventually he was, as they say, institutionalized. But boy could he cook! Even though I was a kid and probably a pain in the ass, he showed me a lot of things in the kitchen. He used to buy a whole leg of veal and show me how he made his own scallopini. The meat he got was so tender, it was a dream to slice.

When you work in a restaurant, your day starts early—there's tons to do before people show up. I would get to work at dawn and start making the dough. Next we'd crush the whole tomatoes through a grinder and season it for sauce, then grate the mozzarella and prepare the other toppings. Then depending on the day, we had certain dishes we made: Monday we'd make gravy (which is tomato sauce with meat in it), Tuesday Veal Scallopini, Wednesday Stuffed Shells or Manicotti, Thursday cutlets, Friday tuna sauce for linguine, or other fish dishes. We made Veal and Pepper Sandwiches from what was left of the leg after the scallopini was sliced, we made meatball heros, subs, Calzones. We'd half-bake the shells and manicotti in their little oven dishes, the same kind

FLATTENING CUTLETS

The usual way to flatten any meat cutlet is to use what they call a "mallet," which is like a wide-headed hammer. You don't really pound the cutlet—you hit it fairly hard and stretch it to make it thinner with each stroke, until the whole cutlet is about the same thickness. Whatever you do, don't use a regular hammer! You'll just make holes.

My favorite way to do it is a little different. I use a meat cleaver or the back of a small, heavy frying pan (like a cast iron one). You lay the cutlet on a cutting board and hit one corner with the flat side of the cleaver or the bottom of the pan. The motion isn't directly down— it's down at a diagonal, which stretches the meat out as you hit it. Turn the cutlet ¼ circle and repeat, until you've hit all four corners the same way. Then flip the cutlet over and repeat on the other side. If the cutlet isn't as thin as you want, flip again and repeat on all four corners (including more of the middle as you go), until the meat is an even thickness (or thinness).

You can cover both sides of the cutlet in wax paper before you do the flattening, but I never do. I find the wax paper often tears and then you have to fish out the bits of it before you cook.

they use today, and we'd freeze them, so when there was an order, they'd go into the hot pizza oven to finish baking and be ready—ba-da-bing!

Serves 4 to 6.

■■■

Fugazy Cutlets

It was from Fat Larry that I learned my first scam. When he couldn't get the veal he wanted or it cost too much, he used to substitute pork. He had the whole neighborhood fooled!

Today I can still con almost anyone who eats my cutlets. Moving around the country later, I was unable to find veal as easily as pork, and when the bankroll was low, pork tasted fine.

I like to serve the cutlets with fusilli, the corkscrew-shaped pasta, that has been tossed with part of the tomato sauce, but you can use whatever pasta you want.

Cutlets:

1½ pounds pork cutlets
1 cup seasoned bread crumbs
½ cup flour
2 teaspoons salt
1 teaspoon black pepper
3 eggs
½ cup olive oil (approx.)
1 pound fusilli or pasta of your choice, cooked and drained (see page 37 for how to cook)

HENRY'S NOTES AND TIPS

If serving with pasta, cook it while cutlets are cooking. Try to time it so the pasta and the cutlets are finished at about the same time.

Sauce:

3 tablespoons olive oil
4 cloves of garlic, minced
1 small brown or white onion, diced
One 28-ounce can plum tomatoes with basil
½ cup dry red wine
¼ cup chopped fresh parsley
2 tablespoons chopped fresh basil
½ tablespoon each salt and pepper

To make sauce:

Heat olive oil in pan over low heat, add garlic and cook, stirring 1–2 minutes. Do not brown. Add the onions and cook, stirring 3–4 minutes or until softened. Add juice from canned tomatoes and the wine and scrape up any bits that are stuck to the pan. Crush tomatoes with your hands or chop well on a cutting board and add to sauce. Bring mixture to a simmer. Add parsley, basil, and ¼ tablespoon black pepper. Simmer 45 minutes, skimming off foam every 8–10 minutes. Season with salt and remaining pepper to taste.

To make cutlets:

To prepare cutlets, first lay them either straight on a cutting board or between sheets of wax paper or plastic wrap on the board and pound until approximately ¼- to ⅛-inch thick. If you don't have a meat pounder, use the back of a heavy pan or a meat cleaver. (See note on page 57 on how to flatten cutlets.) Mix bread crumbs, flour, and a dash of salt and pepper in a bowl or shallow dish. Dip the cutlets in mixture on both sides and lay out on a plate. Beat eggs in a separate bowl, season with salt and pepper, and set aside.

Heat ½ cup olive oil in a large skillet over medium-high heat. Dip each cutlet in eggs on both sides, and slip into pan. Sauté for 1–2 minutes per side, or until golden brown, turning once (don't overcook them). Add more olive oil and reheat if necessary before adding more cutlets. Remove cutlets as they cook to paper towels to drain.

Place the cutlets on plates and top with sauce. If you wish, serve with fusilli tossed with some of the tomato sauce on the side.

WHICH CAME FIRST, THE FLOUR OR THE EGG

My mother always dipped cutlets first in the egg and then in the flour and bread crumbs before frying (she did the same with eggplant for Eggplant Parmigiana). Tommy Bosco did the opposite, starting with the flour and bread crumbs and ending with the eggs, and I picked up the habit. They make for very differently flavored cutlets. The one ending with flour and crumbs is nutty and dark tasting, the one ending with egg is more mellow. The other reason I like ending with egg is when you end with flour and bread crumbs, some of the bread crumbs always fall into the oil and burn, so you have to start over with a new batch of oil after a couple of rounds of frying.

Any food you coat with flour and/or bread crumbs before frying, either in combination with egg or solo (but especially if just coating with flour or bread crumbs), dip it in the flour mixture just before you fry it. If it sits around after being floured, you won't get a crisp crust. Remember the flour and water glue you made in kindergarten? It's the same principal here. When flour comes in contact with moisture, it makes glue in about a minute. The moisture makes the flour stick to the cutlet or whatever you're frying, but if it sits too long you have glue and no crust.

Veal Scallopini and Variations

(Marsala and Piccata)

Fat Larry always took his scallopini from the top round of the veal, for the best quality, and the bottom round for second best. He taught me to cut exactly against the grain with a very sharp knife—if you don't, the veal will curl up and be tough. Also, when you're buying veal, look for paler pieces—they'll have a more delicate flavor.

Veal Scallopini with Marsala Wine

1–1½ pounds veal scallops (scallopini)
8 ounces white mushrooms (optional)
½ cup flour
½–1 teaspoon each salt and pepper
2–4 tablespoons butter
2–4 tablespoons olive oil
¼ medium white or brown onion, or 1 shallot, peeled and diced
  (¼ cup)
½ cup chicken broth
½ cup sweet Marsala wine
1 tablespoon capers (optional)
¼–½ cup chopped fresh Italian parsley for garnish

Lay veal scallops either straight on a cutting board or between
sheets of waxed paper or plastic wrap and pound until about ¼ to ⅛-
inch thick. If you don't have a meat pounder, use the back of a heavy
pan or a meat cleaver. You can also have your butcher do this. (See
details of how to pound meat on page 57.)

Trim stems of mushrooms if using. Rinse them briefly or wipe clean
and slice ¼-inch thick.

Mix flour with ½ teaspoon salt and pepper and put on a plate. Heat
1 tablespoon butter and 3 tablespoons oil in a large skillet over
medium-high heat until hot but not smoking. Dredge veal scallops in
flour on both sides, shaking off excess. Put immediately into pan and
brown on both sides, about 1–2 minutes per side. Remove veal to a platter. Do not crowd scallops—cook veal in two batches if necessary.

If pan is dry, add more butter and olive oil. Add onion or shallot and
sauté, stirring, 2–3 minutes. Add mushrooms and continue cooking,
stirring often, 3–4 minutes, until mushrooms are browned and starting
to soften. Remove to platter with veal.

Remove any excess oil from the pan, leaving 1 tablespoon. Add
chicken broth and Marsala wine. Stir and scrape up any bits that are
stuck to the pan. Once mixture boils, lower heat to medium-low and

HENRY'S	See note above about dredging in flour right before you cook it.
NOTES	Also, don't cook too long on the first side or the second side will get
AND TIPS	moist before it gets browned and won't get crisp. It's better to flip it back

HENRY'S	See note above about dredging in flour right before you cook it.
NOTES	Also, don't cook too long on the first side or the second side will get
AND TIPS	moist before it gets browned and won't get crisp. It's better to flip it back to the first side a second time for another minute if you don't think the veal is cooked through.

cook to reduce slightly, about 3 minutes. Add capers for last minute of cooking. Season with salt and pepper if needed.

Return veal and mushroom mixture to pan, along with any juices they have given off. Heat through. Place scallopini on platter and top with sauce. Sprinkle with chopped parsley and serve.

Serves 4.

■■■

Veal Scallopini with Lemon Sauce

(Veal Piccata)

Veal prepared with a lemon sauce is often called *piccata*, though the term can apply to any meat prepared with a lemon sauce.

1–1½ pounds veal scallops (scallopini)
½ cup flour
½–1 teaspoon each salt and pepper
2–3 tablespoons butter
3–6 tablespoons olive oil
¼ medium white or brown onion, or 1 shallot, peeled and diced (¼ cup)
½ cup chicken broth

HENRY'S	
NOTES	See note for Veal Scallopini with Marsala Wine, above.
AND TIPS	

½ very thinly sliced lemon
2–3 tablespoons fresh lemon juice
¼–½ cup chopped fresh Italian parsley for garnish

Prepare and cook scallopini as above in Veal Scallopini with Marsala Wine.

After removing veal from pan, add ½ cup chicken broth. Cook at a slow boil 2 minutes to reduce slightly, stirring constantly and scraping up any bits that are stuck to the pan. Return veal to pan, coat with the sauce, and top with lemon slices. Cover pan, lower heat to medium-low, and heat through, about 4 minutes.

Remove veal to a serving platter and add lemon juice to the pan. Boil briskly 1–2 minutes. Taste and season with salt and pepper. Pour sauce over veal, sprinkle with chopped parsley, and serve at once.

■■

Makes

2 sandwiches.

Veal and Pepper Sandwiches

2 medium green peppers or 1 red and 1 green
2–4 tablespoons olive oil
½ medium brown or white onion, sliced thin (½ cup)
1–1½ pounds veal, cut in ½" × 3" strips or ½" cubes
1 teaspoon garlic powder
½–1 teaspoon each salt and pepper (to taste)
Two 6–8" Italian rolls, sliced in half lengthwise, lightly toasted if
    desired

Core peppers and remove ribs and seeds. Slice lengthwise in ½-inch strips. Heat oil in a skillet over medium-high heat. Add onion and cook

To me, it's okay if the onion gets dark brown—it just adds flavor. Don't overcook veal or it'll get tough.

HENRY'S

NOTES

AND TIPS

3 minutes, stirring. Add peppers and continue to cook until onion and peppers are starting to brown. Turn heat to high and add veal. Sauté 2–3 minutes, until veal is browned and just cooked through. Stir constantly. Add seasonings. Divide into two portions and serve immediately on rolls, drizzling with any pan juices.

PAULIE

The pizzeria was Paulie's office. Paul Vario was the head of his family, and he and his four brothers were part of the Lucchese crime family. The Varios did a lot of different things for the Luccheses: They ran their local illegal businesses like the numbers business, crap games, loansharking, the construction/labor union business; they collected from the cigarette machines in local restaurants, and the pinball machines and jukeboxes. They also were big-time enforcers for the family and were known as one of the toughest gangs around. And they knew how to eat.

In the front part of the pizzeria were the usual ten or twelve small tables and the counter where you'd order your food. If you went past the counter and the kitchen, you'd come into a much bigger room with lots more tables and an aisle down the middle. Part of Paulie's "office" was a big round table on the right. People would be back there munching their pies and never know how much money was changing hands right across the room.

Paulie and his crew would show up for meetings around 2 or 3 p.m. It was pretty quiet then—lunch was over, dinner wouldn't start for a few hours, so he could do his business in peace. Sometimes they'd just nibble on olives and marinated cherry peppers—they ate them like other guys eat chips. Maybe they'd add salami and cheese, and afterward pastries and espresso. Or sometimes Paulie would want a full meal. He would collect from different groups on different days: the bookies were Tuesdays, the construction workers would pay their Shylock loans on Thursdays and Fridays, etc. People would eat whatever was on the table—except there was a kind of hierarchy, like people paying off Shylocks weren't invited to join in.

The numbers runners had to get their take to their comptrollers every day. They had drop points, a candy store or pizza joint in their area. Paulie ran numbers businesses in Harlem, Jamaica (the city in Queens, not the island), and downtown Brooklyn—all the major Black neighborhoods, and even up in Connecticut. In those days, almost everyone would play the numbers. Even my mom played—just a little. All the housewives did. It was like the lottery.

The runners would drop their take, and once a week their comptrollers would "straighten out" with Paulie. Each comptroller had a bank of, say thirty-five thousand dollars, and no matter how much money they had made or lost, they had to end up with the same amount in the bank at the end of the week.

The runners had to have their take in by 1 p.m., or there was a chance someone would try to fake a winner. That happened to Paulie with his Bridgeport, Connecticut, business. He discovered that the guy who ran his Bridgeport business was faking winners and taking home the profits, right under his nose.

Paulie was livid; he made plans for us to go up there and whack the guy. We all climbed into his car to drive to Connecticut—Paulie and Jimmy Burke in the front, and me and Bobby Brooks, who we called Brooksie, in the back. But as we were starting out, Paulie saw another crew member, Tommy DeSimone, pulled up beside him, and told him to get in. Tommy did as he was told—this was Paulie, after all—but when he asked where we were going, no one answered. He was squished between Brooksie and me in the back seat. He almost died when we turned onto the freeway north. He was such a paranoid, he thought we were going to whack *him*! When we saw how scared he was, we kept the riff going the whole trip.

So Paulie had us stop at his favorite diner on the way—a place known for its delicious fresh-baked ham. That ham was so good, I can still taste it like it was yesterday. The minute they saw Paulie coming, they'd start setting up his plate. Poor Tommy could hardly eat—he thought it was his last meal.

If a big number hit, there was a scramble to cover it. Like one time, there was a freak event. A plane went down at LaGuardia that had a number on the tail, say it was 240. A lot of people saw that 240 and played it—and it hit! The numbers guys and Paulie couldn't believe it—they had to come up with so much money it was scary. So when it got like that, Paulie would have to borrow from the Shylocks himself. He would get money to cover the bets at maybe quarter to half a point. Then he would lend the money to me at one and a half points, and I would lend it to someone else, until the last guy getting the loan would sometimes pay four or five points a week.

That was the way Paulie always worked things—everyone down the line got paid something. Sometimes when I was working in the pizzeria, there'd be cheese wars, and the prices would drop when vendors competed for business. Fat Larry had a great eye—he could always tell the best cheeses, the ones that tasted good and wouldn't burn too fast when they melted—which is a big deal when you're making pizza. The guys who trucked the cheese would have to pay Paulie something to have the route. So would the guys bringing the canned tomatoes—there were more fights about that. Paulie knew when anybody new came into the neighborhood, and if you were going to deal with us, you had to give him something. But the thing was Paulie was a stand-up guy. Once you were on the payroll, unless you screwed it up yourself, you had a steady gig with him.

Paulie loved Larry's cooking. Even when Paulie went to a round of meetings in the City, and I got to go along and run in and out of his car all day with messages, Larry'd send us off with fresh calzones wrapped in butcher's paper to keep warm. Besides our daily specials at the pizzeria, whatever Paulie wanted Larry would cook for him. One of his crew would call up, "Larry, do some bass," or "Paulie could use a little veal." Or he would make lobster. My mom wouldn't make lobster at home very often, but I ate it a lot with the wiseguys. It was sort of a status symbol, like a Cadillac or Lincoln in the driveway.

Makes

6 calzones.

■■■

Calzone

A calzone is really a pizza made into a sandwich. It uses the same dough, and you can put inside whatever you would put on a pizza. They usually also have ricotta cheese in them, but you can make them without.

1 recipe Fat Larry's Pizza Dough, page 70
2–3 tablespoons olive oil
1 pound Italian sausage, hot, mild, or a mix
15 ounces whole-milk or part-skim ricotta cheese
15 ounces grated packaged mozzarella cheese (3–4 cups)
1 cup freshly grated Parmesan or other hard cheese
¼ cup chopped fresh parsley, or 1 tablespoon dried
¼ cup chopped fresh basil, or 1 tablespoon dried
½ tablespoon garlic powder
1 teaspoon granulated onion or onion powder
1 teaspoon dried oregano
1–1½ teaspoons each salt and pepper (to taste)

Prepare pizza dough and set aside to rise. Heat 1 tablespoon oil in a medium-size skillet over medium heat. Remove sausage from casings and add to pan. Season with ¼ teaspoon salt and ½ teaspoon pepper. Brown meat, breaking it into small pieces and stirring occasionally, until cooked through, about 10–15 minutes. Drain on paper towels. Divide sausage into 6 equal parts.

In a large bowl, mix together the cheeses, parsley, basil, garlic and onion powders, oregano, and salt and pepper to taste.

Preheat oven to highest temperature (probably 500°F). If using a pizza stone, place it on a rack in the middle to upper third of the oven before heating. If using baking sheets, lightly flour two and set aside.

After punching down pizza dough and kneading it 1–2 minutes, divide dough into 6 equal sections. Roll each section into a ball and set aside 5 of them, covered lightly with a towel. Put 6th dough ball on a floured board. Roll dough into a rough 6-inch circle using a rolling pin, and then pushing out to form the final shape. Or you can press dough ball into a rough circle and then pick it up on your two fists and turn, stretching dough gently until it is desired size.

Place ½ cup of cheese mixture on half of the rolled-out dough circle, leaving a ½-inch margin. Sprinkle one-sixth of sausage on top of cheese and top with another ½ cup cheese mixture. Fold the unfilled dough over the filling to make a half circle and pinch or roll edges together to seal well. If using a pizza stone, place the calzone on a pizza peel generously coated with cornmeal. (A pizza peel is a large wooden

If you're adding ingredients like spinach, make sure to cook beforehand and get all the moisture out of them you can or it'll make the calzone mushy.

Even though the broil setting on an oven is even hotter than 500°F, don't use it—it will only cook the top of the calzones, and will probably burn them too.

spatula-type object you can also get at a cooking store. They often sell pizza stones and peels in the same package.) If using baking sheets, place calzone on one of the prepared sheets, leaving room for two more calzones. Make two or three 1½-inch slits in the top of calzone.

Prepare two more calzones in the same way. When three are ready, brush the tops lightly with olive oil. If using a pizza stone, slide calzones off the pizza peel and onto the stone, pulling the peel away with a quick jerk. If using baking sheets, place sheet in oven. Bake calzones 20–25 minutes, checking at 15 to make sure they aren't browning too rapidly. If so, cover lightly with aluminum foil.

While first three calzones are baking, prepare the remaining three in the same way as the first.

Serves 4.

Striped Bass or Bluefish for Paulie

Striped bass is one of the best-tasting East Coast fish, and bluefish is a close second. On the West Coast they farm-raise striped bass, which is a little milder. You can use this recipe for almost any whole fish. To cut the "fishiness" of some fish, like red snapper, soak it first in milk (see recipe, page 69).

When topping fish or meat with oil or liquids and spices, always put on oil or liquids first and then spices, or the spices will get washed off.

Most stores sell whole fish scaled and gutted or will do it for you if you ask. If you're cooking fillets instead of whole fish, see variation below.

1 whole 3–4-pound striped bass or bluefish, scaled and gutted but
    with head and tail left on
2 cups milk for soaking (optional)
4 tablespoons olive oil
Juice of ½ lemon + ½ lemon, sliced thin
3 cloves of garlic, minced
2 large russet or red potatoes (optional)
¼ cup chopped fresh Italian parsley
1 teaspoon dried oregano
½ teaspoon salt
¼ teaspoon black pepper
1 medium brown or white onion, peeled and sliced
Lemon wedges for serving

If soaking fish, rinse it well and place in shallow dish. Add milk and soak half an hour in refrigerator, turning once or twice. Remove from milk and drain.

Preheat oven to 350°F. Oil bottom of a baking dish large enough to accommodate fish with 2 tablespoons olive oil and place fish in dish. Cover top of fish with 1 tablespoon olive oil and lemon juice. Peel and thinly slice potatoes (if using) and toss in a bowl with 1 tablespoon oil, half the garlic, parsley and oregano, and a dash of salt and pepper. Scatter around fish in baking dish. Top fish with a single layer of onion and lemon slices and sprinkle with remaining garlic, parsley, oregano, salt and pepper. Cover dish with foil and bake 20 minutes. Remove foil and stir potatoes. Continue to bake 15–20 minutes, depending on size of the fish. Serve fish whole on a platter with lemon slices arranged on top and with potatoes, onion slices, and lemon wedges around it.

Variation for fillets:

Use 2–3 pounds fish fillets. All other amounts are the same as above.

Preheat oven to 350°F. Peel and thinly slice potatoes (if using) and toss in a bowl with 1 tablespoon oil; half the garlic, parsley, and oregano; and a dash of salt and pepper. Place potatoes in oiled baking dish, spreading to cover bottom of dish. Bake in oven about 10–12 minutes.

Place fish fillets (skin side down) on top of potatoes. Drizzle fish with 1 tablespoon oil and the lemon juice and the remaining garlic, parsley, oregano, and salt and pepper. Top with a layer of sliced onions and lemon slices. Cover dish with foil and bake 10 minutes.

After 10 minutes, check pan. Loosen any potatoes that are stuck to the bottom and spoon them over fish. Return to oven and bake another 4–6 minutes, depending on thickness of fillets. Serve as above.

FAT LARRY

The pizza Larry made for the paying customers was excellent! You have to make pizza fast, and only in the hottest oven you can get without burning it. I found out later on how hard it is to make in a normal oven. It doesn't matter what kind of crust you have, the thick Sicilian or the regular thin one, it will burn on the edges and still be underdone in the middle if you can't get the right oven temperature. Larry used pizza stones, which were really asbestos tiles, or pizza screens, or sometimes he'd just move the pizza from the wooden pallet right onto the oven shelf. You just had to sprinkle cornmeal or flour on the pallet before the dough went on so it'd slide off into the oven. See page 220 for my Cookin' on the Run version of pizza dough—it really works! But here, let me give you the real-deal pizza doughs and some of the dishes I learned from Larry.

Fat Larry's Pizza Dough

Basic pizza dough and Italian bread dough often have the same ingredients, you just treat them differently. I can remember times my mom forgot to make pizza dough. She'd send me racing to the baker's before he closed to get bread dough to use instead.

There are a thousand variations on how to make pizza dough. Some add sugar or honey, some use lard or Crisco instead of olive oil, some add milk or an egg. You can let the dough rise very slowly in the refrigerator, leave it on the counter, or even put it in a low-heated oven to make it rise faster. At the pizzeria, we sometimes used what they call a dough retardant to keep it from being ready too soon.

The recipe here is very simple—no sweeteners and only one rising. The same dough is used for Neapolitan style with a thin crust, or the thicker-crusted Sicilian.

1 package dry yeast (2½ teaspoons)
1–1½ cups lukewarm water
3–3½ cups unbleached flour, sifted
1 tablespoon + 1 teaspoon regular olive oil
1–2 teaspoons extra virgin olive oil
2 teaspoons salt
¼ teaspoon dried oregano
1 tablespoon chopped fresh parsley

In a large bowl, dissolve yeast in ¼ cup lukewarm water. Let sit for 10 minutes until it begins to be foamy. Add one cup flour and stir well. Add an additional 1½ cups of flour and ½ cup of water and mix again. Mix in 1 tablespoon of regular olive oil and the salt, ½ cup water, and an additional ¼ cup of flour. The dough should form a ball and be a little sticky. Add more flour or water if it's either too wet or too dry. By this point, you'll probably be using your hands to mix it.

Sprinkle some of the remaining flour onto a board and knead dough on it 8–10 minutes, until smooth and elastic. Form dough into a ball. Oil a large clean bowl with 1 teaspoon regular olive oil and place dough in it, turning so all sides are lightly oiled. Cover with a towel and put in a warm place to rise until doubled in bulk, about 2 hours.

Punch down dough with your fist, turn onto floured board and knead 1–2 minutes. Form dough into either 2 or 4 evenly sized balls, depending on what size pizza you wish to make (either two 12-inch or four 8-inch pizzas). At this point you can freeze the dough balls up to a month, individually well wrapped in plastic. Proceed with unfrozen dough as described below.

Preheat the oven to the highest baking temperature you can (which is probably about 500°F—don't use the broil setting). If you are using a pizza stone (which is really a heavy tile they sell at cooking stores), place it in the oven before heating.

To make the 2 larger crusts: roll out one crust at a time. Place one dough ball back in the bowl and the other on the floured board. (If using a pizza stone, place the dough you are going to roll out on a pizza peel generously coated with cornmeal. Proceed on the pizza peel as you would on the floured board.) Let the dough on the board sit a few minutes—it will be easier to roll out. Roll dough into a rough circle using a rolling pin, and then pushing out to form the final shape, making a slightly thicker rim around the edge. Or you can press dough ball into a rough circle, and then pick it up on your two fists and turn, stretching dough gently until it is desired thinness. Finish shaping on floured board. For thin-crusted pizza, make dough about ¼-inch thick. For Sicilian, about ½ to ¾-inch thick (see below).

If using a pizza stone, put whatever toppings you are using on crust, then put pizza on stone by sliding the pizza peel out with a quick jerk so pizza slides onto the stone. Cook 15–20 minutes.

If baking pizza in a pizza pan or on a baking sheet, lightly oil pizza

HENRY'S NOTES AND TIPS

If you're going to have a lot of toppings, you may wish to prebake the crust a few minutes. This is because in a regular oven not all the ingredients will cook through at the same time and you may end up with a soggy center. (You need a much higher temperature for all the ingredients to get cooked at once.) But don't cook dough more than 3 minutes before adding toppings or it'll get too done. Also, don't roll out dough too thin that's going to have a lot of toppings—I'd make them an inch less in size than described above.

Again depending on toppings, you may want to sprinkle the pizza with different herbs just before you serve it. For example, if you're making a "Designer" Pizza (see recipe on page 76) that has cilantro, sprinkle with a little cilantro at the end instead of parsley and oregano.

CLASSIC PIZZA TOPPINGS
▪▪

The most basic pizza topping is tomato sauce and mozzarella cheese, with a bit of Parmesan and herbs on top. This is often called Pizza Margherita, after Queen Margherita, who it was supposed to have been created for. Traditional pizza toppings to an Italian American range from meats like pepperoni, sausage, sliced meatballs, prosciutto, to spinach, mushrooms, onions, fresh red, green, or yellow peppers, black olives, anchovies, capers, artichoke hearts, and fresh garlic in any way—sliced, slivered, roasted, minced.

pan or sheet and place formed dough on it, adjusting shape to final form you want. Add desired topping and bake 15–20 minutes.

For Sicilian pizza, divide into 2 larger dough balls. Roll out dough no less than ½-inch thick. Proceed as described above for pizza stone or pan baking. The traditional way to cook Sicilian pizza is in a lightly oiled rectangular 9 × 13-inch pan, rolling it into a basic rectangle and then shaping it to fit inside the pan with your hands. Because of the thickness, bake 20–25 minutes with its toppings.

While first pizza is cooking, repeat process with second ball of dough.

Just before serving, sprinkle each pizza with half the parsley and oregano and drizzle with extra virgin olive oil. This gives you a lovely bit of herb and olive flavor right up front.

▪▪

Pizza Sauce

At the pizzeria, we had a tomato grinder. We used canned plum tomatoes and ran them through the grinder to crush them. Most people don't have that kind of kitchen equipment.

Today I make pizza sauce using my recipe for Basic Tomato Sauce on page 13, with one difference: I use either canned crushed tomatoes or, if I use canned whole tomatoes, I drain and chop them in small dice before cooking (but still add the juice from the can). You can use a blender or food processor to chop the tomatoes, but process them only a few seconds or it'll ruin their texture.

To make the sauce thicker, cook uncovered at least 1 hour.

Makes enough sauce for 4 large pizzas (½ to ¾ cup of sauce per pizza).

■■■

Makes

1 large pizza,

about 8 slices.

Pizza Margherita

One 12-inch pizza crust (see recipe on page 70)
½–¾ cup pizza sauce (see recipe above)
½ cup grated mozzarella
3 tablespoons freshly grated Parmesan or Romano cheese
¼–½ teaspoon dried oregano
1 tablespoon chopped fresh parsley leaves
Extra virgin olive oil for drizzling
6–8 whole fresh basil leaves

Follow directions for pizza crust on page 70. Heat oven to its highest setting. When crust is ready to bake, top with a thin layer of pizza sauce, leaving ¼ inch of the edge of the crust unsauced. Sprinkle evenly with mozzarella, Parmesan or Romano, ¼ teaspoon oregano, and ½ table-

HENRY'S NOTES AND TIPS	You may have to adjust the amount of spices you put on your pizza according to your toppings. Like if you're using fresh tomato, I'd add a bit more oregano. And remember, things like tomato, artichoke hearts, and spinach will give off liquid as they cook, so dry them as well as possible before using. The same goes for fresh tomatoes—slice them very thin and pat dry before cooking.

spoon parsley leaves. Bake pizza 15–20 minutes. Just before serving, sprinkle with remaining oregano and parsley, drizzle with extra virgin olive oil and scatter with basil leaves. Slice and serve.

■■

Other Traditional Pizza Toppings

There are many things you can add to a Pizza Margherita for toppings. Italians top pizzas with all kinds of things, even sliced potatoes, which I've never used. Add whatever herbs you like to these ingredients. I love oregano on pizza, but thyme and basil are also very good.

¼–½ pound mild or spicy Italian sausage, crumbled and sautéed in
    1 tablespoon olive oil until cooked through and drained on
    paper towels
¼ pound sliced pepperoni
2 meatballs, sliced (see page 38 for Milly's Meatballs recipe)
2 ounces thinly sliced prosciutto
½ green, red, or yellow pepper, trimmed, seeded, and thinly sliced
    lengthwise
2–4 ounces cleaned and sliced fresh mushrooms
1 cup stemmed spinach leaves, rinsed, dried well, and torn in large
    pieces
½ thinly sliced red or brown onion (½ cup)
4 anchovies, rinsed and cut in large pieces
4–6 cloves of garlic, peeled and thinly sliced
¼ cup sliced black olives
¼ cup marinated artichoke hearts, rinsed, dried, and sliced
½ very thinly sliced large fresh tomato
Thinly sliced zucchini and fresh thyme sprigs

Prepare Pizza Margherita as described above, topping with desired additions before sprinkling with herbs. Bake 15–20 minutes.

"Designer" Pizza

Okay, I could write a whole book about the new pizzas that are around. Nowadays you can top a pizza with almost anything you want— from smoked salmon and caviar to ham and pineapple.

A whole group of traditional Italian pizzas don't start with a tomato sauce base. They're called *pizza bianco*. Italians have always topped pizzas with different kinds of seafood too—shrimp, clams, mussels, scallops, and some they'd cover with vegetables like broccoli or zucchini.

Modern pizzamakers simply expanded the list to include even more possibilities from their varied ethnic backgrounds. They have gotten so creative that it's really a different dish than I grew up eating and making in Brooklyn.

Some of the combos are interesting, some I wouldn't eat if you paid me (well, I might take a bite for a few bucks). I won't even pretend to list all the possibilities, but here's a couple of designer pizzas that look tasty. If you're into making up your own, remember that some things will need to be precooked a bit because they won't cook through in the short time a pizza is in the oven. Like asparagus or broccoli would need to be boiled a minute or two (blanched) and drained before using.

2 roasted red and yellow peppers, ¼ cup goat cheese, ¼ pound sliced onions, ¼ pound cleaned and horizontally sliced shrimp, ¼ cup sliced fresh cilantro

4-cheese pizza—¼ cup each gorgonzola, fontina, cheddar, and mozzarella

½ cup grilled eggplant slices with ¼ cup toasted pine nuts and mozzarella

Asparagus spears with fresh goat cheese and slivered sundried tomatoes (packed in oil or softened in hot water and drained)

No tomato sauce, but basil pesto in its place, horizontally sliced scallops, roasted garlic cloves, and fresh parsley

Smoked salmon, sour cream, caviar, and fresh chives (à la Wolfgang Puck)

CRAP GAME HEROS

When I was still thirteen, my hustling got me another food gig—doing sandwiches and heros for the big Brooklyn crap games. These games would be thirty to forty people at a time, from all walks of life: from dentists to bookies to wiseguys from other families. The guys running the games were professionals just like in Atlantic City, and Paulie and his brothers were in charge of the money. One of my jobs was driving limos for the players so they wouldn't get robbed by local thugs.

At first I bought sandwiches and heros from Al and Evelyn's deli and delivered them to the games for tips. But then I saw an angle: I'd earn more if I made them myself. So I did—damn good sandwiches, too. But after a few weeks, Al and Evelyn saw how much their business had dropped off and got wise. They offered me a deal—they'd give me a nickel for every dollar they got from the games. I didn't respond right away, so they upped it to seven cents. I had my first kickback! And I deserved it, 'cause I could make a great hero.

■■■

Makes two 6-inch

or six 2-inch

sandwiches.

Henry's Kickback Antipasti Hero

One 12-inch good quality baguette
3 tablespoons mustard
3 ounces sliced salami
¼ pound sliced provolone cheese
3 roasted red peppers, peeled, seeded, and sliced lengthwise in wide
   strips
12 black olives, sliced
10–12 fresh basil leaves, stemmed
6 ounces marinated artichoke hearts, sliced
Salt and black pepper

Slice the baguette lengthwise, cutting off about the top one-third of it. Partially hollow out the larger bottom piece to make room for the

Make sure you remove part of the bread before filling. Otherwise, the sandwich is hard to keep together and even harder to get your mouth around.

If you don't have the time, you can serve the hero right when you make it. But it's much better with the refrigeration time.

Use whatever cold cuts and cheeses you like. Improvise!

filling by removing some of the bread inside. You can do this by either cutting it out with a small knife or simply pulling out some bread with your hands. Spread approximately 2 tablespoons of mustard on the bottom portion and 1 tablespoon on the top. Layer remaining ingredients in larger section of bread, seasoning lightly with salt and pepper halfway through the layering process and at the end. Top with smaller piece of bread and push sandwich together firmly. Wrap tightly in plastic wrap and refrigerate 2–4 hours to allow flavors to meld. Cut crosswise in whatever size you want, 2, 4, or 6 inches.

GOING OUT

I didn't spend all my time as a teenager with the big guys. I hung out after hours with Paulie's son Lenny, and some of the Peters and Pauls—almost every wiseguy had sons named Peter and Paul and a daughter named Marie. We were pretty wild, on the loose at fourteen or fifteen, too much energy, too many ideas. I remember coming out of the local nightclub at dawn, totally drunk, knowing I was headed for a beating if I didn't sober up. Just around the corner was Rose's bakery, where Fat Larry worked when he wasn't at the pizzeria. If we timed it right, we'd come rolling out of the club to the smell of fresh-baked bread, just out of the oven. We'd charge into the place and gorge ourselves, slathering the warm bread with olive oil and butter. Nothing could've tasted better. And I'd go home sober as a judge. Almost.

When I started dating, I'd take a girl into Manhattan to really impress her. Little Italy was a big hit. We'd go to Vincent's on Mott Street, a.k.a. Vincent's Clam Bar, and get their great half a loaf of bread "biscuit" and fried seafood. Their sauce is one in a million, but only a true tough guy can handle the hot version. The biscuits are hard as rocks, you could break windows with them. Until you cover them with the seafood and sauce. Then they soften up just right without turning to mush.

In the fall I'd take a special girl to the San Gennaro festival. It's so romantic. They close down the streets to traffic in Little Italy, and it's like a big carnival, booth after booth of things to buy and games to play—loads of fun. And the food! Italy has a big tradition of foods for festivals. Like sausage-and-pepper heros. Every Italian grandmother makes sausage and peppers. At the festival they put it on a nice roll so you can carry it around. The taste takes you back. Or *arancini*, rice balls, which my mom used to make for hot antipasto. You roll leftover risotto into balls the size of oranges, stuff them, then dip them in egg and bread crumbs and fry until they're golden. You can stuff them with whatever you want, enough prosciutto to choke a horse and a bunch of vegetables and cheese, or simply one cube of mozzarella. And there's *sfingi*—they're like yeast donuts coated in powdered sugar. They take no time to cook, so the vendors make tons of them and load them into big plastic bags. We'd buy a bag while they were still warm, the powdered sugar melting into the dough.

■■

Makes

1 sandwich.

Sausage and Pepper Hero

A sausage-and-pepper hero is the essence of Italian-American festival food. I can't imagine San Gennaro without the smell of the sausage, peppers, and onions frying together on a grill. It's not diet food, but it's so satisfying.

1 foot-long Italian hero roll
½ large onion (any kind), sliced thin
½ green pepper, sliced lengthwise in strips
1 tablespoon olive oil
¼–½ teaspoon each salt and black pepper (to taste)
2 Italian sausages, mild or spicy (according to your taste)

You can add some grated cheese like fontina or provolone to the hero if you want—I like mine plain.

Preheat a grill or heat oven to broil.

Slice hero roll down the middle and toast lightly if you want. Set aside.

Toss onions and peppers with olive oil and a bit of salt and pepper and place in a grill pan or on a cookie sheet lined with aluminum foil. Cook until just wilting—about 1–2 minutes. Remove from pan and set aside.

Poke a few holes in the sausages and place them in grill pan or on cookie sheet. Cook, turning, until no longer pink inside (5 minutes per side). Return onions and peppers to pan with sausage and reheat, tossing carefully. Place mixture in sliced hero roll and serve.

Makes about

8 arancini.

Arancini

Arancini are made of leftover risotto formed into balls and stuffed with any number of things, from a cube of mozzarella to almost a full course of chopped meat and vegetables. The name *arancini* comes from their shape and size—they look like small oranges. I like the simple ones my mom used to make for holidays with just mozzarella inside. Risotto is definitely a Northern Italian dish—she must have picked up risotto from a Northern Italian friend in the neighborhood.

HENRY'S

NOTES

AND TIPS

Try to keep the oil at an even temperature. You may have to move the pan off the burner if it gets too hot before continuing cooking.

If some of the bread crumbs fall off into the oil, remove them or they'll turn black and burn.

2 cups regular olive oil
2–3 cups plain bread crumbs
4 eggs, beaten
1 recipe Basic Risotto (see below), chilled
½ pound aged mozzarella, cut in ½" cubes

Heat oil in a large skillet. The oil should be about 1 inch deep. Heat until hot but not smoking.

Put the bread crumbs on a plate and place bowl of beaten eggs nearby.

Fill your palm with about ¼ cup risotto and make a small cup. Place a cube of mozzarella in the center, top with an additional ¼ cup of risotto and seal the edges so the cheese is entirely enclosed in rice. Carefully roll the rice cake until it is a ball, about the size of a small orange. Set aside. Repeat with remaining risotto and cheese until all are made into rice balls.

Dip rice balls in first the egg, then the bread crumbs, and slide into hot oil. Fry rice balls a few at a time until they turn golden brown, turning carefully, and remove to paper towels to drain. Repeat with remaining rice balls.

Serves 4.

Basic Risotto

This is the traditional way to make risotto, the one where you have to stir it a lot while it's cooking. It makes a creamy rice dish that is unlike any other. But if you don't have the time, feel free to use my microwave version, page 276. It'll still be very tasty.

6–8 cups chicken broth (or beef broth if you prefer)
¼ cup olive oil
2 tablespoons unsalted butter
¼ cup chopped onion
1 cup Arborio or other rice, unrinsed
½ cup freshly grated Parmesan or Romano cheese
½ teaspoon each salt and pepper (to taste)

Once you start adding the broth to the rice, the mixture should never get completely dry—the rice should be "swimming" a little. This makes the risotto nice and tender.

Heat broth in a medium-size pot and keep at a simmer on a back burner.

In a large nonstick or regular pot, heat olive oil over medium heat and add butter (do not brown the butter). Add onion and cook, stirring occasionally until onion is translucent, about 5 minutes. Add rice and cook, stirring and tossing, 1–2 minutes. Lower heat to medium low.

Add ½ cup heated broth and cook, stirring constantly until most of the liquid is absorbed into the rice. When the liquid is almost gone, add another ½ cup liquid and repeat the cooking/stirring process. Continue adding liquid, cooking/stirring until the rice is al dente, or almost ready to eat, which should be another 2–3 additions of liquid.

Add an additional ¼ cup of broth when rice is almost ready to eat. Stir well and add cheese and salt and pepper to taste. The rice should be soft but still in a broth that is creamy—not all the liquid should be absorbed. Serve immediately, with additional cheese if desired.

Makes about

2 dozen.

Sfingi

One ¼-ounce packet of dried yeast
¼ cup warm water
2 tablespoons unsalted butter, softened
½ cup sugar
1½ cups milk (any kind but nonfat), warmed
2 beaten eggs
3 cups unbleached flour, sifted
1 teaspoon salt
Canola oil for deep frying (about 3–4 cups)
1–2 cups confectioner's sugar, sifted

Dissolve the yeast in the warm water in a small bowl. Allow it to sit for 5 minutes until foamy on top.

Cream together softened butter and sugar in a large bowl. Stir in warmed milk and yeast, stirring gently to dissolve. Add beaten eggs and combine well.

Mix together sifted flour and salt in a medium-size bowl. Then add the flour mixture one cup at a time to the liquids, mixing well with each addition. Cover the bowl with a towel and allow to rise in a warm place for 1–1½ hours, until puffy.

Heat oil in a deep pan (there should be about 4 inches of oil) to hot but not smoking (when it's ready a drop of water will "spit" when dropped in the oil). Drop by tablespoons into the hot oil and fry, turning, until deep golden brown. Remove and drain on paper towels.

As soon as possible, dust with sifted confectioner's sugar, tossing so *sfingis* are coated on all sides, and serve. Eat while warm or room temperature.

Chapter Three

The Army and Cooking School

■■

I joined the Army when I was seventeen. It was the only way I could figure to get out of a big jam with my father. I'd been loaning my father's
gun to Tuddy at the cab stand and sneaking it back into the house after
he'd used it, but my dad found out. I knew I was in bigger trouble than
I'd ever been with him. So I went to the recruitment office and signed
up for the paratroopers.

My dad was so proud. He thought I'd finally come to my senses, that
I was through with "those bums" at the cab stand.

The wiseguys, on the other hand, thought I was nuts. Why would I
want to leave the crew and go pandy to some stupid sergeant? They
thought like Sonny who lectures his younger brother Michael in *God-
father II* about guys who enlist, "They're saps because they risk their life
for strangers."

It was my first time away from home—ever. What can I say? I was
young and adventurous, I loved every minute of it, even basic training.
To be a paratrooper, they send you to jump school. What a thrill! I was
crazy about jumping out of planes! Yeah, I probably *was* nuts.

When I finished training, they assigned me to the 82nd Airborne in
Fort Bragg, North Carolina. The first day I was there, I was on line for
chow and spotted the mess sergeant serving at the end. I'd already
noticed that cooks got special treatment. So when I got to him I asked

if he needed any cooks. He looked at me hard and said, "You ever been in a kitchen?"

I almost laughed at the guy. Had I ever been in a kitchen? Puh-leese!

But of course he didn't know jack about me. So I filled him in on my background at home and in the pizzeria, and he took me on. His one condition was I had to go back to school, to "learn the basics."

So back to school I went.

The cooking school was like an eight-week commercial course. It was a straightforward restaurant school, not a fancy chef place. It was terrific for me. Though I had lots of hands-on experience, I'd never learned the basics—like the right temperature to cook different meats, all the sauces, which spices go with what. I was into it. They taught us some complicated stuff too, like ice sculptures for buffets—ask me how much I've used that skill.

I also learned how to bake, which I'd never done. When I was growing up, my mother and sisters did all the baking. It was a lot of work and took forever. I was never interested—who had the time? Even my sisters agreed it was a pain in the ass. Other than my mom making bread, they usually just made treats for holidays. The rest of the time they'd get Aunt Nina to stop by the local bakery and pick up a few items.

My favorite thing when I was young was sneaking some of those goodies Aunt Nina brought before dinner. I loved to grab 'em right from under my mother's nose and get away with it. Mom'd be stirring the sauce, giving me jobs to do, and I'd be working away, but all the while my hand was slipping unnoticed in and out of the pastry box. When it came dessert time, I'd try to sneak out, but mostly I'd catch holy hell.

Cannoli

Cannoli Shells

3⅓ cups sifted unbleached flour + additional for rolling
4 tablespoons cold butter, lightly softened
2 tablespoons Marsala wine
1 cup water
Light oil for deep frying
3 egg whites, beaten

Filling and Decoration

32 ounces mascarpone cheese
8 ounces ricotta cheese
½–¾ cup sugar (to taste)
2 teaspoons rum or flavored extract of your choice
8–16 ounces semi- or bittersweet grated chocolate
16 ounces unsalted unshelled pistachios
½ cup confectioner's sugar for dusting

To make the filling:

Combine cheeses and sugar to taste (start with ½ cup) and rum or extract in the bowl of an electric mixer and blend, using the whip attachment, until mixture begins to look smooth, approximately 2 minutes. Grate or shave approximately 8 ounces of chocolate and fold approxi-

HENRY'S **NOTES** **AND TIPS**	It is important to seal the dough before deep frying or the cannoli will fall apart in the hot oil, and you'll have butterflies instead of tubes (though I have found these "mistakes" disappear very fast, especially if you coat them with confectioner's sugar).

mately 4 ounces into the cheese mixture. Set aside. If you are not finishing the cannoli until the next day, cover and refrigerate.

To make the cannoli shells:

Place flour and butter in the bowl of an electric mixer (or if you don't have a mixer, in a large bowl). Using the paddle attachment, beat on medium speed until the mixture resembles small pebbles, approximately 2 minutes (a fork works well if you're doing this by hand). Gradually add Marsala wine and water. The dough should be moist but not sticking to your hands. Cover the bowl with a paper towel and let dough sit for 5 minutes.

In a large pot, heat oil for deep frying. The oil is ready to use when a small piece of dough dropped in it sizzles and rises to the surface immediately.

Lightly flour a cutting board and rolling pin (or whatever you are using—a spare cannoli tube, for example). Break off a small piece of dough and roll out on the board. With a sharp knife, cut a 3-inch square in the dough and return the scraps to the original piece of dough. Roll the square thinner, trim into a 3-inch square again, and continue rolling and trimming until the dough is nearly translucent (you can almost see through it). Turn dough square so its corners are north, south, east, and west, like a diamond. Lightly oil a cannoli tube, and place it horizontally on the square. Bring the north and south corners together over the tube, overlap them and rub together to seal lightly. Brush the overlapped section with egg white and rub again to make sure the seal is complete.

Holding the dough-covered tube with tongs, carefully slide the cannoli into the hot oil (watch for hot oil splatters!). Allow to cook until light brown (they will be partially cooked). At first this will only take about 2 minutes. The time will get shorter for remaining batches.

Remove cannoli tubes to paper towels to drain. Let cool slightly, then slide the cannoli off the tube carefully by holding one end of the tube with a pot holder and quickly gliding the shell off (don't burn yourself in the process). Return the tubes of dough to the oil to finish cooking until golden brown on all sides, then remove with tongs to cool and drain on paper towels. You can fill shells as soon as they are cool, or let them sit uncovered overnight (this will make them crisper).

To assemble cannoli:

Fill a large pastry bag fitted with a large star tip halfway full with filling for cannoli. Pipe the mixture into cannoli shell from both ends until full, finishing with a star of the mixture on both ends. Dip ends in either grated pistachios or finely grated chocolate and dust the top with confectioner's sugar before serving.

Sicilian Easter Bread with Colored Eggs

This bread was always the centerpiece for the Easter dinner table. My mom would also insist they make small crosses and little nests that would hold only one egg. It used to drive my sisters crazy.

> 5 or 6 pretty Easter-colored hardboiled eggs
> 2 packets dry yeast
> ½ cup warm water
> 1 cup sugar
> ¾ cup butter, softened + additional for greasing
> 1 teaspoon salt
> Zest of one lemon, minced or grated
> 6 eggs, 3 of them separated, reserving both yolks and whites
> 5 cups of flour
> ½ cup scalded milk, room temperature

Dissolve yeast in warm water and stir in a teaspoon of sugar. Let stand about 15 minutes.

Cream butter and sugar and add salt and lemon zest. Beat mixture until fluffy. Add 3 eggs and 3 yolks one at a time. Add yeast mixture. Add flour a little at a time, beating, and continue adding until mixture is stiff (you may not need all the flour).

Form mixture into a ball and knead about 15 minutes until the dough is very smooth. Place the dough ball in a buttered bowl and let rise until dough has doubled (about 1 hour). Punch down dough and knead 5 minutes. Form mixture into a ball again and place the dough ball in the bowl. Let rise again until it has doubled a second time (about 1 hour).

Preheat oven to 325°F. Butter a large cookie sheet. Separate dough into 3 parts. Shape each part into a rope about 25–30 inches long. Line the ropes up next to each other on the pan. Starting at the top, gently braid the dough ropes together and then curve the braid into a ring shape. Try not to pull or stretch the dough as you braid. Close the ring by pinching dough ends together. Position the colored eggs all around the braid where the strands cross. Gently separate the braid a bit so the eggs can fit—you want the bread to hold the egg in place. Lightly brush the entire bread, including the colored eggs, with lightly beaten egg whites. (The egg whites limit the amount of dye that runs onto the dough and make the baked bread golden brown.)

Bake about 45–50 minutes until bread is golden brown.

■■

Makes

3 dozen cookies.

Italian Yeast Cookies

My mother used to make what my niece called "cookies for all the nuns" on holidays or any day she felt she needed atonement (which she never needed, but who can tell what she felt she'd done wrong!). This is close to the cookies she gave them, a recipe from the Sicilian grandmother of a friend who grew up in the U.S. of A.

1 stick unsalted butter
½ cup vegetable shortening like Crisco
2½–2¾ cups sifted all-purpose flour
¼ cup warm milk
1 teaspoon sugar
1 teaspoon vanilla
½ fresh yeast cake
1 egg, beaten
½ pound confectioner's sugar

You may want to bake just a few cookies first to see how long is right for your oven.

Place butter and shortening in a large bowl with 2½ cups of the flour. Using two knives, cut butter and shortening into the flour by slicing them into it until the mixture is fine as cornmeal. Or you can place flour, butter, and shortening in a food processor and pulse until it resembles the texture of cornmeal.

Combine milk, sugar, and vanilla in separate bowl. Stir in yeast until it is dissolved. Add yeast liquid to flour mixture. Add egg and beat. If mixture is very soft, add a bit more flour.

Knead dough briefly. Let it rise until double in bulk (about 2 hours).

(NOTE: When it rises, dough will not be smooth and elastic like bread dough, but a little cracked on top.)

Preheat oven to 375°F.

Coat cutting board with a layer of powdered sugar.

Break off pieces of dough about the size of a small golf ball. Roll each piece of dough in sugar and place on the cutting board. Shape into a crescent by rolling back and forth under your palm until dough lengthens into a tube about ½ inch high and 2 inches long. It should be a bit thicker in the middle. Bend the ends of dough toward each other to form the crescent shape. Add more sugar if necessary, but not too much or the dough will fall apart.

Place each crescent as it is formed on a greased baking sheet. When baking sheet is full, bake cookies for 12–15 minutes. Check at 12 minutes so you don't overbake.

Serves

about 10.

Ricotta Cheesecake

This is not like American cheesecake—it's not as sweet and has less calories. It doesn't even need a crust, which saves you time.

Butter and flour to prepare a 9- to 10-inch springform pan
1½ pounds ricotta cheese (regular or lowfat)
1 cup sugar
3 tablespoons flour
3 eggs
1 teaspoon vanilla extract
1 teaspoon grated lemon zest
1 teaspoon grated orange zest
½ cup golden raisins (optional)

Preheat oven to 300°F.

Butter and flour the springform pan and set aside. For the smoothest ricotta, place cheese in batches in a blender and blend 1 minute, then push through a sieve into a large bowl. Or you can use an electric mixer and beat on low-medium speed 1–2 minutes before putting cheese through the sieve. (Don't beat too long or cheese will get too much air in it.)

Combine sugar and flour in a small bowl and stir into ricotta, mixing very well. Add eggs one at a time, stirring thoroughly after each addition. Add vanilla and lemon and orange zests, then gently fold in optional raisins.

Pour mixture into the prepared pan, using a rubber scraper to clean the bowl. Bake 1¼ hours, or until the top is a light golden brown. Remove from oven and let cool to room temperature. Cover with plastic wrap and refrigerate until thoroughly chilled.

Just before serving, remove sides of pan and slice.

You can make this two days ahead—it'll keep fine in the refrigerator.

HENRY'S NOTES AND TIPS

Italian Macaroons

(Amaretti)

This is what the classic macaroon you can buy at any number of Italian delis comes from. The difference is these are fresh and soft, and don't need to be dipped anywhere to taste great.

7 ounces almond paste
1 cup sugar
2 medium beaten egg whites
½ teaspoon almond extract
½ cup granulated sugar for dusting
⅛–¼ cup flour

Preheat oven to 350°F. Line a cookie sheet with parchment paper and dust lightly with flour.

Break almond paste into small pieces and place in a mixing bowl. Using the paddle attachment, combine with sugar, beating on low speed until mixture is very fine granules (about 5 minutes). Add half the egg whites and continue mixing 1–2 minutes. Add remaining egg whites and mix another 1 minute. Add almond extract and mix briefly to combine evenly.

Cut off one corner of a sealable plastic bag and fill about half full with cookie dough. Pipe dough onto lined cookie sheet in small rounds about ½ to 1 inch in size and ½ inch apart. When sheet is full, wet your fingers and gently press down on each cookie to flatten tops slightly. Do not flatten completely as they will continue to spread out while cooking. Sprinkle each cookie with a bit of granulated sugar.

HENRY'S NOTES AND TIPS	If some cookies refuse to come off the parchment paper, reverse the paper and brush it lightly with water—they should then come off easily. You can use the parchment paper twice for baking, but shake off the old flour and sprinkle it with fresh.

Bake in preheated oven about 15 minutes until cookies are light brown. Remove to a rack and cool completely before peeling off paper. Brush off any excess flour from the bottom of the cookies.

If there is cookie dough remaining, repeat piping/baking process with fresh parchment paper dusted with flour. Store cookies in an airtight tin or plastic container.

LIFE IN THE ARMY

The cooking school was in Virginia, near Fort Lee. My cousin Jimmy happened to be stationed there. And he had a car. While I was in school, we'd bomb up to Brooklyn every weekend. We'd take off as early as we could Fridays and come back as late as we could Sundays. We'd go back to the neighborhood and hook up with the crew, catch up on gossip, go into the City and get juiced, pick fights—the usual. I felt like I was living at home and just visiting the Army.

But after I finished cooking school and returned to Fort Bragg, there were long stretches I was away from Pitkin Ave. First off, I was busy earning. The Army always either overordered or just didn't think. Weekends? Out of 250 guys, half left base on leave. That's 125 steaks for me. I started selling the extra to restaurants in Bennettsville and McColl, little towns across the border in South Carolina. To my mind, I was doing the Army a favor—all the extra they bought was getting used instead of tossed. So what if I was making a few bucks off the deal?

Also, I was having a serious good time with my buddies down there. Truth is, my time in the Army was a romp. I can't begin to tell you the stunts we pulled, the rules we bent. Even the things we were required to do we turned into games.

Like to keep paratrooper status, we had to jump out of a plane once a month. Everybody else's jumps were scheduled, but cooks could go whenever they wanted. And we were allowed to jump "Hollywood style," which means we didn't have to carry our gear, just our rifles. The other dolts would be sitting there miserable, waiting to jump with a couple hundred pounds on their backs—watching us fool around, free as birds. We clowned the whole time. We'd hook guys to the plane without them knowing it, we'd tie our chutes together and jump as a pack. Danger? Never heard of it.

I had an Army pal named Joe Palozzi. We had a lot of adventures together. We were both cooks and were often on the same shift. We were both part Italian, and both our families had eight kids. We did some crazy things.

We hitchhiked everywhere. After our shift one night, we just started hitching and ended up in a town in South Carolina called McColl. It was about fifty miles from Fort Bragg. We went to a bar and ended up having a great time, getting drunk, meeting some girls. Somehow we got back in time for our next shift.

But once we started going to McColl, we went every night. We'd wake up hungover, and Joe would swear, "I'm not going there tonight, not tonight, I'm gonna get some rest tonight." And every night, we'd end up down in McColl. We used to "borrow" the sergeant's car sometimes. Or we knew this real doofus who had a car. We bribed him to drive us to McColl with promises of girls, girls, girls. He was salivating.

When we got there, we fixed the doofus up with Mona, the owner of the bar where we hung out. But later when we looked around, the kid had disappeared. I feared the worst—he'd been dragged upstairs by the proprietor. But no, we finally found him hanging face down over the propane tank outside, half frozen. He must have gone out to pee and was so drunk he never made it back. Believe me, he was lucky to escape Mona.

On weekends, we'd go to Myrtle Beach, South Carolina. The Strand in Myrtle Beach was where you'd go if you didn't want to go as far as Miami. It was beautiful and undeveloped in those days, virgin territory. We'd go to a high-class club that had a big outdoor patio and dance floor. It was all lit up with paper lanterns. We'd drink and dance the Peppermint Twist for hours. That's right—me, doing the Peppermint Twist. There were tons of girls around, they were coming out our ears. The myth is true—there's nothing like a uniform to attract the broads. We'd finish the evening at a local motel with any number of girls in tow. The room would put us back a whopping seven dollars a night. Joe claimed he screwed every girl in town. Probably did.

What adventures Joe and I had! We were sent on winter maneuvers to Canada, where they tried to teach us how to ski—a total disaster for a Brooklyn boy like me. So we snuck out of the barracks and hitched our way to Montreal. Nobody spoke English, only French. We couldn't understand a word, and we didn't have a dime on us. We tried to hitch back to camp, but it started snowing like crazy. We couldn't see our hands in front of our faces. We were in the middle of nowhere. Finally, we spied a light—there was a tiny store that was open, and the lady took us in for the night. All we could think was how were we gonna tell her that we couldn't pay her.

The next morning, the lady even made breakfast for us. Now we really felt guilty. We finally got up the courage and explained to her (by acting it out) that we had no money. We offered her our dog tags as collateral—when we got back to the base, we'd mail her money, and she would mail back our tags. The lady looked at us, she looked at the tags. Then she showed us a picture of a young man in a uniform—her son was in the army, too! Then she basically tried to say (as far as I could tell) that if he ever needed help, she hoped someone would be kind to him the same way she'd been to us. She even gave us packs of cigarettes. Who'd believe people could be so nice.

Joe and I even went AWOL together. Joe was supposed to get transferred to Germany. He didn't want to go. He tried to get me to smash his leg with a cinderblock so they wouldn't take him, but I couldn't make myself do it. So we hitched down to McColl, and we just stayed. I was seeing this girl down there, and I hid out at her house. Joe stayed with whatever girl he was seeing that night (he told me later he probably saw ten girls in two weeks). Eventually, the local cops picked us up for the MPs. My feet were sticking out from under the curtain or something. Actually, they knew where we were long before they picked us up, but they didn't really care. The longer we were away, the more fines we got, and the more they docked our pay. They threw us in the stockade and took away what stripes we had. But we still had girls flocking to see us every day.

The girl I hid out with was named Peggy. I fell in love with her. Hey, I was what, eighteen, nineteen? Love at that age—do I have to draw you a map?

Peggy was a beautiful American-Indian girl. She had this shiny black hair that went all the way down her back. I was smitten. She was a couple of years older than me, and married to a guy in prison. But I didn't care. I spent every minute I could with her.

She worked at a restaurant/bar that sold whiskey under the counter. She lived in one of those dry southern counties where everybody drinks but nobody admits it. At her bar I met a plumbing contractor I hung out with, a big friendly southern guy. He loved to cruise around all day in his Caddie with his girl and a pal or two getting juiced. It was my type of fun. It reminded me of Brooklyn.

In a few weeks Peggy and I were almost living together. Once again, being a cook had its privileges. Normally, I'd work a twenty-four-hour shift, and then have two days off. So I started pulling double shifts, which meant I had four days in a row to spend with my girl. Yes!

And of course, I was cooking for her. Listen, when it comes to women, all guys are jamokes lookin' for an angle. And Peggy had never tasted anything like my cooking. In the Carolinas in the '60s, "Eye-tal-yun" food consisted of overcooked spaghetti and undercooked pizza. I showed her different. And I don't think it hurt.

Serves 4–6

as an appetizer.

Stuffed Mushrooms

12 ounces fresh medium to large mushrooms
½ cup olive oil + 1 tablespoon for coating pan
1 cup seasoned Italian bread crumbs
1 cup freshly grated Parmesan cheese
½ teaspoon pepper
¼ cup chopped fresh Italian parsley or 1 tablespoon dried
1½ tablespoons finely chopped garlic

Preheat oven to 350°F. Wipe or rinse mushrooms and pat dry. Pull out the stems, leaving caps whole. Use 1 tablespoon olive oil to coat bottom of a baking pan large enough to hold all the mushrooms in one layer (about 8 × 8-inch square or 10-inch round). Place mushroom caps stemmed sides up next to each other in pan.

HENRY'S NOTES AND TIPS

Add an anchovy or two for a stronger flavor. Rinse it in water and mince fine with the garlic. You may also want to drizzle with a bit of lemon juice if you add the anchovies.

Mix together remaining ingredients in a bowl. Cover mushrooms with bread crumb mixture. With a spoon, stuff each mushroom with enough bread crumb mixture to form a small mound covering the entire mushroom. Cover pan with foil and bake in oven 30 minutes or until mushrooms are tender when pierced with a fork. Remove foil, turn oven to broil, and broil mushrooms for 1 minute to crisp top.

Serves 2.

■■

Chicken Breasts Parmigiana with Capellini

6–8 cloves of garlic, minced
½ cup olive oil
One 28-ounce can plum tomatoes
One 28-ounce can crushed tomatoes
12 large fresh basil leaves, torn in large pieces, or 1 tablespoon dried
¼ cup finely chopped fresh Italian parsley or 2 teaspoons to 1
    tablespoon dried
1 tablespoon fresh oregano or 2 teaspoons dried
½ teaspoon each salt and pepper
1 cup flour
1 cup seasoned Italian bread crumbs
2 large beaten eggs
2 skinless boneless chicken breasts (about 1–1½ pounds)
1 cup grated fresh Parmesan or Romano cheese

In a large skillet or medium-large wide pot, cook garlic briefly in olive oil over medium-low heat (do not brown). Add the juice from the canned plum tomatoes to stop the garlic cooking. Crush tomatoes with your hands or chop well on a cutting board and add to the pan. Add crushed tomatoes, basil, parsley, oregano, and half the salt and pepper to sauce. Bring to a boil, stir once thoroughly, then reduce heat to a low simmer. As the acid from the tomatoes flows to the top, skim it off every 10–15 minutes. Check for seasoning and add the rest of the salt and

Heating the cutlets with just the tomato sauce allows the sauce to seep into the cutlets, making them even tastier. The cheese will burn if it's added at the beginning of the baking process.

You'll find flattening chicken cutlets is much easier than flattening veal or beef. It only takes a minute or two.

pepper if desired. If you want a very smooth sauce, purée it in batches very briefly in a food processor—but not too long or the mixture will get air into it and ruin the texture of the tomatoes.

Place flour, bread crumbs and a dash of salt and pepper in a bowl or shallow dish. Beat eggs in a separate bowl, season lightly with salt and pepper and set aside.

Flatten chicken breasts (see page 57 for how to flatten meat). Heat oil in a large skillet until very hot but not smoking. Dip the cutlets first in flour/bread crumb mixture, then in eggs and slip into pan. Sauté until golden brown, turning once. Add more olive oil and reheat if necessary before adding more cutlets. As they cook, remove cutlets to paper towels to drain.

Heat oven to 350°F. Place cutlets in a roasting pan and top with a few tablespoons of tomato sauce. After about 10 minutes, add a sprinkling of grated cheese and continue heating until the cheese melts, about 10 minutes.

Serves 2.

Italian Green Salad and Dressing

I like a very simple salad, like most Italians. Of course you can add whatever you want to a salad, but in my tradition, a salad complements a meal, it doesn't take over.

10 ounces mixed greens—whatever lettuces you want to use
2–3 radishes, washed and trimmed, sliced thin
¼–½ medium-size cucumber, peeled if you like, sliced thin
1 small tomato, sliced or cut in wedges

Don't put the dressing on the salad until just before serving or it'll wilt the greens.

¼ cup extra virgin olive oil
2 tablespoons lemon juice or red wine vinegar
1 teaspoon dried oregano
1 tablespoon fresh parsley leaves, chopped
¼ teaspoon salt and pepper + a few grindings of fresh black pepper

Place greens in a bowl. Top with sliced radishes, cucumbers, and tomatoes.

In a small bowl, whisk together olive oil, vinegar or lemon juice, oregano, parsley, salt, and pepper. Toss dressing with salad, add a little fresh black pepper, and serve immediately.

Serves 10.

Chocolate Walnut Orange Torte

This makes a nice moist cake. For real decadence, serve it with a dollop of whipped cream.

1 stick unsalted butter, softened + extra for greasing pan
¾ cup flour + ⅛ cup for pan
10 ounces semi- or bittersweet chocolate (1¾ cups)
1 teaspoon baking powder
⅛ teaspoon salt
1½ cups chopped walnuts
7 eggs, separated, reserving both yolks and whites
¾ cup sugar
1 tablespoon orange zest
¼–½ cup confectioner's sugar
Whipped cream to serve (optional)

Preheat oven to 350°F.

Butter bottom and sides of a 9-inch round cake pan. Cut out a circle of waxed paper the size of the pan and place in bottom. Butter paper and then coat bottom and sides with flour, tapping pan upside down to remove extra flour.

Break chocolate into pieces (or use chocolate chips) and melt in a double boiler or a small bowl set over a pan of hot water. Stir until smooth and cool to room temperature.

Combine flour, baking powder, salt, chopped walnuts, and orange zest in a bowl.

Using an electric mixer, cream together stick of butter and sugar until slightly fluffy. Add egg yolks one at a time, and beat until pale yellow. Add chocolate mixture and beat 1 minute until well mixed. Stir in flour mixture and combine thoroughly.

Beat egg whites to stiff peaks. Fold into cake mixture. Pour or spoon into prepared pan and bake 1 hour. Cool to room temperature on counter or a wire rack. Place a plate over pan, reverse it, and tap bottom to remove cake onto plate. Place confectioner's sugar in a sieve and shake to cover top of cake. Serve with whipped cream on the side if desired.

DISCHARGED

The end of my Army career was pretty screwed up. I got drunk and started a fight that turned into a huge brawl; and when they called in the sheriff, I snitched his car and drove it all the way to Brooklyn. Not smart. My last days in the Army were spent in the brig.

I had a lot of time to think while I was locked up. Peggy and I had split up when her husband got out of prison, but she'd come back to me. I wasn't sure where I was headed next. I knew I could get a job cooking—I had lots of restaurant contacts from selling Army food. So I lined up a job at a local restaurant, a place right on Route 301.

Route 301 used to be part of the main route to Florida, but they'd built the interstate and now it was quieter. So the restaurant served mostly locals, which was fine by me—I like places where it feels like family. I'd met the owner where Peggy worked. He was a great guy and I was glad to work with him.

When I started, they were serving the usual American restaurant fare—which in the '60s meant lots of meat and potatoes—steaks, meatloaf, pork chops, all with some kind of gravy, baked or mashed potatoes, and usually overcooked vegetables or an iceberg lettuce salad. Being in the South meant you had options like macaroni and cheese or hush puppies if you wanted. It didn't take me long to start slipping in some Italian classics—lasagne, simple pizzas, some *good* spaghetti and meatballs (my aunt Milly's) instead of the tasteless stuff they were used to. The customers loved it.

██

Serves 8–10.

Classic Lasagne

Most American lasagne recipes have ground meat added to the tomato sauce. My mom's version is basically her Sunday Gravy, using the meatballs and sausage as the meat in the casserole. This version will knock you out. Don't plan on doing anything after eating this—you'll be very full.

12 ounces lasagne noodles (preboiled if you can find them)
½ recipe Sunday Gravy (meat sauce), page 33
Two 15-ounce containers ricotta cheese
¼ cup chopped fresh parsley or 2 teaspoons dried
¼ cup chopped fresh basil or 2 teaspoons dried
¼ teaspoon black pepper
8 ounces mozzarella, grated
1 cup freshly grated Parmesan

Preheat oven to 350°F.

If using dried lasagne noodles, prepare them by following Cooking Pasta directions (see page 37), but cook only until *barely* al dente. Remove from water carefully and drain completely.

If using preboiled noodles, soak in a large bowl of warm water 5 minutes until they soften slightly. Drain completely.

Carefully remove meatballs and sausage from tomato sauce to a bowl. Cool to room temperature. Slice meats in ¼-inch-thick rounds. Thin tomato sauce with ½ to 1 cup of water if very thick.

Combine ricotta, parsley, basil and pepper in a bowl.

To assemble lasagne:

Coat the bottom of a 10 × 13-inch pan with a thin layer of tomato sauce. Make a layer of lasagne noodles on top, covering sauce and slightly overlapping noodles. Cover noodles with another thin layer of tomato sauce (½–¾ cup). Add a layer of one-third of ricotta mixture, then meatballs and sausage, mozzarella, and finally a sprinkling of Parmesan. Repeat layering of noodles, tomato sauce, meats, ricotta, mozzarella, and Parmesan two more times. You should have a few noodles left over to place generally on top (they will not cover the layer below completely). Cover with what's left of tomato sauce and sprinkle with remaining Parmesan. Cover pan with foil. Either bake immediately or refrigerate up to 24 hours. Bake 30 minutes covered, then remove foil and bake an additional 15–20 minutes more, until lightly browned on top. Let sit at least 10 minutes before cutting into squares and serving.

THE END

I was happy cooking at the restaurant. But it wasn't enough for me, and Peggy and I started having problems. We were drinking like fish and squabbling more and more. Finally one night we got into a huge fight, and she put her fist through a plate glass window. When the cops showed up, I was the one who got thrown in jail. That was it for me, I'd had enough. I headed North as fast as I could.

But it wasn't the last time I saw her.

For my twenty-first birthday, I bought my first new car—a 1964 Bonneville. Me and my neighborhood pal Johnny Pazzole drove my new wheels to Florida with a shipment of silk summer blouses. Our store contacts there paid us royally. Johnny insisted we go straight to a local racetrack, where we blew the whole wad. I always liked Johnny, but he could never hang onto a dime. He definitely had a problem with the gambling.

So we started driving back North, broke and miserable. And then fate stepped in. In South Carolina, I hit a deer. It was nuts—we were twenty miles from where Peggy lived! I called an auto mechanic I knew in McColl and had the car towed there. Then I called her up.

She looked terrific. And she'd finally gotten completely free of her deadbeat husband. My heart leapt.

But she'd remarried. And she was pregnant.

Like I said, she looked terrific.

The car was going to take a while to fix, so Johnny and I took the train back to Brooklyn. A week or two later, I went back to get the Bonneville.

This time, I didn't call. We'd already said good-bye. And though I didn't know it yet, I was about to meet Karen.

KAREN

For those of you who don't know the book *Wiseguy* or the movie *GoodFellas*, Karen became my wife. We were together for a lot of years of craziness, both in the Mob and after. We met on a blind date I didn't want to go on and I hurried her through. Our next date I didn't even show. But she found me and bawled me out in front of the whole neighborhood for standing her up. A few months later we eloped.

Karen was Jewish. It was a big deal to her family that I wasn't. When we were first married, we lived with her parents. It was pretty tense, but I worked at smoothing things out. I wanted them to like me. The kitchen was the perfect place. I knew a little about Jewish food because Pitkin Avenue was a very mixed neighborhood. But I'd never seen it made firsthand. I was full of questions, I wanted to know why this, why that, how did you make that brisket so tender. After a while, I could get even the grandmother to smile.

Potato Latkes

4 medium baking potatoes (russet or Idaho, about 2½ pounds)
1 large onion, grated (1 cup)
¼ cup all-purpose flour
2 large eggs, beaten
½ teaspoon salt
¼ teaspoon black pepper
3 tablespoons vegetable oil
Sour cream and applesauce for serving

Preheat oven 200°F.

Wash, peel, and grate potatoes. Combine with onion in a bowl. Add flour, eggs, salt, and pepper and stir well.

Heat oil in a large skillet over medium-high heat. Scoop up large spoonfuls (about ¼ cup) of batter and drain them slightly before dropping into skillet. Flatten pancakes a little. Cook about 2 minutes per side, or until both are crisp and golden brown. Remove to paper towels to drain, transfer to ovenproof platter and keep warm in oven. Repeat with remaining batter. Serve with sour cream and/or applesauce.

Chapter Four

The Restaurants

■■

By the time I was twenty-five, I had a family to support. Though I was earning with Paulie, I never knew if it was going to be a lot or a little. I needed a legitimate business with a steady income. Karen was all for it. I knew a Shylock named Raymond Montemurro, who also worked part-time as a waiter at Mike's Steak House. He was with Tommy Agro's crew. We'd done some jobs together, and he had an uncle who worked at Gilly's and used to get us tickets when Sinatra was in town. Ray knew of a wiseguy selling his pizzeria in Long Beach, Long Island. It was next to a movie theater, which meant steady business. So Ray and I went in on it. I think we paid four thousand dollars total, all in cash.

Back then, Long Beach was a summer resort type place right on the ocean. I was counting on lots of business from May to September and then it being quiet the rest of the year except for some movie-going folk. That way, we'd make money in the summer and the rest of the year be free for jobs with our crews.

Our first season went great. I made the usual pizzeria fare I had learned from Fat Larry—pizzas, calzones, veal and pepper sandwiches—and used my mom's recipes for others—manicotti, meatballs, baked ziti.

That summer the place was hopping, and business fell off after Labor Day, just like I thought. But we started making book out of the joint. Ordinarily we wouldn't have gotten much business in the winter but Long Beach is a stone's throw from Kennedy Airport and a lot of airport workers lived there—cargo handlers, dispatchers, foremen. We'd used a bunch of them as insiders on airport jobs—hijacking cargo—so when they found out we owned the place, they showed up in droves. On the way home to the wife and kids, they'd stop and have a slice and lay down a bet or two. And on Fridays they'd bring us whatever swag they'd lifted from the airlines for a little weekend cash.

Now all of a sudden the pizza place was turning into a year-round gig. On top of which, I was doing a lot of work with Jimmy Burke, one of Paulie's main guys. Jimmy was a bona fide nut—I think he loved killing people. He'd as soon whack you as look at you if you said the wrong thing, and now he started going crazy with hijacking jobs. He was like an organ grinder and I was his monkey. Pretty soon I was spending all my time racing back and forth between the restaurant and airport hijackings. And Ray had gotten busy with Tommy Agro. The restaurant was getting stuffed with swag from the airport workers. We didn't even have time to figure where to move it. No one was watching over the place. But we were making so much money from other schemes that we didn't care if it turned a profit. After two summers, we were glad to unload it. Success—what a headache.

But I still loved being around the cooking, I loved having a restaurant. So when a chance came up not much later, I got myself a real restaurant, in Queens.

THE SUITE

When I tell people today I had a restaurant in Queens, they turn up their noses. But back then Queens was in. All the wiseguys hung out there—Paulie and his crew, John Gotti's *capo* Aniello Dellacroce, upon whose death Gotti had Paul Castellano whacked so he could take over—lots of guys. It was out of Manhattan, so it was safer. It wasn't just the wiseguy bosses. Big politicians and mayors would come to Queens for crap games. There were clubs and restaurants, late-night joints. It was the cool place to be.

I got The Suite from a wiseguy who had gambling debts. It was on Queens Boulevard not far from Forest Hills. It's what we called a "supper club," which means there was a big bar and a disco, about 18 tables, food if you wanted. It was a place to hang out, whether you were drinking, eating, or romancing some broad.

Of course to me the food was most important. I hired a good cook and really dove into getting it right. I wanted it to be a top-notch place. I stole ideas from "rug joints"—the deluxe restaurants catering to money—I used to go to in the Five Towns on the Island and places like the Bamboo Lounge and Don Pepe's Vesuvio, which was a class act—it was the Rao's of Brooklyn then. Everybody who was anybody went to Don Pepe's.

■■■

Serves 6.

Minestrone

Minestrone means "big soup," from *minestra*, soup, and the *one* or *oni*, large (just like *cannelloni* means large stick or tube). Everybody has their own recipe. What they have in common is a variety of vegetables and some kind of bean. Pretty much everything else is up to the maker. It's a great way to use up leftover vegetables and the perfect place for any tough old green beans you were going to throw out. You can use water or chicken broth, but it's most flavorful made with beef broth.

PREPARING LEEKS
■■■

Leeks need to be very well washed. They catch all kinds of dirt between their layers. Cut off the top greenest part and bottom end, slice into at least 4 sections lengthwise and separate the layers. Soak them in a sink full of water a few minutes and rinse well before draining and chopping.

3 tablespoons olive oil

¼ pound bacon or pancetta, diced

1 large or 2 medium brown or white onions, peeled and coarsely chopped

2 medium carrots, peeled and diced

2 large stalks celery, diced

1 leek, white and pale green parts, diced

4 canned, peeled plum tomatoes and ¼ cup of their juice

Two 14-ounce cans beef broth and 2 cups water (or more as needed)

A large handful of green beans

½ pound green or Savoy cabbage, sliced and cut in 2-inch pieces

2 medium potatoes, peeled and cut in large chunks

2 small zucchinis, diced

¼ cup chopped fresh parsley or 2 teaspoons dried

1 teaspoon dried basil, marjoram, or thyme

1 bay leaf

One 2-inch piece of Parmesan cheese rind, wax removed

Salt and pepper

Grated Parmesan cheese (optional)

Other Vegetables (optional):

Green peas

Swiss chard

Spinach

Broccoli

Cauliflower

Turnips

HENRY'S NOTES AND TIPS

You don't have to chop all the vegetables before you start—do them as you go along. In other words, cut up the bacon or pancetta, and while that's cooking chop the onion, and when that's cooking chop the carrots, celery, and leeks, etc.

Minestrone tastes even better the second day and freezes very well (up to two months). It gets thicker as it sits, so you'll probably need to add more broth or water when reheating.

Peppers
Red onion
Whatever's about to go bad in the refrigerator

Heat oil in a large pot. Add bacon or pancetta and cook, stirring, over medium heat 5–8 minutes, or until browned but not crisp. Add chopped onions and cook 5 minutes (do not brown). Add carrots, celery, and leek and cook 5 minutes, or until all vegetables are soft. Crush or chop tomatoes. Add tomatoes and juice, broth and water to the pot and stir well. Bring to a boil, then lower heat to a simmer. Snap off ends of green beans, break into approximately 2-inch pieces and add to pot. Add remaining ingredients and salt and pepper to taste (do not over-salt—it will get saltier as it cooks). Simmer for 1 hour, stirring occasionally. Taste for seasoning. Continue cooking 1 hour. Add water if soup gets too thick, and stir thoroughly to avoid scorching. At the end, add salt and pepper to taste, and serve with optional cheese and warm crusty bread.

■■

Serves 6–8

as an appetizer.

Fresh Mozzarella, Tomato, and Basil

(Insalata Caprese)

This is usually a "starter" salad, just something to nibble on at the beginning of the meal. Use the freshest ingredients you can for this, especially the tomatoes. In fact, you can use tomatoes that are almost overripe—the ones that are in the "cheap" boxes at farmer's markets. If you can still slice them, you can use them.

4 medium-size ripe tomatoes
8–12 ounces fresh mozzarella, drained
12–16 fresh basil leaves
¼ cup extra virgin olive oil
⅛–¼ teaspoon salt (to taste)
¼–½ teaspoon freshly ground black pepper (to taste)

Don't drown in olive oil. Use less rather than more.

Some people make a salad dressing of the olive oil, a tablespoon of lemon juice or red wine vinegar, and salt and pepper and pour that over the tomatoes and cheese. I think plain olive oil brings out the flavors best.

It's easiest to slice tomatoes with a serrated knife.

Rinse, core, and slice tomatoes ¼ inch thick. If they are very liquidy, drain by slightly tilting a plate, holding back tomatoes. Slice mozzarella ¼ inch thick. Remove all stems from basil leaves. Arrange tomato and mozzarella slices, overlapping, on a platter, tucking basil leaves between layers. Drizzle with olive oil and sprinkle with salt and freshly ground pepper. Let sit at room temperature at least 15 minutes and up to 2 hours before serving.

Serves 6.

Manhattan Clam Chowder

This is my version of the classic tomato-based soup that's a meal in itself.

1 tablespoon olive oil
2 ounces salt pork or bacon, diced
1 large onion, chopped (½–¾ cup)
1 large carrot, peeled and diced (½ cup)
1 large stalk celery, diced (½ cup)
Two 28-ounce cans peeled plum tomatoes and their juice
3 sprigs fresh thyme or 1 teaspoon dried
1 bay leaf
5 stalks fresh parsley
½ teaspoon salt and pepper (to taste)
4 dozen cherrystone or littleneck clams, or 2 dozen large "chowder" clams, or 1½ pints shucked clams with their juice (clam "liquor")

1 large peeled russet potato or 3 unpeeled medium-size red potatoes
   (¾ pound), cut in large dice
One 8-ounce bottle clam juice (if needed)
1 tablespoon minced fresh parsley leaves

In a large pot, heat olive oil over medium-high heat, add salt pork or bacon and cook 5 minutes or until pieces are crisp, stirring to keep from scorching. Remove bits of browned salt pork or bacon and set aside, and remove all but 2 tablespoons of grease. Add onion, carrot, and celery and cook, stirring, until onion is translucent, 3–5 minutes. Coarsely chop tomatoes and add them with their juice, along with the thyme, bay leaf, parsley stalks, salt, and pepper. Bring to a boil and lower heat to a simmer.

Place unshucked clams in a large pot or skillet and add about ¼ inch water. Cover tightly, bring water to a boil, and cook about ½ minute. Remove any clams that have opened, cover, and reheat any remaining clams. Continue removing and reheating until all or almost all clams have opened. Throw away any that don't open (give them as much as 5–8 minutes to open—some are just stubborn!). Either strain the liquid left in the pan and add it to tomato mixture, or simply spoon it out, leaving any grit in the bottom.

Remove clams from their shells, coarsely chop, and add to tomato mixture. If using shucked clams, chop coarsely and add them and their

ABOUT CLAMS

What kind of clams you get depends on where you live. For stuffed clams or Clams Casino, you can use any small clams. You can get littlenecks or cherrystones on the East Coast, and there are Pacific littlenecks that are just as good.

For a sauce, even the larger clams are fine—steam them as you would the smaller ones and chop before adding to a sauce.

If using unshucked clams, scrub clams and soak, covered, with cold water and a tablespoon of salt dissolved in it for a few hours or overnight (refrigerated if overnight).

juice to the pot. Bring to a boil, lower heat, and simmer, covered, one hour, stirring occasionally.

After an hour, remove thyme and parsley stems and bay leaf. Add diced potatoes. Simmer until potatoes are tender, about 20 minutes, stirring occasionally. If soup is very thick, add bottled clam juice and/or water to desired consistency and heat an additional 5–10 minutes. Adjust seasonings and stir in minced parsley just before serving.

Serves 6 as an

appetizer.

Bruschetta with Fresh Tomatoes & Basil

10 large garlic cloves
One 2-foot baguette
5 large fresh tomatoes, diced
12 fresh basil leaves (about ½ cup loosely packed), sliced thin
¼ cup extra virgin olive oil
1 teaspoon salt
½ teaspoon black pepper

Peel garlic. Slice 7 cloves thinly and place in a bowl. Set aside remaining 3 cloves. Slice baguette in ¼- to ½-inch rounds. Toast bread slices in 400°F oven on a cookie sheet or in a toaster oven until light brown (about 2 minutes, but check earlier). Rub bread with whole garlic cloves while still warm. The garlic should melt into the bread. Set aside.

Add diced tomatoes, basil, olive oil, salt, and pepper to bowl with garlic slices. Stir to combine well. Let sit at room temperature at least ½ hour up to 3 hours.

Serve tomato mixture with a small spoon for topping bread slices.

MOZZARELLA

There's a big difference between fresh and aged mozzarellas. I don't usually use the fresh to cook, just the aged. The fresh is great just sliced or cubed by itself or with tomatoes and basil as above. The aged is good with anything cooked—on pizza, in pasta, or baked in lasagne.

Or top slices with about 1 tablespoon tomato mixture on each and arrange on a platter to serve.

Serves 8–10.

Lasagne with Eggplant and Roasted Peppers

This is a vegetarian lasagne that a lot of people swear has meat in it!

1½ pounds eggplant, trimmed and peeled
2–4 tablespoons olive oil
¼ teaspoon garlic powder
¼ teaspoon each salt and pepper to season + ¾ teaspoon for ricotta mixture
8–12 ounces lasagne noodles (preboiled if you can find them)
15 ounces ricotta cheese
¼ cup chopped fresh Italian parsley or 1 tablespoon dried
5 large fresh basil leaves, chopped, or 1 teaspoon dried
1 recipe Basic Tomato Sauce (3–4 cups; see recipe on page 13)
6 Roasted Sweet Peppers (see recipe on page 23)
8 ounces packaged grated (not fresh), mozzarella
1 cup freshly grated Parmesan

Cut eggplant lengthwise in slices about ¼ to ½ inch thick. To cut the eggplant's bitterness, place the slices in a large bowl of salted water and soak the eggplant slices in it for 1 hour, weighted with a plate or pan so they're submerged. (See page 27 for other ways to prepare eggplant.) Remove from water and pat slices dry with paper towels.

Heat 2 tablespoons of oil in a skillet over high heat until hot but not smoking (oil will ripple slightly). Season eggplant slices on both sides with garlic powder, salt, and pepper and cook in batches in skillet about 1 minute per side. (Add more oil and reheat if necessary.) Do not cook slices completely. Drain on paper towels.

If using dried lasagne noodles, prepare following Cooking Pasta directions on page 37, but cook until only *barely* al dente. Remove from water carefully and drain completely.

If using preboiled noodles, soak in a large bowl of warm water 5 minutes until they soften slightly. Drain completely.

Preheat oven to 350°F.

Combine ricotta, pepper, parsley, and basil in a bowl.

To assemble lasagne:

Coat the bottom of a 10 × 13-inch pan with a thin layer of tomato sauce. Make a lengthwise layer of lasagne noodles on top, slightly over-lapping and covering sauce. Cover noodles with another thin layer of tomato sauce (about ½–¾ cup). Add a layer of one-quarter of ricotta mixture, then one-third of eggplant slices and one-third of roasted peppers, one-quarter of mozzarella and Parmesan, and sprinkle with a bit of remaining black pepper. Repeat layering of noodles, tomato sauce, ricotta, eggplant, roasted peppers, mozzarella, and Parmesan and pepper two more times (use up all the eggplant and roasted peppers). You may have enough noodles left for an entire top layer, or you may have just a few to place on top. Cover noodles with remaining ricotta, then tomato sauce, cheeses, and a sprinkling of pepper. Cover pan with foil. Either bake immediately or refrigerate up to 24 hours. Bake 1 hour, removing foil for last 15 minutes to lightly brown top if desired. Let sit at least 10 minutes before cutting into squares and serving.

Veal Chops with White Wine and Sage

This is very tasty, has only a few ingredients, and takes about fifteen minutes to make. The hardest part is finding good veal. I don't know, maybe it's me, but what you get in the grocery stores today doesn't seem to have much flavor—it's very different from what we could get in Brooklyn. Go to a good butcher, he may carry farm-raised veal, which is much better tasting. Use thin chops for this dish. I've allowed one chop per person, but you may want to make more.

2 tablespoons olive oil
2 tablespoons unsalted butter
4 veal chops on the bone
½ cup flour seasoned with ¼ teaspoon each salt and pepper
2 medium-size sprigs fresh sage + 4 more fresh leaves for garnish
½ cup dry white wine
½ cup canned chicken broth
2 tablespoons flour (if needed)

In a large skillet, heat oil and butter over medium-high heat. Dip veal chops in seasoned flour, shake off the excess and slip them into the pan. Add sage sprigs. Brown on both sides, cooking for a total of 8–10 minutes. Don't overcook, or they'll get tough.

Remove chops from pan and set aside. Add white wine and deglaze pan. Reduce, stirring constantly, for about 1 minute. Add chicken broth and lower heat to a simmer. Cook down 1–2 minutes. If sauce isn't as thick as you want, whisk in 1–2 tablespoons flour. Remove sage sprigs and return chops to pan. Reheat chops, season with salt and pepper to taste and serve, garnished with one sage leaf per chop.

If you want to make up to eight chops, don't double the rest of the ingredients, use the same amount as listed above—with maybe the exception of adding a bit more wine and chicken broth if you want more sauce.

HENRY'S NOTES AND TIPS

Linguine with Clam Sauce

Fresh clams, tomato, and oregano—a perfect combination! If you use fresh clams, keep in mind they give off a lot of juice, which is why you add more tomato paste when using them.

    2–3 dozen fresh clams in their shells or three 8-ounce cans
        chopped clams
    ½ cup chopped white onion
    ¼ cup olive oil
    6–8 cloves of garlic, minced or thinly sliced
    1 small carrot peeled and grated (¼–½ cup)
    1½ 4-ounce cans tomato paste (1 can if using canned clams)
    Three 28-ounce cans peeled tomatoes, drained, reserving juice
    ½ cup dry red wine
    12 large basil leaves, torn in large pieces, or 1 tablespoon dried
    ½ cup finely chopped fresh parsley
    ½ teaspoon chopped fresh oregano
    ½ teaspoon crushed red pepper flakes
    ¼–½ teaspoon salt
    ½ teaspoon black pepper
    1 tablespoon olive oil
    1 cup bottled clam juice
    2 pounds cooked and drained linguine (see page 37 for how to
        prepare)
    1 cup freshly grated Parmesan for serving (optional)

If using fresh clams, scrub their shells briefly with a brush and soak them covered in cold salted water for about 2 hours. The clams will clean themselves in the water as they soak. Rescrub and rinse well before using.

One and a half hours before serving, cook onion 3–5 minutes in a large pot, with olive oil, over medium-low heat until translucent. Add garlic and cook 1 minute. Do not brown, or it will get bitter. Add the grated carrot and cook, stirring 2 minutes. Add tomato paste and stir, then the juice from the canned tomatoes and wine and stir to combine. Crush tomatoes with your hands or chop well on a cutting board and add to sauce. Add basil, parsley, oregano, red pepper flakes, and half of salt and pepper to sauce. Bring to a boil, reduce heat to a low simmer. As the acid from the tomatoes flows to the top, skim it off every 10–15 minutes. Cook sauce 1 hour. It will be quite thick.

If using fresh clams, rinse and drain. Heat 1 tablespoon olive oil in a large skillet over medium heat and add clams in a single layer. Cover and steam clams until they open, about 2 minutes. Remove clams from pan and add liquid in pan to tomato sauce, stirring sauce briefly to combine. Take clams out of shells, reserving 10–12 unshelled. If clams are large, chop in large pieces and add to sauce. If small, add whole. Add up to 1 cup of clam juice if necessary.

If using canned clams, drain, reserving liquid, and add to sauce. Add reserved juice if sauce is too thick.

Reheat sauce 5 minutes, or until heated through. Add remaining salt and pepper to taste. In a large serving bowl, toss about 2 cups of sauce with linguine, top with more sauce and reserved clams in shells (if using), and serve with optional Parmesan on the side.

THE SUITE GETS OUT OF HAND

The original idea was that The Suite would be legit and not a crew hangout like Robert's Lounge. But that didn't last long. At first people would drop by for a late-night drink, but eventually everyone was there so much we used it for special occasions like birthday parties and wedding receptions. With this group, some of those special occasions got out of hand.

Like one night, it was Jimmy Burke's birthday. We had a singer/piano player, and he'd sung "Happy Birthday" to Jimmy a zillion times already. Around one in the morning, someone asked for him to sing it again, and the guy said forget it, he was sick of it.

By then, Jimmy and the crew were totally boozed and drugged up and crazed—so they beat the shit out of him. And I mean they really did him over big time. So there was a huge brouhaha, the cops showed up and took the guy to the hospital, and then to the station for questioning.

Well, he refused to tell the grand jury who beat him up, so *he* got thrown in jail for thirty days. But I tell you, that guy was smart—thirty days in jail was a lot better than getting whacked, which would have happened easily. And he earned respect for being smart enough to keep his mouth shut—it ended up a big career move for him.

Chapter Five

Busted:
Cooking in Prison

....

I GET BUSTED BIG-TIME

When you're in the Life, there's always a chance you'll get a major sentence. But some wiseguys go their whole life without serving more than a few months at a time. I thought I would be one of them. I was always careful, and I'd gotten away with so much for so long. On top of which, what they put me away for was almost a joke compared to what I'd done.

Some guy owed gambling money to a pal of ours, Casey Rosado, who was head of the waiters' and bartenders' union at Kennedy. So one weekend Jimmy, Casey, and I went down to Florida where the guy lived and leaned on him some. At first he acted real tough, so we popped him a few times. He gave up pretty quick. But he was bleeding a lot, so we took him to the back room of a bar Casey's cousin owned and called a doctor to take care of him. After a few hours arranging things, Casey got his money. No big deal. We partied for a day or two with Casey and went home.

It should have been that simple. What we didn't know was the guy's sister worked for the FBI; and she was so upset, she broke down and told the whole story to the agents she worked with. She even ratted on her own brother. Weeks later back in New York, the Florida FBI came down on us like a ton of bricks. After two trials and a whole rigamarole, we each got sentenced to ten years.

I couldn't believe I was going away for that long. Karen was losing her mind. Not only would I be gone, but as far as we knew, there'd be no money coming in. I tried to get things set up so she and the kids wouldn't starve. I did all kinds of hustles—from selling swag to stolen credit cards to arson.

I also had to deal with time owed to Nassau County from an earlier arrest. When I left to do the Nassau time, The Suite was still running, but by the time I got out, the IRS had closed it down. Karen had no choice but to go along with them—we had no cash to cover the debt.

When I got out, I broke into The Suite and took everything out of it but the dust. I wasn't going to give the IRS the satisfaction of auctioning off my stuff to line their pockets.

ROGER'S PLACE

Besides the hustles, I was looking for a restaurant to give Karen and the kids steady money. I knew a guy named Roger who owned a bar on Queens Boulevard, and next door was a building that was perfect for a restaurant. So I made a deal with Roger—I'd open the restaurant as part of his establishment, he'd get the bar money and I'd get whatever the restaurant brought in.

We redid the tiny kitchen and upgraded the interior and opened it up. It was way different from The Suite—I made sure of that. I didn't want the crew hanging out like they did at The Suite and racking up debts. So we made it a family kind of restaurant, a place you could take your kids. I've always been a big seafood fan, so we specialized in seafood.

Clams Casino

This is a classic. I love the combination of the smoky meat and the sweet sea taste of the clams. The bacon or prosciutto add all the salt you need.

2 dozen littleneck or cherrystone clams
¼ pound bacon (about 4 strips) or prosciutto
1 cup dry white wine or ½ cup dry vermouth
¼ cup + 2 tablespoons chopped fresh parsley leaves
1 large clove of garlic, peeled and halved
2 tablespoons olive oil
2 tablespoons unsalted butter
¼ medium onion or 1 large shallot, minced (2 tablespoons)
¼ medium red pepper, chopped (2 tablespoons)
Dash Worcestershire sauce
1–1½ tablespoons lemon juice (to taste)
¼ – ½ teaspoon pepper (to taste)

To remove grit from clams:

Scrub clams well. Dissolve 2 tablespoons of salt in a large bowl of cold water and add clams (the water should cover them). Soak 2–4 hours or overnight (refrigerate if longer than 2 hours). Remove clams from water, rescrub their shells, rinse, and drain.

Cut bacon or prosciutto in 1-inch pieces (to fit on top of clams). Set aside.

Place wine, 2 tablespoons parsley, garlic and clams in a large pot, cover and heat to a simmer. Cook 5–8 minutes, or until all clams are open (discard any that don't open). Remove clams and set aside. Strain liquid in pan through a fine sieve or a sieve lined with cheesecloth and reserve.

Heat olive oil and butter in a large skillet over medium heat. Add onion or shallot and red pepper and cook, stirring occasionally, until onion is translucent, about 5 minutes. Add liquid from cooking clams,

If you usually buy clams from the same place and they don't have a lot of grit, skip the soaking and just scrub the shells well.

If you prefer your bacon well done, precook the slices in a small frying pan until half done before cutting in pieces. Prosciutto doesn't need to be precooked at all—you could eat it straight out of the package and it'd be fine.

and cook until almost all liquid is gone. Remove from heat and discard garlic. Combine in a large bowl with parsley, Worcestershire sauce, lemon juice, and pepper to taste.

Preheat oven to 450°F.

Place a large sheet of aluminum foil on a baking sheet, crumpling to make "nests" in the foil to hold the clams flat. Remove clams from shells and separate top and bottom shells. Return clams to bottom shells and place on baking sheet in "nests." Top each clam with a large teaspoon of onion and pepper mixture and place a piece of bacon on top. Bake clams in oven about 5 minutes, raise oven temperature to broil and broil clams 1–2 minutes, or until bacon starts to get crisp. Serve immediately.

Serves 4–6

as an appetizer.

Baked Clams

When we were low on cash, my mother made baked clams with the clams chopped and she'd double the other ingredients. It's a completely different flavor, but it still tasted fabulous. This is the recipe I made for the wiseguys at the restaurant—they were never counting their pennies.

2 dozen littleneck or cherrystone clams
1 cup dry white wine
2 cups seasoned Italian bread crumbs
½ cup freshly grated Parmesan or Romano cheese

2 tablespoons olive oil
¼ cup chopped onion
3 large cloves of garlic, minced
¼ cup chopped fresh parsley leaves
1½ teaspoons chopped fresh oregano or ½ teaspoon dried
Dash of cayenne pepper
¼–½ teaspoon each salt and black pepper (to taste)
1 large egg, beaten
Dash Tabasco sauce (optional)
½–1 tablespoon lemon juice (if needed)
1 lemon cut in wedges for serving

To remove grit from clams:

Scrub clams well. Dissolve 2 tablespoons of salt in a large bowl of cold water and add clams (the water should cover them). Soak 2–4 hours or overnight (refrigerate if longer than 2 hours). Remove clams from water, rescrub their shells, rinse, and drain.

Place wine and clams in a large pot, cover and heat to a simmer. Cook 5–8 minutes, or until all clams are open (discard any that don't open). Remove clams and set aside. Strain liquid in pan through a fine sieve or a sieve lined with cheesecloth and reserve.

Put bread crumbs and cheese in a large bowl and mix well. Set aside.

Heat olive oil in a large skillet over medium heat. Add onion and garlic and cook, stirring occasionally, until onion is translucent, about 5 minutes, being careful not to brown garlic. Add all but ¼ cup of strained cooking liquid, raise heat, and cook down until liquid is reduced by half. Add parsley, oregano, cayenne pepper, salt, and black pepper to taste. Sauté 2 minutes, or until parsley begins to wilt. Cool to room temperature and combine thoroughly with bread crumbs and cheese. Add egg and optional Tabasco and mix very well. If you want a moister mixture, add a small amount of lemon juice.

Preheat oven to 400°F.

Place a large sheet of aluminum foil on a baking sheet, crumpling to make "nests" in the foil to hold the clams flat. Remove clams from shells and separate top and bottom shells. Return clams to bottom shells and place on baking sheet in "nests" or in a baking pan that will hold them in a single layer. Top each clam with a tablespoon of bread crumb mixture (you can pile it up a bit) and drizzle with a little of reserved clam cooking liquid. Bake clams in oven about 5 minutes, raise oven temperature to broil and broil clams about 2 minutes, or until bread crumbs are golden brown on top. Serve with lemon wedges and Tabasco sauce if desired.

■■

Serves 4 people

about

6 caps each.

Shrimp-Stuffed Mushrooms

These were big sellers at Roger's Place. And easy to make, because we had so much shrimp for shrimp cocktail around, we'd just grab a bunch of them and add the other filling ingredients—a snap.

For a home cook, I'd recommend you buy shrimp that's already cooked to save you the work. Just make sure it's fresh.

¼ cup olive oil + 1 teaspoon for greasing baking sheet
½ cup finely chopped shallots or onion
1 tablespoon minced garlic
¾–1 teaspoon chopped fresh rosemary or ½ teaspoon dried, crumbled
8 ounces peeled, deveined, and cooked shrimp, chopped coarsely
½ cup plain bread crumbs (fresh or packaged)
⅓ cup freshly grated Parmesan cheese
4 tablespoons mayonnaise
½ teaspoon each salt and pepper (to taste)
8–12 ounces fresh white mushrooms (about 20–24)
2 fresh lemons

Preheat oven to 350°F.

Heat oil in large skillet over medium heat. Add shallots or onion and sauté 5 minutes. Add garlic and rosemary and continue cooking, stirring occasionally, 3 more minutes. Cool slightly and put in bowl. Add shrimp, bread crumbs, Parmesan, and mayo to the onion mixture. Season with salt and pepper. Set mixture aside.

Remove mushroom stems (save stems for stock if you wish). Rinse or wipe clean tops. Grease baking sheet with 1 teaspoon oil and place mushroom caps on it, stem side up. With a spoon, fill each mushroom cap with shrimp mixture, pressing mixture into caps. It's okay to overfill them a bit.

Bake mushrooms for 30–35 minutes or until they start to brown. Cut a lemon in half and squeeze the juice onto mushroom caps (run lemon juice through your closed fingers to hold back the seeds). Cut the second lemon in quarters and serve alongside caps.

Serves 4.

■■

Shrimp with Roasted Peppers

You can cook this with floured or unfloured shrimp, depending on your taste (or your calorie count). Serve them with bread or white rice. In a pinch, you can use jarred roasted red peppers. But freshly roasted ones will have much more flavor and they're easy to make.

6 large red peppers
2½ pounds medium or large shrimp (20–35 per pound), peeled and
    deveined, reserving shells
1 cup white wine
1 medium onion, coarsley chopped (1 cup)
2 cups chicken broth (or more)
3 large cloves of garlic, one peeled and halved, the others minced
1 bay leaf
1 sprig each rosemary, thyme, and tarragon + ½ tablespoon dried
    rosemary leaves, slightly crumbled
1 large tomato, coarsely chopped (½–¾ cup)
Dash salt and black pepper
1 cup flour (optional)
½–1 teaspoon salt and black pepper (to taste)
¼–½ teaspoon cayenne pepper (optional)
¼ cup olive oil
½ cup chopped fresh parsley

To roast peppers:

Preheat broiler or the oven to broil setting (or the highest temperature you can if no broil setting). Rinse whole peppers and place on a cookie sheet or broiler pan lined with foil and place in broiler or oven. Roast peppers, turning with tongs or large spoons as they blacken until all sides are dark. Place in a large bowl and cover with foil from cookie sheet, sealing on all sides. Let sit for 15–20 minutes (longer is okay). Discard tops, peel off skins, and remove seeds and veins. Save any liquid the peppers give off. Slice peppers lengthwise into thin strips.

While peppers are roasting, place shrimp shells in a medium saucepan along with white wine and onion. Bring to a boil and then simmer until liquid is reduced by half. Add 2 cups of chicken broth; the halved garlic clove; bay leaf; sprigs of rosemary, thyme, and tarragon; tomato; and a dash of salt and pepper (to taste). Bring to a boil and then cover and simmer about 15 minutes. Add more chicken broth if liquid gets too low (you should have about 1½ cups of liquid). Taste broth after 10 minutes and if flavor is weak, remove cover and reduce to strengthen the taste. Cool slightly and strain liquid. Set broth aside and discard solids.

Season flour with salt, black pepper, and optional cayenne pepper and place on a plate. Heat olive oil in a large skillet over medium-high heat until hot but not smoking. Dredge shrimp in seasoned flour and sauté in pan until just pink, about 3 minutes per side. Lower heat and add roasted pepper strips, dried rosemary, and broth. Simmer an additional 3–5 minutes and serve immediately over rice or with chunks of good bread to sop up the sauce. Garnish with fresh parsley.

Variation:

If making without flour, toss shrimp in a bowl with salt, black pepper, and optional cayenne pepper and sauté until pink, 2–3 minutes per side.

Seafood Salad

This is one of the many seafood dishes my mom would serve on Christmas Eve. I adapted it for Roger's Place, where I served it as an appetizer or part of an antipasto.

1 pound shelled mussels or 2 pounds mussels in their shells
1 dozen fresh clams
1 pound fresh calamari, cleaned and cut in pieces
½ pound fresh shrimp, peeled and deveined
One 6-ounce can scungilli (conch), drained and cut in large pieces
    (optional)
½ pound cleaned and sliced octopus (optional)
1 large stalk celery, chopped (1 cup)
½ cup coarsely chopped red onion
½ cup finely chopped white or other sweet onion
2 tablespoons capers + 1 tablespoon caper juice
½ cup chopped fresh parsley
1 tablespoon chopped fresh oregano leaves
2 tablespoons sliced kalamata olives (optional)
1 cup extra virgin olive oil
Juice of two lemons
1 teaspoon salt
½ teaspoon black pepper
1–2 teaspoons crushed red pepper flakes (to taste)

If using fresh mussels, scrub and debeard them and soak covered in cold water for 1 hour. Scrub and soak clams in same bowl.

Don't overcook shrimp; they turn to rubber.

HENRY'S NOTES AND TIPS

Place mussels (shelled or unshelled), clams, calamari, shrimp, and optional scungilli and octopus in a large pot of water. Bring water to a boil and immediately turn off heat, drain seafood in a colander and rinse in cold water. (As soon as shrimp turn pink, the seafood is done!) Allow to drain well a few minutes while preparing other ingredients.

Combine seafood and all other ingredients in a large bowl and toss well. Refrigerate until very cold and serve.

PRISON WITH PAULIE

I kept my lawyers appealing the sentence. It was almost two years before the lawyers told me there was nothing more they could do. It was time for me to go in.

Meanwhile, I'd done a ton of research on what I could do inside to get my time reduced and which prison I should try to get assigned to. I decided on Lewisburg Federal Penitentiary in Pennsylvania. It happened that a bunch of wiseguys were already there, including Paulie, who was in for two and a half years for tax evasion. At least I'd have company. I bribed one of the prison officers and he saw to it I got to go where I wanted.

I was right about Lewisburg—it was the best choice I could have made. When I finally went in, scared as could be, I was met by Paulie, Johnny Dio, and Fat Andy Ruggierio. They acted like I was coming to a big party.

In some ways being in prison wasn't so different from being outside. It was all about working the system, seeing what you could get from it, just like outside. But being in prison was also very different from outside. The wiseguys call jail time "vacation." I started to see why. Nothing is ever simple on the outside. In prison things were very clear—you knew who you had and who you didn't. You knew exactly who you were dealing with and what you were trying to get around. It was almost easy.

Lewisburg wasn't like any other time I've been in prison. The wiseguys had it all set up. They had tons of guards and officials on the take. They had hired big, tough cons to protect them. We were so well cared for that at one point when there was a riot and some killings, the hacks put us all in solitary so we'd be safe.

Of course, we had to spend a bundle. Before long, I was shelling out a few hundred a week, and Paulie and some other guys paid much more. It was how you survived.

The money wasn't just for protection. A lot of it went for food and booze. The wives and mistresses would smuggle in care packages at the visiting area, but we had to eat it there, we couldn't bring anything into the prison itself. To get food inside we paid the hacks big-time. They'd bring us all kinds of stuff: steaks, shrimp, fresh basil. We paid them twenty to thirty dollars for a pint of booze. We hired everybody. We even had the priest. Yeah, the priest—we were getting him laid. We'd send him to New York to get laid. He snuck in whiskey every day in his briefcase, and he'd get us these huge scallops that Johnny Dio was nuts for.

I'd been in maybe two months when a wiseguy got released. He had lived in the "honor dorm" with Paulie and all the other wiseguys—Vinnie Aloi, Joe Pine, Tommy DiSimone, a bunch of guys—and when he left, I got the spot. It was a whole different life there. We had it pretty good, considering it was prison.

There were some real advantages. Like the fact that Vinnie Aloi, the head of his family, was in charge of the prison bakery. Which means we had access to the kitchen almost any time we wanted. In the middle of the afternoon, we could tell the guards, "Gotta ice the cakes," and go down and cook sauce for dinner. But it was a pain to cook downstairs, you always had to deal with the guards over your shoulder, so we'd borrow pots and pans and cook on one of the stoves upstairs that Paulie had rigged up—he was a nut for making stoves. Paulie made great stoves. I mean, the best. He also used to make "stingers." They were like those coils they sell to heat up your coffee or tea water. We'd use them for espresso after dinner. You tie two spoons together, run a wire from it and hook up a plug. It worked great.

As much as possible, we'd cook in our room, which we weren't supposed to do. The guard station was down a stairway right near us, and to keep the smells out, we'd get someone to stand outside our cell and blow baby powder into the air. The odors would grab onto the powder, and the air would just smell sweet from the powder. All it would cost was a plate of whatever we were cooking.

The baby powder didn't always work. The smells would drift down to the guards, and they'd come charging up, all upset, and probably pissed off 'cause it smelled so good. They'd "confiscate" all the pots and pans we'd lifted from the kitchen. But it wasn't a big deal—we'd just go back and resteal them a few days later, and the whole rigamarole would start all over again. I think it gave the guards something to do.

We lived four guys to a room in the honor dorm. You really get to know each other in a situation like that. At dinner, it would all come out. I knew everybody's habits, especially about food.

A lot of American guys won't set foot in the kitchen. The only cooking they'll even consider is outside on the barbecue. Italian men look at cooking very differently. To them it's a sign of strength. It's both sexy and very "manly" to be a good cook. Their recipes are a source of great pride. I've seen a million fights over how you cook sauce.

So we all had our ways to cook, and more than a few opinions. Like Johnny Dio, who was in for blinding a reporter with acid, he used to have this thing—you couldn't put wet basil in the sauce. And if he saw you do it, he would go friggin' nuts. You had to pat the leaves dry. Vinnie Aloi, he put way too many onions in the sauce, to my mind. It tasted almost like the sauce the street vendors use on hot dogs. I hated it. But Paulie was smart—he gave us all assignments to keep the peace. He'd slice the garlic (paper thin with a razor) and do the chopping, I'd assist him, Vinnie Aloi got the sauce, and Johnny Dio cooked the meat.

The food was like a religion. When we couldn't get ingredients for some dishes, we'd talk about them, on and on. I've seen Paulie almost in tears talking about his mom's osso buco.

Serves 4.

■■

Osso Buco

When made right, this dish has a sweet, dense flavor that you can't stop eating till you've wiped the last of the sauce from your plate. It's traditionally served with Saffron Risotto, so I've included that recipe below—they're fabulous together! Some people won't eat Osso Buco without Lemon Gremolata—it's a matter of taste. I think it overwhelms the veal.

4 veal shanks, about 3" thick
1 teaspoon salt and pepper

½ cup flour, seasoned with ¼ teaspoon salt and pepper
¼ cup olive oil
2–3 large carrots, diced fine (1½ cup)
1 medium onion, diced (1 cup)
2 celery stalks, diced (1 cup)
4 sprigs fresh thyme or 1–2 teaspoons dried
One 28-ounce can peeled plum tomatoes with juice
3–4 cups chicken stock
2 cups dry white wine
3–4 cloves of garlic, minced (1 tablespoon)
1 cup chopped fresh parsley or 3 tablespoons dried
Lemon Gremolata (optional; see recipe below)

Preheat oven to 375°F.

Use a large ovenproof pan or casserole that will hold all the shanks in one layer if possible. Season shanks all over with ½ teaspoon salt and pepper. Season the flour and place on a plate.

Heat the olive oil in the pan over high heat until very hot but not smoking. Lightly coat each shank with flour and shake off excess. Place shanks in olive oil and brown well on all sides. (Turn on the fan!) Remove shanks and set aside. Lower heat to medium and add carrot, onion, celery, and thyme. Cook until vegetables are softened and lightly browned, about 8 minutes. Add tomatoes, chicken stock, and wine and bring to a boil. Return shanks to pan. The liquid should half-cover them. Add more stock if necessary. Add garlic and parsley. Cover the pan with lid or aluminum foil. If using foil, make sure you seal it well. Cook in oven for 2½ hours. Shanks should be very tender. Carefully remove shanks and heat remaining sauce over medium heat, reducing it until thick and dark, about 15–20 minutes. If you used fresh thyme, remove the twigs—the leaves will have disappeared into the sauce. Return shanks to pan and heat through. Adjust salt and pepper (you may not need salt). Add Lemon Gremolata if desired and heat 1 minute. Serve with Saffron Risotto (recipe follows) and warm bread.

Lemon Gremolata

2 teaspoons lemon peel
2 large garlic cloves, coarsely chopped
2 tablespoons fresh parsley leaves

Combine all ingredients in a food processor and pulse briefly until well chopped but not mushy. Add to osso buco and heat briefly, or serve it on the side for those who want to eat it.

Serves 4–6
as a side dish.
For hearty eaters,
make 1½ times
the recipe.

Saffron Risotto

Risotto is mainly a Northern Italian dish, but my mother used to make it—I don't know, she must have picked it up in the neighborhood. It's even more demanding than pasta—you have to eat it the minute it's done or it turns to glue.

Cooking traditional risotto means you stir it the whole time—a pain in the neck! See page 276 for my microwave version that you can walk away from.

2½ cups beef broth
2 tablespoons olive oil
1 slice bacon, chopped
2 tablespoons chopped onion
1 tablespoon butter (optional)
1 large garlic clove, minced
1 cup Arborio rice (do not rinse!)
½ teaspoon saffron strands, coarsely chopped and dissolved in
   ¼ cup hot water
½ teaspoon salt and pepper (if needed)

Heat beef broth in a small pot and keep simmering on the burner.

Heat the olive oil in a medium-size pot over medium heat and add the chopped bacon. Cook, stirring, until bacon is browned. Remove bacon bits. Lower heat to medium-low and add onion and optional butter. Cook about 5 minutes, or until onion is translucent. Add garlic and cook briefly, stirring. Add rice and cook, stirring constantly, 2–3 minutes. Add ½ cup of beef broth and cook, stirring constantly, until almost all liquid is absorbed into rice. Add a second ½ cup of broth and repeat process until liquid is absorbed. Add saffron and its liquid and an additional ½ cup of broth, stirring. Repeat, adding ½ cup liquid and cooking and stirring until liquid is absorbed, then test for doneness. Season with additional salt if necessary. If rice needs more time, add more liquid, cook, and stir until done. If you run out of broth, add a ¼ cup of water. The rice should be cooked and thick, but should have a little bit of creamy sauce.

■■

Serves 4.

Oven Penitentiary Sauce with Sausage

Sometimes we had to cook sauce in the oven in the kitchen. That would be after the hacks retrieved the pots and pans we'd "borrowed." For a couple of days we could get only hotel pans—those big metal pans they use to keep food warm on buffets. You can't put a hotel pan on top of the stove—they're too thin, they burn right through. So we'd sneak down to the kitchen and make the sauce in the oven. You just have to watch to make sure the sauce doesn't get too thick too fast. One of our crew was the baker for the prison, so when they pulled our stoves, we'd go down to the kitchen and announce to the guards that we were "baking cakes."

But this sauce turned out to be so good I've made it many times on the "outside." Baking a sauce in the oven with the meat makes the sauce really rich and the meat tender. I had to go to prison to learn this?

1 pound mild or spicy Italian sausage
¼ cup olive oil
6–8 cloves of garlic (about 2 tablespoons)
Two 28-ounce cans peeled plum tomatoes with basil, drained,
    reserving juice
12 large basil leaves, torn in large pieces, or 1 tablespoon dried
¼ cup finely chopped Italian parsley or 2 teaspoons–1 tablespoon
    dried parsley
1 cup dry red wine
1 teaspoon each salt and pepper
Grated Parmesan or Romano cheese
Fresh Italian bread slices
1 pound pasta of your choice, cooked and drained

Preheat the oven to broil. Poke sausages all over and place on baking sheets covered with aluminum foil. Grill sausages, turning when
browned, 10–15 minutes, until barely cooked.

Reduce oven heat to 350°F. Add all remaining ingredients to a large
baking pan and mix very well. Place pan in oven. Cook 15 minutes (but
watch your back!). Add sausages, and continue cooking, skimming off
any grease that rises to the top, for 45 minutes or until sauce has thickened and sausage is tender. Serve with 1 pound cooked pasta if you can,
and fresh bread to sop up the sauce, or just bread if you can't get to a
stove to boil the pasta.

HENRY'S NOTES AND TIPS	You don't have to cook the sausages through because they'll finish baking in the sauce. And if they're not fully cooked, they'll add fat and flavor to the tomatoes.

Pasta e Fagioli

There were times the hacks couldn't get us anything good and we were stuck with what we could scrounge from the kitchen. They use lots of dried and canned foods in prison, so we'd make things like Pasta e Lenticchie (pasta and lentils), Pasta con Sarde (pasta with sardines). Or the classic Pasta e Fagioli (pasta and beans). We almost came to blows over this recipe. This is true comfort food for a cold night. It's also one with a lot of variations, depending on what part of Italy you're from. One of the wiseguys in Lewisburg had a fit when I didn't put any tomatoes in. They had to pull him off me.

2 tablespoons olive oil
2 ounces salt pork in one piece or 2 slices bacon, cut in 1" pieces
1 large onion, diced (1½ cups)
8 garlic cloves, minced (2 tablespoons)
1–2 large stalks celery, sliced thin (1 cup)
1 large carrot, peeled and diced (¾ cup)
Two 15-ounce cans cannellini or small white beans
4 cups chicken broth
2 cups beef broth
1 bay leaf
1 sprig fresh rosemary or ½ teaspoon dried (optional)
Parmesan cheese rind about 1 × 3" (optional)
1 cup dried macaroni or other small pasta
¼ teaspoon black pepper
Dash cayenne pepper
Grated Parmesan for serving

In a large pot, heat oil over low heat. Add salt pork or bacon and cook 3–4 minutes, stirring (do not brown). Remove excess oil, leaving 1–2 tablespoons. Add onion and cook, stirring 5 minutes until translucent. Add garlic, celery, and carrot and cook 5 minutes more, stirring.
Raise heat to medium. Stir in beans and their juice, chicken and

Don't salt this at all. The salt pork or bacon and the cheese rind (if you use it) will be more than enough. On top of which, if you use canned broths—which is easiest—they have tons of salt. Use low-salt ones if you can.

beef broths, bay leaf, rosemary and cheese rind if using. Heat to a boil, then lower to simmer and cook 10 minutes. Add pasta, black and cayenne pepper, and cook just until pasta is al dente, about 5 minutes, stirring occasionally. Adjust seasonings and serve with Parmesan on the side.

Serves 4.

Pasta e Lenticchie

This is very simple, tasty, and comforting food. You can add sliced fresh fennel if you can find it or half a cup of white wine and reduce before adding broth to intensify the flavor.

½ pound lentils, rinsed
2 tablespoons olive oil
1–2 ounces salt pork or bacon, cut in large pieces
½ cup chopped onion
2 large garlic cloves, minced
½ cup chopped celery
1 medium-size carrot, peeled and diced (½ cup)
2 cans canned chicken broth (about 4 cups)
¼ cup chopped fresh parsley or 2 teaspoon dried, crumbled
3 fresh thyme sprigs or 1 teaspoon dried, crumbled
½ teaspoon salt and black pepper (to taste)
½–1 teaspoon cayenne pepper (to taste)
½ pound cooked curly pasta—fusilli or rotelli (see page 37 for how to prepare)
1 cup freshly grated Parmesan or Romano cheese for serving

Soak lentils in cold water to cover 15 minutes and discard any that float to the top. Rinse and drain.

Heat oil in a medium-size pot over medium low heat. Add salt pork or bacon and cook, stirring occasionally, 5 minutes. Add onion, garlic, celery, and carrot and cook an additional 3–5 minutes. Turn up heat, add lentils, and cook, stirring, 2 minutes. Stir in chicken broth, thyme, parsley, salt, black pepper, and cayenne pepper and bring to a boil. Lower heat and simmer, covered, about 20 minutes, or until lentils are just done (you don't want them overcooked and mushy!). Adjust seasonings, add pasta, and toss. Reheat and serve, topping each serving generously with cheese and a bit of freshly ground pepper.

Serves 4.

Pasta con Sarde

In Italy and sometimes in Brooklyn you can get fresh sardines. Sicily is famous for its fresh sardine sauce. Most of the time they're very hard to find in America, and in prison, are you kidding? So I came up with a version in prison that is nowhere near the fresh sardine sauce, but it's pretty darn good and reminded all the gang of the fresh stuff, which is what it's all about in prison.

2 large garlic cloves, minced
2 large anchovies, minced
½ cup olive oil
1 large onion, finely chopped (1 cup)
1 teaspoon fennel or anise seeds, crushed lightly on a cutting board
2 tablespoons pine nuts
Three 3–4 ounce cans sardines, canned in water if possible or if canned in olive oil, rinsed and dried
½ cup canned chicken broth
1 pound cooked and drained pasta of your choice (see page 37 for how to prepare)

Place garlic and anchovies on a cutting board and mince fine, or place in a mortar and pestle and crush well.

In a large skillet, heat olive oil to medium heat. Add onion and cook 5 minutes, or until onion is translucent. Add garlic/anchovy mixture and cook 2 minutes longer (do not brown garlic). Add fennel seeds and pine nuts and cook briefly. Stir in sardines and toss gently. Add chicken broth and heat well. Toss with cooked pasta and serve.

Chapter Six

The End

■■

FIXING GAMES IN BOSTON

When I got out of prison four years later, I was close to broke. I needed to start earning again—and fast. At Lewisburg I'd hooked up with a guy from Pittsburgh named Paul Mazzei. Inside, we were in business selling pot and pills. And despite Paulie's ironclad rule against it, I started dealing with him outside too. The money was just too easy.

I used to go to Pittsburgh a lot to pick up stuff. Paul Mazzei and I would do our business and then go to dinner. He had a favorite restaurant. He never wanted to go anywhere else. He wanted to go to the same restaurant, sit at the same table, and eat the same things. He always started with wedding soup, which is a chicken-based soup with pastina in it. I used to push him to try something else, life is short, where's your sense of adventure? Nope, it was always wedding soup, wedding soup. It drove me crazy. Though I gotta admit, that soup was darn good.

Serves 2–4.

Wedding Soup

This soup will take you twenty minutes to make, and it's absolutely delicious.

½ cup pastina (also called egg pastina or *acini de pepe*)
6 cups chicken broth, homemade or canned
3 eggs
¼ cup chopped fresh parsley
⅓ cup freshly grated Parmesan or other hard cheese
½ teaspoon salt
¼ teaspoon freshly ground black pepper

Bring a pot of salted water (1 teaspoon salt) to a boil. Add pastina, stirring. Cook until al dente, about 4–6 minutes. Drain and reserve.

Heat broth to boiling in a large pot. Lower heat and add pastina to broth. Cover and keep at a simmer.

Put eggs in a bowl and beat until well combined but not frothy. Stir in parsley, Parmesan or other cheese, salt, and pepper.

Bring broth back to a boil and slowly add egg mixture, stirring gently so eggs break up. Remove from heat as soon as eggs begin to look cooked. Serve immediately, with additional black pepper if desired.

HENRY'S NOTES AND TIPS	Pastina is the only pasta I can think of where it's okay to be cooked more than al dente. You need to make sure the center is done as well as the outside.
	Don't add the egg mixture until the very last minute—if your guests are lingering over the antipasto, hold off. This soup has a lovely creaminess when the eggs are just done.

BOSTON

It was through Paul Mazzei that I got involved in fixing college basketball games. Paul's best friend was a bookie named Tony Perla. Tony's brother Rocco had been close pals ever since high school with Rick Kuhn, who was then playing basketball at Boston College. Tony said that Rick was willing to shave points—not lose games, but shave points, for a few thousand a game, and that he had another player on the team, Jim Sweeney, who was interested. We could clean up if we could get down enough bets.

I told Paulie and Jimmy about the scheme, and we had a meeting with Tony Perla and Paul Mazzei. So far, so good. But I needed to check out these kids and see who we were really dealing with. So Paul Mazzei, Tony, Rocco, and I met the two players at the airport in Boston. It was just a quick thing so we could eyeball each other.

A couple of weeks later, and three days after the Lufthansa heist at Kennedy, we flew up to Boston again for the real-deal meeting. For the occasion, we got two rooms and a suite at the Sheraton in the Prudential Center—very swanky, very high class. The players were impressed, and a little edgy. But not so edgy they didn't order room service lobsters for dinner. Not cheap.

I could have lobster any day with the wiseguys. My Irish half was more interested in some real Boston fare, so I got the New England clam chowder and corned beef and cabbage. The chowder was excellent, but my brother Joe's corned beef can't be beat. He does it in an electric frying pan. It cooks all night, very slowly, and it comes out so tender you don't even need a knife to cut it.

Serves 6–8.

New England Clam Chowder

Will the real-deal chowder please stand up? Are you red, or are you white? I spent most of my life eating the red one, Manhattan, but to tell the truth, I like 'em both. And Beantown sure knows their version. You can make this chowder with the toughest clams around, tough as elastic bands, it'll still work. I think that's why they started making it—they didn't want to waste the flavor the tough clams still had.

2 tablespoons vegetable oil
3 ounces of salt pork, diced
1 large onion, diced (1½ cups)
1 stalk celery, sliced thin (⅓ cup)
4 cups clam juice or 2 cups clam juice + 2 cups chicken broth
¾ pound red potatoes, scrubbed and cut in 1–2" pieces
2 pounds canned or frozen clams, chopped
Dash mace
½ teaspoon black pepper (to taste)
2 cups half and half
¾ cup milk
3 tablespoons flour
2 tablespoons butter
Oyster crackers

Heat oil in a large soup pot over medium-low heat. Add salt pork and cook, stirring often, 5–10 minutes, until salt pork begins to brown. Add ¼ cup water and stir to scrape up any bits stuck to the pan. Add onion and celery. Cook 5 minutes. Add ½ cup water and continue cooking over low heat for 20 minutes, stirring occasionally in case mixture starts to stick to the pan.

Add clam juice and/or broth and potatoes and cover pot. Simmer until potatoes are just tender (10–15 minutes). Do not overcook potatoes! Add chopped clams, mace, and pepper. Cook 5–10 minutes. Stir in half and half, milk, and add flour, whisking to incorporate. Cook a few minutes, stirring, until it reaches desired thickness. Stir in butter. Adjust seasonings. Serve with traditional oyster crackers or any crackers or bread if desired.

Joe's Corned Beef and Cabbage

I love corned beef, but almost never have it except on St. Patty's Day. It's such a deal then, who could pass it up? You'd pay more for a can of dog food than for a six-pound corned beef on March 17th. Why don't they put prosciutto on sale on Columbus Day?

One 5–6 pound corned beef with pickling spices
One 12-ounce can of beer
10 peppercorns
1 bay leaf
6–8 medium potatoes
1 small head of cabbage
2–3 medium onions
6–8 medium carrots
½ teaspoon salt and pepper

Mustard Horseradish Sauce:

¼ cup prepared horseradish
¼ cup mayonnaise
1½ tablespoons Dijon-style mustard or ½ teaspoon dry
1 teaspoon honey
¼ teaspoon black pepper
½ cup whipping cream

Place corned beef and pickling spices in a deep electric frying pan or a Crock-Pot. Add beer, peppercorns, bay leaf, and water to cover. Cook 4–5 hours over very low heat. If using a pot, simmer 3 hours. Check occasionally to make sure water still covers meat.

Prepare vegetables during last hour of cooking. Scrub and halve potatoes. Rinse cabbage and remove tough outer leaves. Core and cut in quarters. Peel onions and quarter. Trim and peel carrots and cut in large chunks. Add to corned beef. Cook 20 minutes and check vegetables.

Remove with a slotted spoon to a bowl when they are just done (the carrots even a bit crunchy if you like). Toss with salt and pepper.

To make Mustard Horseradish Sauce:

Combine all ingredients except cream in a medium bowl. Whip cream until it forms soft peaks and fold into mixture. Cover and refrigerate until serving.

Check corned beef for tenderness—a knife or fork should slide into it easily. When done, remove from water and drain well in colander.

Place beef on a cutting board and cut across the grain into ½-inch slices. Arrange on a platter and surround with vegetables. Serve with Mustard Horseradish Sauce on the side.

HENRY'S

NOTES

AND TIPS

Normally you can count on a half pound of meat per person, but I find corned beef disappears very fast. Allow three-quarters to one pound per person. If you have leftovers, it makes great sandwiches.

Joe uses the flat-cut corned beef, but the point cut, which is cheaper and fattier, is very tasty. It's not as healthy, but the extra fat adds flavor.

If your corned beef didn't come with a packet of spices, you can buy pickling spices in most spice departments. Use one tablespoon.

SHAVING POINTS

So we fixed a few games, and no one knew. Red Auerbach, the great Boston Celtics coach, once said, "There's no way you can tell if a referee or player is shaving points—absolutely no way." We got away with it, and at the end of the season, we came out ahead, by maybe seventy-five or one hundred thousand dollars.

But it wasn't easy. In fact, it was frustrating and nerve-racking. We would win one, and encouraged by that, would bet bigger on the next game, and lose that. Which would mean we'd have to bet bigger next time just to get even. When the bookies started to suspect something was going on, they made it even harder for us to make a buck. Sometimes we'd lose by missing the spread by as little as three or four points. It just made me madder and madder. And Jimmy Burke would lose his mind when we lost. So I gotta say, I was glad when the season was over. And no one ever suggested we try it again.

FLORIDA

When I was in the Life, sometimes Paulie, Jimmy, and I went to Florida in the spring for "vacation." We'd take our families. I didn't always get to stay—I made a lot of trips back to New York to take care of different schemes, back and forth, back and forth. But it was worth it to even get a few days in the sun down there. It made you feel so good.

Of course there's great seafood in Florida. They have fish and shellfish I'd never even heard of. Like mahimahi, which is also called dolphinfish (even though it's not a dolphin). Or there's stone crabs. I thought all crabs were alike, but there's different kinds all over the world. These crabs have shells that are hard as rocks—that's why they call them stone crabs. If you break their claws off, they grow back in a year or two, and you can do the same thing all over again. Their claws are nothing but meat. They taste unique, like a cross between lobster, abalone, and crab. Delicious!

Paulie would go nuts for stone crabs. After a few drinks, he'd start demanding, "Stone Crab Joe's, Stone Crab Joe's." Which is where we'd end up going for dinner and getting their stone crabs with mustard sauce.

The place was really called Joe's Stone Crab, but Paulie always reversed the name, especially as he got older. By then, Paulie would get stupid on three or four beers. When I first met him, he could down two bottles of Chivas a night. Now after three tall necks, he'd be out of his mind drunk. A 300-pound marmaluke, he'd be spitting and slobbering. People would laugh at him. It was sad.

■■■

Stone Crabs with Mustard Sauce

Serves 2
(6 claws
per person).

Stone crabs are available only a few months a year. In season you buy them already cooked at the fish market—that's the way they sell them. I've never even seen them sold uncooked. And what you're really buying is the claws, which are removed from the crabs and will grow back by the next season. They're so pretty, a kind of light peach color tipped with black, you almost don't want to eat them. Not that that ever stopped me from eating something delicious. But since you know they didn't have to kill the crabs and the claw will grow back next year, they taste even better.

Make sure you get the fishmonger to crack them for you or you'll be in for a long night with a hammer.

2 pounds stone crabs claws, cracked (about 12 claws)

Serve stone crabs chilled with Mustard Sauce on the side. Make sure you have cracking implements to finish the shelling job and bowls for shells, and lots of napkins!

Makes 1 cup.

Mustard Sauce

1 cup mayonnaise
1–2 tablespoons dry mustard (or more)
2–3 teaspoons Worcestershire sauce
2 tablespoons cream, half and half, or milk
⅛–¼ teaspoon salt and pepper (to taste)

Place mayonnaise in a large bowl and whisk in mustard until smooth (2–3 minutes by hand, or 1 minute with an electric mixer on medium-low). Then whisk in 1 teaspoon Worcestershire sauce and cream or milk, one at a time. Taste for seasoning, adding salt and pepper and more mustard and Worcestershire if desired. Serve chilled.

THE END

I guess my real last day in the Mob was the day I got busted for dealing. Even though Paulie had told me he wouldn't stand for it, I had continued working with Paul Mazzei, and our business had really taken off. We were selling everything: coke, heroin, uppers, downers, you name it. I'd even gotten Jimmy Burke involved, which was another thing Paulie didn't know about.

I'd also become a good customer of my own wares. To keep the business going, I was doing more and more coke. It was the only way I thought I could keep up.

It was the biggest hijack in Kennedy Airport history—we stole $6 million in cash. But there were other crazy things going on. Like the big Lufthansa heist. I had helped set it up by giving Jimmy the information about the goods being at Kennedy. Then, after the heist, the people who had been involved in the theft were dropping like flies. By the time I got nabbed, there was hardly anybody left alive who had done the heist except Jimmy and me. It made me very nervous. I knew what a nut he was, how crazy he'd been acting since the heist, and how easy it was for him to whack people.

So when I got arrested, it was almost a relief. I was probably next on his hit list.

THE LAST SUPPER

The day I got caught, I made a major meal, not knowing what was about to happen. I had great rolled veal cutlets to start, my brother Michael's favorite sauce with pork butt, veal shanks, and ziti, green beans with olive oil and garlic. When I was in prison, I thought about those dishes and how lucky I was to have had them before the Feds got to me.

Rolled Cutlet Canapés

These are like mini-*braciole* made with veal or pork. They're a delicious hot appetizer and also good as a main dish with a lightly sauced pasta and salad.

3 ounces provolone cheese, cut in strips
3 ounces grated packaged mozzarella cheese
½ cup freshly grated Parmesan cheese
2 tablespoons chopped fresh parsley or 1 teaspoon dried
4 garlic cloves, minced (1½ tablespoons)
1 teaspoon black pepper
1 cup flour
½ teaspoon salt
2 pounds thinly sliced veal or pork cutlets (about 16 small cutlets)
4 tablespoons olive or vegetable oil
Lemon wedges for serving (1–2 lemons)

Put cheeses, parsley, garlic, and ½ teaspoon pepper in a bowl and mix together well. Combine flour, salt, and remaining pepper and put on a plate.

Pound cutlets one at a time until evenly ⅛-inch thick (see page 57 for how to pound cutlets). Lay out each cutlet and place about 1 tablespoon cheese mixture in a stripe down cutlet, a bit closer to one side rather than down the middle. Roll cutlet tightly and secure with one or two toothpicks. Don't worry if ends are not totally closed—the cheese will ooze out a little if they're not, no big deal. Coat cutlets in flour on all sides and set on a plate.

HENRY'S
NOTES
AND TIPS

You can make this with any combination of cheeses—a simpler version is just the mozzarella and Parmesan. If you use only two cheeses, add more of each to make up three more ounces.

Heat oil in a skillet over medium-high heat. Cook cutlets, browning on each side, 8–10 minutes. Serve immediately with lemon wedges.

■■

Michael's Favorite Ziti with Meat Sauce

Makes enough sauce for 4–6, depending on their appetites.

This was my brother Michael's favorite pasta recipe. He'd sit in his wheelchair and stir the sauce lovingly all day to make sure it didn't stick. It uses some meats which are hard to find now. If you can't find them, substitute a version of them and it'll still be fine.

¼ cup olive oil
1 pound pork butt (or shoulder), in one piece
1 pound veal shanks
6–8 cloves of garlic, minced or thinly sliced (about 2 tablespoons)
Two 28-ounce cans peeled plum tomatoes with basil, drained, reserving juice
12 large basil leaves, torn in large pieces, or 1 tablespoon dried
¼ cup finely chopped Italian parsley or 2 teaspoons–1 tablespoon dried parsley
¼–½ teaspoon each salt and pepper (to taste)
1 recipe Milly's Meatballs (see page 38 for recipe)
1 pound cooked and drained ziti (see page 37 for how to prepare)

In a large pot, heat oil over medium heat. Add pork butt and veal shanks and brown on all sides. Remove meat from pan.

In the same pan, cook garlic over medium heat until soft (do not brown) and add tomatoes, basil, parsley, salt, and black pepper to taste. Bring tomatoes to a boil, breaking them up, and stir once thoroughly, then reduce heat to a low simmer. As the acid from the tomatoes flows to the top, skim it off (after 10–15 minutes).

Remove bones from veal shanks and coarsely chop meat.

After 15–20 minutes of cooking, return meat to tomato sauce. Continue cooking at a low simmer, skimming when necessary and stirring briefly right after skimming for about 4 hours (this was my brother

Michael's job). One half hour before serving, add the 6 prepared meat-balls (see recipe for meatballs, page 38) and continue cooking.

When ziti is cooked al dente, place in a large bowl and toss with the meat sauce. Serve immediately with grated Parmesan or Romano cheese on the side.

Serves 4.

■■■

Green Beans with Garlic and Oil

To make green beans tender, I usually boil them first, then add them to a skillet with the other ingredients for flavor.

1 pound green beans, snapped (meaning you take off the bud end
    and snap in half if they're large)
2 tablespoons olive oil
2–4 cloves of fresh garlic, minced
¼ cup white raisins (optional)
¼ cup pine nuts (optional)
½ teaspoon salt and pepper (to taste)

Bring a large pot of water to a boil and add tablespoon of salt. Stir and bring back to a boil.

Add snapped beans and boil 5–8 minutes, depending on the size of the beans. (Test one bean after 5 minutes. They should still be bright green and almost tender.) Drain and rinse in cold water to stop them cooking.

In a large skillet, heat olive oil over medium heat. Add garlic and cook 1 minute, being careful not to burn. Add cooked beans, optional raisins and pine nuts, and sauté 1–2 minutes. Season with salt and pepper and serve immediately.

HENRY'S NOTES AND TIPS

Leave out the raisins and pine nuts for a simpler dish.

I ROLL

When they first arrested me, I thought it was only a speed bump, I'd be back on the street in a day or two. Didn't turn out that way. I thought, "Paulie'll pull some strings, I'll be free again." But the Feds knew they had me on a major bust. Twenty-five years to life.

This wasn't simply a question of Paulie paying somebody off. He would have had to call in some big favors to get me out, and he wasn't about to. He'd warned me about the drugs. He didn't want any part of them. I'd fucked up. In his mind, it was the worst thing I could have done.

And Jimmy was still in his pocket. My guess was Jimmy wanted me dead—I knew too much about Lufthansa, I knew too much about everything. I could put them away forever if I talked. Alive, I was a dangerous guy.

I got out on bail briefly, but even then I knew I was in more danger on the street from Jimmy, and Paulie too. Paulie would use Jimmy to get rid of me. They knew I had to go back in. They knew there was a good chance I'd roll on them, facing all that time. No matter how long we'd been together, no matter that they were almost my father and my brother, they thought they couldn't trust me.

And I knew I couldn't trust them. After what I'd done with the drugs, Paulie had turned his back on me. If I didn't rat them out and got back on the street somehow, or even if I went to prison, I'd be walking into a death trap. Jimmy'd find a way to whack me no matter where I was. It was life in prison if I said nothing, or it was a bullet in my head on the street, or even death from some wiseguy in prison if I didn't talk.

I had no choice. I rolled. I put myself, and my family, in the Witness Protection Program. I said good-bye to life as I knew it. And I've missed it ever since.

SECTION TWO:
ON THE RUN

A NEW LIFE

The Feds took me into the Program Memorial Day weekend 1980. Their job was to find a town in America that was safe from the wiseguys who wanted to kill me, a place they didn't have spies who could report where I was. But it also needed to be near a major airport, because I had to roundtrip it to New York a lot to add to my testimony.

It took them a number of weeks to get all the paperwork done to relocate us. In the meantime, they had to keep moving us around. We lived all over Connecticut and New Jersey. Every couple of days, we'd be in a new place. We wouldn't even bother to unpack. It was Bonnie and Clyde time.

We couldn't go anywhere. We couldn't make a phone call. And we were scared to death. We were still on the East Coast—much too close to Paulie and Jimmy for me. They had never hesitated to whack somebody who crossed them. And I wasn't just going to cross them, I was going to put them away for the rest of their lives—if I lived to testify.

The Feds did everything they could to make us comfortable. Any requests we had they tried to grant. The sky was the limit as far as what we spent on food or other life "necessities." Fine by me. We were gonna eat like kings.

I started cooking for everyone—not just Karen and the kids, but all the marshals and agents who were around. I'd plan the night's menu in the car while they moved us from one town to another, and the minute we arrived, I'd get a guy to go to the grocery store.

At one point, they took us to the Hamptons. Maybe this wasn't going to be so bad after all. I mean, who doesn't like the Hamptons? And what would you eat in the Hamptons but seafood? I asked the Feds if they could get us some lobsters.

One of the agents named Tom looked shocked. I asked him what was wrong. He confessed he'd never had lobster. Never had lobster! What kind of life was that? He'd grown up shanty Irish, eating nothing but cabbage, potatoes, a little corned beef, a leg of lamb once a year on Easter. His family could never afford lobster.

His story was too familiar. I think my mom had lobster only a few times, and that was because I brought them home from a wiseguy connection at the fish market. I felt terrible for Tom. So I made us a ton of Lobster Fra Diavolo. He loved it.

Serves 3–6,

depending on

your appetite.

Lobster Fra Diavolo

A lot of wiseguys were crazy for lobster. They'd have the bugs two, three times a week. "Fra Diavolo" is one of my favorite ways to do it. The lobster gets cooked in a spicy tomato sauce ("diavolo" means devil), and the lobster flavor gets all through the sauce and makes it fabulous— you'll need lots of bread to sop it up.

   1 cup olive oil
   1 tablespoon garlic, minced
   Two 28-ounce cans peeled plum tomatoes with juice
   ¼–½ teaspoon dried oregano (to taste)
   ¼–½ teaspoon dried red pepper flakes (to taste)
   3 live lobsters, about 2 pounds each
   ¼–½ teaspoon each salt and pepper
   1 pound pasta, cooked and drained (optional, see page 37 for how
      to prepare)

Heat 2 tablespoons oil in a large skillet over medium heat. Add garlic and cook 2 minutes to release its flavor—do not brown. Add juice from the tomatoes, stir quickly to stop garlic cooking, crush tomatoes in your hands, and add to garlic. Add oregano, red pepper flakes, and ¼ teaspoon salt and pepper and lower heat to a simmer. Simmer sauce 20 minutes, occasionally skimming off any foam or oil that rises to the top.

Meanwhile, kill the lobsters by stabbing them quickly in the back of the head right behind the eyes with a sharp knife. (You can lull them a bit beforehand by stroking the back of their heads—it makes them dopey and sleepy.) Cut lobsters in half through the underside and take out the green stuff (tomalley) and the stomach sac. Remove the legs and set aside. Lightly rinse lobster halves and shake off excess water.

Break legs in half and put in a small saucepan with 1½ cups water. Bring to a boil, and cook uncovered over medium-high heat until the water is reduced to about 1 cup. Strain and add ½ cup of the water to the tomato sauce for flavoring. Save the rest for thinning if necessary.

Don't overcook the lobsters or they'll get tough. They're done as soon as the meat has lost its "sheen" when you cut into it.

If you don't want to bother with boiling the legs, don't. Add up to one cup of bottled clam juice to the tomato sauce instead.

"Fra Diavolo" isn't limited to lobster. You can use it for other shellfish—shrimp, clams, mussels, or even meats. Use your imagination!

Heat remaining oil over medium heat in a pot large enough to accommodate a couple of lobster halves at a time. Sear halves in batches in the oil, shell side down, until they turn bright red. The lobsters are now basically cooked and will finish in the tomato sauce.

Remove halves and drain on paper towels. When all halves are done, add them to the tomato sauce, spooning the sauce over them. Cook until lobsters are heated through, about 5 minutes. Add more salt and pepper if desired. Serve with bread and optional pasta, tossed with about 1 cup of sauce.

RULES FOR COOKING ON THE RUN

It was during those first weeks in the Program that I realized my cooking was going to have to change—evolve, whatever you want to call it. I mean, they didn't have the same stuff in grocery stores in Connecticut as they had in the Italian delis in Brooklyn. I was stuck with what I could find.

But I learned some things pretty quick, partly because I'd been cooking so much of my life. I discovered that as long as I kept a few ideas in mind, I could make good food, and it'd have some Italian flavor. And I was really going to need those cooking ideas for wherever they moved us next.

Henry's Rules for Cooking on the Run:
HOW TO MAKE GOOD ITALIAN FOOD ANYWHERE

Rule 1: Use fresh ingredients whenever you can. It's a European tradition to shop every day for the freshest ingredients, and Italian Americans—or at least my family—still do that. Me or one of my sisters would go to the store every day for fresh tomatoes, escarole, fresh fish or meat. Today you can get all kinds of ingredients mailed to you from all over the country, even all over the world. But the stuff that was picked or caught that morning around the corner from you is always going to taste the best.

Rule 2: Cook with the Italian "Quartet." Sicilian food almost always includes the same four things: garlic, olive oil, parsley and basil. They are in so many dishes I think of them as one ingredient. If you use these four, your food is almost sure to taste Italian. Oregano and rosemary are also around a lot, but not as much as the "Fab Four."

Chapter Seven

Omaha

■■

The first place they relocated me and my family to was Omaha, Nebraska. It's a pretty safe bet there's not a lot of wiseguys there.

But there are a lot of cows—feeding pen after feeding pen after feeding pen. They raise them in Omaha and send them up to Chicago to get whacked. Oh, and there's something else. Corn—cornfield after cornfield after cornfield. To feed all the cows.

I thought I'd landed at the end of the world. It was like a foreign country where they happened to speak English. I hadn't spent much time west of the Mississippi. I'd been up and down the East Coast, always for some scheme: running cigarettes from North Carolina, down to Miami on business for Paulie. But I was never in those places long— I'd do my job and leave. This was completely different.

The first thing I noticed was the sky. It was huge. It took up more than half of what you saw anytime you looked around, it never seemed to end. Except that the place was so flat that the land never seemed to end either. There was nothing to cut off the flat land but the sky, and there was nothing to cut off the sky but the flat land. No tall buildings, no clubs, no subways, no street signs, no noise even to break up the monotony. Just a bunch of cows.

The Feds stashed us in this tract house in the middle of a lot of other tract houses. The houses were so alike, I had to count from the beginning of the block so I'd to go to the right one.

My whole family was miserable. We were completely separated from everything we'd known all our lives. Karen was miserable without Fortunoff's, the kids had no interest in the 4-H Club.

I had a lot to learn. I didn't even know how to write a check or read the phone book. Stand on line at the grocery store? Me?

When I feel bad, the first place I turn for comfort is food. I thought here at least I could cook us up some good meals—a good Italian sauce, a little pasta, find a good bakery for bread, maybe we'd start to feel at home. No matter how awful things could get in Brooklyn, no matter how many bodies they found or what craziness I was involved in with Paulie, Jimmy, and Tommy, the food was always there. It made a lot of things okay.

So I headed to the grocery store.

And I hit a brick wall.

I guess I was stupid. I knew I wasn't going to be able to find some things, but it never crossed my mind it could be *this* bad. When I checked out the biggest grocery store in Omaha—and you have to remember this was twenty years ago; things have changed a lot since then—I found almost *nothing* Italian. There were aisles and aisles of crap—TV dinners, frozen this, prepackaged that. The only lettuce in the vegetable section was that watery iceberg stuff, which I had never eaten in my life, and the only tomatoes were those rock hard ones that have been injected with something weird and have no taste. Puh-leese!

I tracked down a grocery clerk and asked if they had basil and parsley. First he took me to the spice aisle and showed me the dried stuff. When I said, "No, I want fresh, you know, the leaves," he was astounded. He had never seen fresh basil, he didn't even know it came like that. He did have parsley, and took me to their supply: a few ratty bunches of curly parsley, way past their prime.

I was getting exasperated. I asked if he had any Italian food, and a light bulb went off. He took me to an aisle with store brand spaghetti next to the Minute rice and instant mashed potatoes. When I still wasn't satisfied, we went to an area in a back corner of the store. There, tucked away, was a small section labeled specialty foods. It was about two feet wide and maybe covered three shelves, and everything they considered "international" was all jammed together: soy sauce, chick peas, sardines from Norway—and hiding among dusty cans of Devil's Food Liver Pate and beef Bovril paste was a sight for sore eyes: Ronzoni, the brand my mother always used! Lasagne noodles, an exotic pasta shape! There were also a couple of boxes of fettuccine.

I bought them out. Hiding behind the pasta were some cans of Greek green olives and tiny jars of pimientos (which you can use for red pepper flavor)—they went in the basket too. As well as some tiny bottles of olive oil that cost an arm and a leg.

There were other disappointments. The only Parmesan cheese was the dried stuff in a shaker, which never melts, just sits on top of the food like pebbles; a tiny piece of yellowed, old mozzarella was ridiculously expensive; and of course there was no prosciutto, not a chance of an artichoke. I kept thinking, what do these people eat? How do they survive?

Henry's Rules for Cooking on the Run:
HOW TO MAKE GOOD ITALIAN FOOD ANYWHERE

Rule 3: Cheap can be expensive. Use good quality canned, frozen or dried when you can't get fresh. Good canned tomatoes are worth the extra pennies, believe me.[1] My mother always used canned scungilli, which is conch, because it was too expensive to buy fresh, but she used a good brand.

Rule 4: Check dried spices for freshness. If you use your grandmother's ancient dried oregano, you'll be wasting your time. If the spice doesn't have much smell when you rub it between your fingers, don't bother adding it. Get a new jar or leave it out. I have used garlic powder when I couldn't find fresh, but I don't use garlic salt—it's almost all salt and little garlic. Use about ¼ teaspoon garlic powder for one normal clove of garlic.

Rule 5: If you don't see what you want, ask. Grocers can order things for you. That's if you are thinking ahead and can wait for it to show up. My way is usually to need something right away. But if you have the time, this can work.

---

[1]For canned goods, I like Progresso or San Marzano the best for tomatoes, but there are other good brands available. Try them and see what you like.

They eat beef. In every form possible. And potatoes from nearby Idaho. And corn when it's in season. Omaha does have the freshest and tastiest beef in the country, made from all those cows. A salad to them may be a hunk of iceberg smothered in Thousand Island dressing, but their burgers are delicious.

Okay, I resigned myself to going with the flow—beef it would be, and everything else would be cooking by the seat of my pants. But I also sought out the manager to see if any special orders were possible. A few weeks later, my cans of Progresso tomatoes arrived, and I was a much happier man. Meanwhile, there was dinner to make.

Serves 2–4.

Steak Oreganato

Oregano is a spice I use mostly with fish or on pizza. But I guarantee you'll love the flavor it gives the beef here.

2 tablespoons olive oil
¼ teaspoon salt
½ teaspoon black pepper
1 teaspoon dried oregano, crumbled
2 garlic cloves, chopped
4–6 tablespoons red wine vinegar (¼ cup)
⅛ cup soy sauce
Two 8–12-ounce steaks, such as rib-eye, T-bone, New York strip, porterhouse (whatever's on sale is my rule, but T-bone is a little heartier and good for this recipe)

HENRY'S NOTES AND TIPS

You can marinate the beef longer than two hours, but don't leave it overnight. Beef combined with acid (like vinegar or lemon) starts to break down after a while.

Combine all ingredients except steak in a nonreactive pan or bowl large enough to hold all the steak in one layer (glass or stainless steel, not aluminum). Or mix together all ingredients except steak in a bowl and pour into a large sealable plastic bag. Add meat to marinade and turn (or lightly shake bag) to coat all sides. Marinate for 20 minutes to 2 hours (how much time you got?).

Preheat broiler or grill. Broil to desired doneness and serve.

ABOUT BEEF

Everybody has their favorite steak or cut of beef. There are no rules as to which you should buy. But here's some simple information about beef that may help you in cooking it.

Bones enhance the flavor of beef—even "bone dust" left by the saw adds to it. Don't rinse it off; it's so slight you won't notice once the beef is cooked. I always buy steaks on the bone.

Filet mignon (or tenderloin) has no bone. It isn't even really a muscle. It's expensive because it's one small piece out of a whole side of beef and it's very very tender. But it's not as flavorful as a steak on a bone. Its tenderness makes it great for carpaccio, which is raw beef pounded very thin and seasoned.

To cook steak on a stovetop, I try to use a cast iron skillet. Sear the meat over high heat at the beginning of cooking. The European method is to sear meat on top of the stove and then finish cooking in the oven. I think it's fine to do all the cooking on the burners.

Cheaper cuts of meat need moist heat to bring out their flavor, and usually more time to tenderize. I often marinate cheaper cuts—the liquids will tenderize them and the spices will add flavor.

▪▪

Steak Pizzaiola

As you'd think from the name, this is a steak cooked with a pizza-type sauce. Which also means you can add different vegetables you would put on a pizza and top it with cheese, or you can have it bareback, just the steak and tomato sauce. Either way, it's satisfying the way a pizza and a steak both are.

3 tablespoons olive oil (not extra virgin)
One 3-pound steak (T-bone, porterhouse, rib-eye), about 1" thick
½ cup dry red wine
4 cloves of garlic, minced (1 tablespoon)
One 28-ounce can crushed tomatoes and their juice
1 teaspoon dried oregano, crumbled
1 teaspoon each salt and black pepper (to taste)
3 tablespoons grated Parmesan or Romano cheese (optional)

Optional vegetables:

½ medium red or green pepper, seeded and diced
½ medium brown or white onion, peeled, trimmed, and sliced
4 ounces white mushrooms, trimmed and sliced
¼ cup sliced black olives (American or brined)
3 ounces canned or jarred artichoke hearts (not marinated)

Heat oil over medium-high heat in a skillet large enough to hold steak. Season steak lightly with salt and black pepper on both sides. Brown steak on one side about 3 minutes, flip, and brown an additional 3 minutes on second side. Remove steak to a plate.

Lower heat to medium. If adding peppers or onions, add to pan and cook 3–4 minutes, stirring. Add the wine to the skillet and scrape up any bits from the bottom of the pan. Add garlic, tomatoes and juice, oregano, and salt and pepper to taste. Cook 15 minutes, stirring occasionally, until mixture starts to thicken. If using mushrooms or

ABOUT OREGANO

My mother never used fresh oregano, only dried. She thought the fresh was bitter. It was many years before I used fresh, and I was surprised how much I liked it. It's a very strong herb, so when you use fresh you don't need a lot (a lot of it *will* taste bitter). I use it in main-course dishes that are baked, many fish and seafood dishes, and on pizza. Unlike basil or parsley, you can easily substitute dried oregano for fresh.

black olives, add after 10 minutes. Return steak to pan. Add artichoke hearts if using. Cook until steak is heated and cooked to your taste (rare, medium rare, etc.) Adjust seasoning of tomato sauce. Remove steak to a carving board and cut in serving pieces. If topping with cheese, in the last 2 minutes of cooking, sprinkle cheese over steak and cover pan. Heat until cheese melts, and then move to carving board to cut. Serve topped with tomato sauce and additional sauce on the side, or toss 1 cup of the sauce with 1 pound cooked and drained pasta of your choice—capellini recommended (see page 37 for how to cook pasta).

Serves 4.

Italian Goulash

I call this goulash because it reminds me of a Hungarian goulash I used to get in New York. You can make this dish with any type of steak; it doesn't have to be expensive. The liquid from the tomatoes will tenderize the meat.

Americans like more meat in their sauce than Italians—don't skimp on the protein! If anything, add extra.

2 tablespoons olive oil
1 tablespoon garlic, minced
1–1½ pounds steak (any kind), cut in ½ × 2" pieces
2 medium or large red peppers, cored, seeded, and diced
One 28-ounce and one 14-ounce can plum tomatoes + their juice
¼ cup chopped fresh parsley or 2 teaspoons dried
½ teaspoon salt
¼ teaspoon black pepper
Dash cayenne or red pepper flakes
½ cup dry red wine
1 pound penne, cooked and drained, reserving 1 cup pasta water
    (see page 37 for instructions on how to cook)
Grated Parmesan for serving

Heat oil in a large skillet over medium-low heat. Add garlic and cook 1–2 minutes (do not brown). Add steak pieces, raise heat to medium, and cook until almost done (barely pink inside). Remove steak to a bowl.

GENERAL RULES FOR PASTA WITH RED MEAT

Red meat mixed with pasta is a hefty combo. It'll satisfy the biggest appetite around. A few things to think of when making a meat sauce:

1. Usually you need more time to cook pasta sauce with red meat than one with chicken or seafood. The meat needs to cook in the sauce about half an hour for the flavors to meld, and you can cook it much longer than that. For example, to make a *ragù Bolognese*, which is a Northern Italian dish, you simmer the sauce about three hours, even four. The longer the meat cooks in the sauce, the more the sauce will be flavored by it.
2. Americans like more meat in their sauce than Italians. If you're using more than one kind of meat (see my recipe for Michael's

Favorite Ziti with Meat Sauce, on page 149), you can use four ounces per person per meat. If you have only one meat, it's a *minimum* of six ounces per person, unless you know you have light meat eaters.

3. Always brown meat before adding to sauce. The browning brings out the flavor of the meat. You don't have to, but I brown prosciutto briefly in a tablespoon of olive oil. It gives it a slightly nutty taste.

4. Things to jack up the flavor if you're short of time cooking a meat sauce (based on one twenty-eight-ounce can of tomatoes):

   1 tablespoon of tomato paste—make sure to add early to cut the paste's acid

   ½ cup of red wine—add to pan after browning meat and scrape up any bits from bottom of pan (called deglazing) or add to sauce later to enrich flavor

   ½ cup of beef broth

   ⅛ ounce porcini mushrooms (if dried, soaked in warm water and water drained through a sieve)

   ½ diced red pepper or a tablespoon of pimientos

   ⅛–¼ teaspoon fennel seeds—careful, they can overshadow every other flavor!

   1 whole clove

   A pinch of dried red pepper flakes

Add red peppers to remaining oil in skillet. Cook 2–4 minutes until beginning to soften. Drain tomatoes and add juice to peppers. Either crush tomatoes well in your hands or chop fine on a cutting board and add to skillet along with parsley, salt, black pepper, and cayenne or red pepper flakes. Cook 2 minutes. Return meat and any juices in the bowl to the pan. Cook 20 minutes, skimming off any oil or foam that rises to the top and stirring occasionally, until tomatoes are beginning to break up and get "saucy." Add red wine and reduce sauce, stirring, about 4 minutes. Sauce should be medium thick. If it gets too thick, add ½–1 cup pasta water. Adjust salt and pepper seasoning. Toss steak and tomato mixture with pasta and serve immediately with Parmesan on the side.

POLENTA

I sure ate different things in Omaha. I got introduced to the real American barbecue, not the Italian-style one I knew. I ate coleslaw, burgers, and lots and lots of corn on the cob. The only thing I could think to do with all that corn was use cornmeal and make polenta.

If you're from the South, you'd call polenta "grits." I've even used boxed grits to make it. They don't eat much polenta in Sicily—they don't grow much corn. Both it and risotto are classic Northern Italian dishes, but I knew them from Brooklyn and Italian festivals.

Polenta is cheap and delicious, but the best thing about it is you can cheat. You're supposed to stand there and stir the damn stuff for almost an hour, but you don't have to. I found you can make it with a minimum of stirring on the stovetop, or even in the oven with no stirring. Nowadays you can also buy instant polenta, which cooks in 5 minutes, or it's sold already cooked and packaged. I think the instant kind is too grainy, but it'll do in a pinch. The precooked kind is fine, but costs a lot more than cornmeal.

Serves 6–8.

Basic Stovetop Polenta

6 cups water
1 teaspoon salt
1 cup coarse-grained cornmeal or polenta
1½ tablespoons butter
1½–1 teaspoon black pepper (to taste)
4 tablespoons freshly grated Parmesan cheese (optional)
1 tablespoon olive oil (optional)

Put 3 cups water in a heavy-bottomed pot and the other 3 cups in a regular saucepan. Add salt and polenta to the water in the heavy-bottomed pot and stir well, using a wire whisk to start and then a wooden spoon as the polenta starts to thicken. Heat the water in the saucepan to a boil and keep heated at a simmer.

Heat the polenta mixture over high heat to a boil, stirring constantly. When it reaches a boil, lower heat and cook at a simmer, stirring occasionally, for 10 minutes. When the mixture starts to thicken, add one cup of the heated water from the saucepan and stir well. Stir constantly for about 2 minutes. Cover the pot and let mixture cook about 10 minutes, until it begins to thicken. The polenta should be simmering fast but not boiling. Remove lid, and stir well for about 30 seconds. Re-cover and allow to cook another 10 minutes before stirring for another 30 seconds. If mixture is too thick, add ½ cup of heated water from the saucepan at a time, stirring well. (You probably won't use all the heated water.) Repeat process once more (for a total of 30 minutes). The polenta should be pulling away from the sides of the pan when you stir it. If not, stir well and cook an additional 5-10 minutes. It should have a smooth, not grainy texture.

If serving immediately, remove polenta from heat and stir in butter and pepper, then add optional cheese. Stir well to combine and serve.

If making firm polenta to use later, cook an extra 5 minutes to thicken a bit more. Lightly oil a 1–1½ quart casserole and spoon warm polenta into it, smoothing the top with a spatula or knife. Cool to room temperature, cover with plastic wrap or foil and refrigerate at least 1 hour. Polenta will get firm as it cools.

As noted, you won't use all the hot water on the side. The basic ratio for polenta to water is four to one. The extra water is in case the mixture gets too thick.

HENRY'S NOTES AND TIPS

Fried or Broiled Polenta

Cold polenta slices nicely and can be fried or broiled, and then served different ways—as is, topped with many things like mushrooms, artichokes, and different sauces, or as part of a sandwich or a salad. It's even terrific alongside a couple of eggs for breakfast, the way you might have grits.

For frying:

1 recipe Basic Stovetop or Basic Baked Polenta (see page 168 or
        171), refrigerated at least 1 hour, or one 16-ounce package
        precooked polenta
½–1 teaspoon each salt and pepper (to taste)
2 tablespoons olive oil
2 tablespoons butter

Slice polenta into ½-inch-thick slices. Salt and pepper both sides. Heat oil and butter in a large skillet over medium heat and when hot but not smoking, slip in polenta slices. Don't crowd the polenta; cook in batches if necessary. Cook on one side until it begins to look golden, turn with a spatula, and repeat on second side. Drain on paper towels and serve, adding whatever topping you choose.

HENRY'S NOTES AND TIPS

You can coat polenta with flour to keep it from sticking to the frying pan. Mix a quarter cup flour with a quarter teaspoon each salt and pepper and place on a plate. Dredge polenta slices one at a time on both sides in flour, shaking off excess, before adding to pan.

If frying more than one batch, make sure that you add more oil and butter and reheat before cooking second batch.

I've had trouble grilling polenta. It sticks to the grill and makes a mess. You have to have a completely clean, well-oiled grill. To me, it's not worth the effort.

For broiling:

Replace the butter with up to 2 tablespoons additional olive oil. Slice polenta into ½-inch-thick slices.

Preheat broiler. Brush a baking sheet with olive oil, place polenta slices on it (do not crowd), brush tops with olive oil and season lightly with salt and pepper. Broil until polenta starts to turn golden, turn slices using a spatula, season second side with salt and pepper, and grill until second side is also golden. Serve with topping of your choice.

▪▪ *Serves 6–8.*

Basic Baked Polenta

This is a no-work version of polenta, baked in the oven.

4 cups water
1 teaspoon salt
1 cup coarse-grained cornmeal or polenta
½–1 teaspoon black pepper (to taste)
1½ tablespoons butter (optional)
4 tablespoons freshly grated Parmesan cheese (optional)
1 tablespoon olive oil (optional)

Preheat oven to 350°F. Put water in a 1–1½ quart casserole. Whisk in salt and then polenta and black pepper to taste. Stir until smooth.

Place casserole in oven and bake 35 minutes without stirring. At 35 minutes, check polenta for doneness and stir, adding optional butter and cheese. Cook an additional 10 minutes if needed. Serve immediately, topping as you choose, or follow steps to prepare firm polenta as written in Basic Stovetop Polenta, above.

Baked Polenta with Sausage and Tomato Sauce

This uses the polenta almost like lasagne noodles. It's a real crowd-pleaser, and easier to make than lasagne.

¼ cup olive oil
1 pound hot or mild Italian sausage (or a mix), casings removed
   and crumbled (or ground seasoned pork sausage)
One 28-ounce can peeled plum tomatoes, or 1 pound fresh, cored
   and diced
½ medium onion, peeled and diced (½ cup)
4 garlic cloves, peeled and minced (1 tablespoon)
¼ cup chopped fresh basil or 2 teaspoons dried, crumbled
½ teaspoon dried red pepper flakes (optional)
½–1 teaspoon each salt and black pepper (to taste)
1 recipe Basic Baked Polenta (see page 171), cooled in refrigerator
   for an hour, sliced in ½"-thick slices or one 16-ounce package
   precooked polenta
½–1 cup grated fresh Parmesan or Romano cheese (or a mix of
   both)

Heat 2 tablespoons oil in a large skillet over medium heat. Add sausage and cook, stirring occasionally and turning to brown on all sides, about 8 minutes. Remove sausage and drain on paper towels. Remove all but about 1 tablespoon fat from skillet.

Strain juice from canned tomatoes into a separate bowl. Reheat fat over medium-low heat. Add onion and cook, stirring, 5 minutes. Add garlic and cook, stirring 1–2 minutes (do not brown garlic). Add juice from canned tomatoes, then crush canned tomatoes with hands or chop on a board and add to mixture. Or if using fresh diced tomatoes, add to onion-garlic mixture.

Raise heat to medium and add basil, optional red pepper flakes, and salt and black pepper to taste. When mixture begins to bubble, lower to simmer and cook 15 minutes, skimming off any oil or foam that rises to the top and stirring occasionally. Return sausage to pan and heat 3 or 4 minutes. Adjust seasoning.

Preheat oven to 350°F. Lightly oil a 1–1½ quart casserole dish with olive oil. Cover bottom of casserole with a layer of one-quarter of the polenta slices, topped with ½ cup of sausage/tomato mixture and sprinkle with ¼ cup cheeses. Make two more layers in the same way, ending with a layer of polenta topped with a light sprinkling of cheese.

Cook casserole in oven 20–25 minutes, until sauce is bubbling around the sides and top is golden. Let rest a few minutes out of the oven before cutting into squares and serving.

■■■

Serves 6–8

as an appetizer

or light lunch.

Mushroom Topping for Polenta

This makes a great hot appetizer, or serve with a salad for a light lunch.

¼ ounce dried porcini mushrooms (see Henry's Notes and Tips, below)
4 tablespoons olive oil
3 medium garlic cloves, peeled and sliced thin lengthwise
8 ounces white mushrooms
8 ounces mixed other mushrooms, such as shiitake or brown cremini
¼ cup chopped fresh Italian parsley or 2 teaspoons dried, crumbled
2 sprigs fresh rosemary leaves, minced, or 1 teaspoon dried, crumbled
½–1 teaspoon each salt and pepper (to taste)
¼ cup dry white wine
1 recipe fried or broiled polenta slices (see Basic Polenta recipes, pages 168 and 171)
½ cup freshly grated Parmesan cheese for serving (optional)

If you can't find dried porcinis, try substituting a combination of one tablespoon tomato paste dissolved in one cup heated beef or chicken broth (I prefer beef). Add this when you would add the porcini liquid with the white wine. Reduce a minute or two longer to allow the tomato flavor to mix in with the mushrooms.

Soak porcinis in 1 cup of hot water for 10–15 minutes, until soft. Drain through a fine sieve (or a strainer lined with cheesecloth), reserving soaking liquid. Rinse porcinis carefully to remove any sand or grit and chop coarsely. Set aside.

Rinse or wipe both kinds of mushrooms clean and trim off any tough stems. Slice in ¼-inch-thick slices. Set aside.

Place polenta slices on an oiled baking sheet and warm in the oven (at no more than 200°F).

Heat oil in a medium skillet over medium-low heat. Add garlic slices and cook 2 minutes (do not brown). Raise heat to high and add porcinis, white and mixed mushrooms, parsley, rosemary, and salt and pepper to taste. Sauté 3–4 minutes, or until mushrooms give off their liquid. Reduce heat to medium. Add porcini liquid (leave sediment at bottom of container) and white wine. Reduce liquid until it begins to get "saucy," about 5 minutes. Adjust seasoning.

Place polenta slices on individual plates or a large serving platter and top with hot mushroom mixture. Serve immediately, topped with Parmesan if desired.

Black Olive Appetizer

Believe it or not, this appetizer tastes great with plain old American canned olives. If you like a stronger olive taste and can get brined olives, use the second recipe. And if you can't find pine nuts or fresh parsley, make it anyway. It's still fabulous.

Two 6-ounce cans pitted American black olives
4 whole garlic cloves
½ cup fresh Italian parsley leaves (see Henry's Notes and Tips, below)
¼ cup pine nuts (optional)
8 tablespoons olive oil
½ cup grated Parmesan cheese
½ cup grated mozzarella cheese
Salt and pepper to taste
Crackers or toasted baguette slices

Put all ingredients except crackers or bread in food processor and pulse until coarsely chopped (don't overprocess—you want it a bit chunky). If you don't have a food processor, place olives, garlic, parsley, and pine nuts on a cutting board and chop together fine. Place in a bowl and stir in olive oil, cheeses, and salt and pepper to taste. Serve with crackers or toasted baguette slices.

For a little more zing, add an anchovy and/or a tablespoon of lemon juice.

Dried parsley needs to be cooked to taste okay, so it doesn't work as a substitute here.

HENRY'S NOTES AND TIPS

Black Olive Appetizer with a Bite

One 6-ounce can kalamata or other brine-cured black olives, pitted
One 6-ounce can American pitted black olives
6–8 whole garlic cloves
1 cup loosely packed fresh Italian parsley leaves (see Henry's Notes
    and Tips to previous recipe, page 175)
4 anchovies
½–1 cup olive oil
1 large tablespoon capers, drained
Salt and pepper to taste
Crackers or toasted baguette slices

Place all ingredients except crackers or bread in a food processor
and pulse until coarsely chopped. Or mix olives, garlic, parsley, and
anchovies on a cutting board and chop fine. Put in a bowl and stir in
olive oil and capers. Season with salt and pepper to taste. Serve with
crackers or toast.

HENRY'S NOTES AND TIPS

Start with a half cup olive oil and add more if needed to moisten.
Both recipes serve eight to ten as an appetizer.

Oven-Dried Tomatoes

I discovered this when I couldn't find any sundrieds and I couldn't
stand the cardboard tomatoes' lack of taste. It takes hours to cook on
very low heat, but the result is very tasty. Their flavor is different from
sundrieds—not as dark and earthy, more like a jacked-up tomato flavor.

1 pound fresh plum tomatoes (or any beefy kind of tomato)
1–1½ teaspoons salt
½ cup olive oil or to cover
2 garlic cloves, peeled and halved

Heat oven to 200°F. Wash tomatoes, trim stem ends and cut in half lengthwise. Place on a foil-lined cookie sheet cut side up and sprinkle generously with salt. Bake in oven 6 hours. Tomatoes should be darker and wrinkled all around the edges, but not completely dried out. (They won't get as dark as sundrieds.) Cool to room temperature. Place in a glass jar and add garlic pieces and olive oil to cover. Refrigerate 2 days before using, shaking jar occasionally. They'll last a couple of weeks in the fridge.

■■

Serves 4.

Oven- or Sundried Tomato Marinara

4 ounce oven or sundried tomatoes (½ cup packed) in oil
3 cloves of garlic, minced
⅓ cup carrot, chopped fine
⅓ cup celery, chopped fine
One 28-ounce can peeled plum tomatoes with juice
¼ cup chopped fresh parsley
½ teaspoon fennel seeds, lightly crushed (optional)
½ cup dry white wine
½–1 teaspoon salt (to taste)
¼ teaspoon black pepper
1 pound pasta of your choice, cooked and drained, reserving 1 cup
    pasta water (see page 37 for how to cook)
Freshly grated Parmesan cheese for serving

Drain dried tomatoes well in a strainer, reserving oil, and slice in thin slivers. Heat 3 tablespoons of reserved oil in a large pot over medium heat. Add garlic and cook 1 minute, stirring. Do not brown garlic. Add carrot and cook 3 minutes, stirring. Add celery and cook an additional 2 minutes, making sure garlic doesn't brown or burn (turn down heat if necessary). Add juice from canned tomatoes to stop cooking process. Crush canned tomatoes with your hands or chop well on a cutting board and add to sauce, along with dried tomatoes, parsley, and fennel seeds (if using). Lower heat to simmer and cook 20 minutes, skimming sauce occasionally. Add white wine, salt, and pepper and cook down 5 minutes. Stir in up to 1 cup of pasta water to reach desired consistency. Adjust seasonings. Serve over chosen pasta with Parmesan cheese on the side.

NEW YORK TIME

When I first entered the Program, the Feds were flying me to New York every week to stay a few days at a time to testify. It was grueling. In the Program, I never flew directly anywhere. To go twenty-five hundred miles, sometimes I'd fly fifty-five hundred, with five to six hours in layovers. The flights gave me the time change blues. I never really left New York time—I still haven't twenty years later. I'd get up in Omaha at 4 or 5 a.m. and be ready for the day. And I was hungry. So I'd cook a little something—often a frittata, which is almost an egg pie, with different vegetables, potatoes, onions, some parsley, cold cuts, and cheese. I'd eat some and leave the leftovers for Karen and the kids for their breakfast when they got up.

Serves 4.

Henry's Insomnia Frittata for Four
(Or, Clean the Fridge Frittata)

I hate to waste food. This is a great way to use up leftovers—that single slice of cheese, those mushrooms that are getting old. The ingredients are suggestions (except for the eggs, of course)—you can add just one or two things or all of them.

4 tablespoons olive oil

1–2 potatoes, peeled and sliced

¼–½ teaspoon salt and black pepper (to taste)

1 small or ½ medium onion, sliced thin or chopped

¼–½ red or green pepper, sliced or diced

Sliced fresh mushrooms if available (¼–½ cup)

Cold cuts from the refrigerator: cured sausage, salami, mortadella, or other meat cold cuts, diced (about ½ cup)

6 eggs

¼–½ cup whatever cheese is on hand: provolone, Swiss, cheddar, jack, or mozzarella, grated or cubed

⅛–¼ cup chopped fresh Italian parsley, or 1 teaspoon dried

Heat olive oil in a large skillet over low heat. Add potatoes, season lightly with salt and pepper and sauté 5 minutes, stirring with a spoon or spatula to keep from sticking. Add onion and cook and stir until translucent. Add peppers and mushrooms and cook a few minutes. Add cold cuts. (If mixture is sticking, add a tablespoon of water and scrape the bottom of the pan to loosen.) Beat eggs seasoned with salt and pepper in a small bowl, add 2 tablespoons cold water, and whip air into eggs (this will make frittata light and puffy). Pour eggs into potato mixture and stir lightly. Cook a couple of minutes until eggs are set. Cook until potatoes are tender, about 5 minutes. Sprinkle with grated cheese and parsley. Either cover and cook briefly or put under broiler for 30 seconds until cheese melts.

Variation:

Fry potatoes over high heat to crispy before adding onion (turn heat to low). This gives the frittata a great crunch.

Most cold cuts and cheese are already salted, so go light on the salt. This is a rare recipe in which I don't use garlic. There's such a thing as too early for garlic.

HENRY'S NOTES AND TIPS

SOCIAL LIFE

Meanwhile, Karen had found a social group she liked in Omaha—she joined a Jewish country club. She and the kids spent a lot of time there. Everyone was in the insurance business—we didn't have much in common with them, but they were nice people. When they asked me what I did for a living, I told them I was an arson investigator. That way, when I went back to New York all the time, nobody would question where I was. "Well, there was this fire up in Milwaukee, and my company sent me to check it out . . ."

■■■

Serves 2

as a main course,

or 4 guys

who've been scarf-

ing chips while

watching

the game.

Halftime Linguine

Football is a big deal in Nebraska. Nothing interrupts it—even eating. You eat your meals in front of the TV if a big game is on. So I had to accommodate. My insurance friends were impressed when I started making this pasta at the end of the second quarter and we were taking our first bites as the third quarter began.

Sundried or oven-dried tomatoes are very different from fresh tomatoes. They have a rich, earthy taste. A little goes a long way to flavoring a dish. Feel free to adjust the amount of dried tomatoes and anchovies according to your tastebuds.

½ cup olive oil
4 large garlic cloves, sliced very thin or minced (1½ tablespoons)
4–6 flat anchovy fillets in oil
¼–½ cup sundried (or oven-dried) tomatoes in oil, cut in strips
    (see recipe on page 176 to make oven-dried tomatoes)
½ cup chopped fresh Italian parsley leaves or 2 teaspoons dried
8 ounces linguine, cooked and drained (see page 37 for how to
    cook; do not salt water), reserving one cup pasta water
¼–½ teaspoon black pepper
Grated Parmesan cheese for serving

ANCHOVIES

▪▪▪

Anchovies have a bad reputation—probably from people not liking their flavor undiluted on pizza. When they are mashed and stirred into a sauce, they lose a lot of their fishiness and add a depth and richness of flavor. To cut their saltiness, you can rinse them in cold water. If you still find them too strong-flavored, soak in milk 10–15 minutes, rinse, drain, and pat dry before using.

Heat olive oil in a skillet over medium-low heat. Add garlic and cook, stirring 1 minute. Add anchovies with their oil and mash them in the pan with the back of a spoon until they melt into the oil. Stir in tomatoes, parsley, ½ cup reserved pasta water, and black pepper and cook, stirring, 3–5 minutes. Add more of pasta water if desired. Toss quickly with linguine and serve immediately with Parmesan on the side.

THE TORNADO

At first my insurance pals would tease me about cooking. Keep in mind, these were guys who only went in the kitchen to get a beer or a dish of ice cream. But they loved my food. I could see them trying to figure it out—a macho-type guy who can cook? It made me laugh.

Things were getting better. I was barbecuing for our friends a lot; Karen and the kids had friends from the country club. Old Omaha was getting to be okay.

And then the tornado hit.

I had never seen anything like a tornado. We had hurricanes in the East, I could deal with them. It would rain a lot, it would be real windy for a while, some thunder and lightning. But this was serious. Like God was talking to us. And he wasn't happy.

One morning, I looked out the kitchen window. The tract houses across the street weren't finished, nothing was built yet. It was just empty fields, and you could see for miles. It was very still outside, weirdly quiet, and when I looked out, I could see this big dark funnel moving along the horizon. I thought my life was over. I'd been scared in the Mob, but this was much bigger than anybody who wanted to whack me. The tornado didn't care who I was; if it came close, I was a goner.

The twister passed us by—it hit a few miles away. We could continue our new life. But when the Feds told us not much later that we had to move, I can't tell you how happy I was.

Chapter Eight

Kentucky

▪▪

Our move from Omaha was as fast as you can spit. We got a phone call from the marshals: "We'll be there in half an hour. Pack enough for three to four days. We'll explain later."

The Feds had warned us something *might* happen and we'd have to be ready to drop everything and go. But the first time, it was a shock. We were just starting to feel at home. Our furniture had finally arrived from New York, we had cars in the garage. We had to leave everything, except the dogs and a pet bird. The rest would catch up with us later, if we were lucky.

How do you face stuff like that? Karen and the kids were real troopers. They did it with a smile. When the marshals arrived, we piled in as fast as we could and drove off—to wherever they were taking us.

First we went to the marshals' headquarters, where the head marshal told us what had happened. Jimmy Burke, one of the most dangerous of my wiseguy colleagues, was overheard saying, "We know that rat bastard Hill's somewhere in the Midwest" (it's a safe bet he called me something worse than a rat bastard). That was enough to freak the marshals out, and me too. I knew what horrible things Jimmy could do, and he had a lot of connections to make things happen.

Then we were driven to what they called a "safe house." Safe? It really means a place where they think they can protect you for more than an hour. In this case it was a hotel/motel sixty to eighty miles from

Omaha, like a Regency Suite. It was a kind of live-in place with a small kitchen. We were there maybe two weeks before they decided where to move us more permanently.

During those two weeks, we were all on edge. It was like we were back to square one. Someone could come around the corner and we'd all be dead in a second. So once again, we couldn't go anywhere. We were cooped up just like those cows in Omaha waiting for the slaughter-house.

No one had an appetite, but I was determined we would eat or we'd be even worse off. Besides which, just about my only entertainment was thinking about what to cook. We couldn't order groceries in (what d'ya think, they had Pink Dot and Internet Home Grocer then?). So I had to give my shopping list to one of the marshals. At first he couldn't figure out what some of the things were and he'd roll his eyes like it was a big pain in the neck. But once he tasted the food, he started getting interested, asking me about the ingredients, watching me cook. Hey, for all I know, the guy's a chef by now.

Serves 2.

Aglio e Olio

This is a classic way to cook pasta. It's the cheapest, quickest pasta you can make and it tastes great. You can't go wrong with it.

½ cup olive oil
6–8 cloves of garlic, minced (about 2 tablespoons)
½ pound dried pasta of your choice (I like linguine or capellini)
⅓ cup finely chopped Italian parsley
¼–½ teaspoon salt
¼ teaspoon black pepper
Grated Parmesan cheese (optional)

Heat oil in small saucepan or skillet, add chopped garlic and cook over medium-low heat until garlic is very lightly colored—don't brown it or it'll lose its sweetness. Cook pasta according to Cooking Pasta directions, page 37, reserving 1 cup of pasta water. Toss drained pasta with garlic/oil mixture and parsley. If mixture is too dry, add part of reserved pasta water. Season with salt and pepper and retoss. Serve immediately with grated Parmesan on the side.

Variations:

There are a zillion variations on this one. Here are a few:

Some people peel the garlic cloves but leave them whole. I burp them all night. You can also cook the cloves whole in the oil but take them out before you combine the oil and pasta, so you just get the garlic flavor.

For a real strong garlic taste, add a large clove of minced raw garlic when tossing with garlic and parsley. (Talk about burping!)

While the pasta is cooking, dip out ¼–½ cup of the pasta cooking water and add it to the garlic mixture (slowly to avoid splatters). Simmer over low heat until pasta is done.

My sister Lucille likes to add a tablespoon of grated lemon zest. Toss with pasta when adding garlic and parsley.

Add ½–1 cup of any of your favorite vegetables, or whatever's in the refrigerator: sliced peppers, zucchini (julienne cut to look like pasta), sliced mushrooms, a little spinach. Sauté vegetables in garlic/oil mixture briefly or simply add them to pasta water for last minute of pasta cooking.

Serves 4–6.

On-the-Run Pasta with Canned Tuna

I've made this "on the run" many times. If you cook it with capellini (angel hair), it'll be done before the cops (or the wiseguys) hit the door.

You may not think of canned tuna as an Italian ingredient, but the truth is, they eat a lot of canned tuna in Italy. For many it's a staple on the antipasto platter. Italians don't smother it in mayonnaise, but instead may add some chopped parsley and drizzle it with lemon juice.

Some people add cheese to this dish, but I usually don't mix the two. I think the cheese overwhelms the taste of the fish.

1 pound dried linguine (cappellini in a hurry)
6 cloves of garlic, minced
6 tablespoons olive oil
½ red pepper (if on sale), seeded and chopped
Two 6-ounce cans tuna in oil (Italian if you can get it)
6–8 large black olives, chopped or sliced (optional)
1 tablespoon capers (optional)
¼ cup chopped fresh parsley
1 tablespoon lemon juice (optional)
¼ cup fresh or dried toasted, seasoned bread crumbs (optional)

Cook the pasta to al dente according to directions on page 37. Drain, reserving 1 cup pasta water. In a large skillet, sauté garlic in oil over medium-high heat 1–2 minutes, add red pepper, and cook 30 seconds. Add tuna and pasta water to garlic and pepper. Break up tuna into large pieces with a fork. Bring to a boil. Add pasta to skillet, along with black olives and/or capers if using, toss to combine and heat through (1–2 minutes). Add parsley and optional lemon juice and retoss. Sprinkle each serving with toasted bread crumbs if using.

Serves 4.

Beef and Vegetable Soup with Horseradish

Very simple and very good. Don't skip the horseradish—it makes the dish.

2 tablespoons olive oil
½ large onion, diced (1 cup)

1 carrot, peeled and diced (1 cup)
½ pound stewing beef, cut in large pieces
¼ teaspoon each salt and black pepper
6 cups beef stock or canned broth
½ pound potato, scrubbed and diced
½ pound green beans, stem ends trimmed and broken in 2" pieces
1 small tomato, diced
⅛–¼ cup prepared horseradish

Heat olive oil in a large pot over medium high heat. Add onion and carrot and sauté 5 minutes, stirring. Add beef, season with salt and pepper, and sauté, stirring until meat is browned and the vegetables are slightly caramelized. Add 1 cup of stock and stir, scraping up any bits sticking to the pan. Add remaining stock and potato. Cook until potato can be pierced with a fork but is not too soft, about 10 minutes. Add green beans and tomato and cook 5 minutes. Serve with horseradish on the side, allowing each person to add as much or as little as they want.

■■■

Serves 2.

Pan-Fried Steak

I like my steak medium rare—seared on the outside, pink and tender in the middle. Hotels and motels almost always have electric stoves, not gas. Even on broil, an electric oven doesn't get hot enough to really sear it right for medium rare, so I'd cook steaks on a burner.

1 tablespoon olive oil
2 whole cloves of garlic
Salt and pepper
1 pound steak (porterhouse or T-bone are my favorites here)
½ onion, peeled and diced
4–5 mushrooms, brushed and sliced

Put olive oil and garlic in a frying pan and cook briefly over medium heat. Turn the heat to the highest you can get on the stove. Salt and

HENRY'S **NOTES** **AND TIPS**	It's okay if the garlic burns a little here. It adds to the flavor.

pepper one side of the steak and put that side down in the pan. Salt and pepper top side. Cover the pan with a lid and cook for 5 minutes. Flip the steak and cover the pan again. After 3 minutes on the second side, uncover pan and add the onions and mushrooms, adding more salt and pepper if needed. Cook an additional 2 minutes and serve.

LEXINGTON

It wasn't until we were in the air on our way out of Nebraska that they finally told us where we were going: Lexington, Kentucky.

Fine, Lexington, Kentucky. But something was nagging at me. Why had I heard of Lexington, did they hold the Derby there or something? It kept bugging me until it hit me why it was so familiar.

There was a huge Federal pen in Lexington.

I probably knew twenty wiseguys doing time there. Their wives and kids came to visit a lot. I'd even heard of whole families that had relocated to Lexington to be near their loved ones. If we lived in Lexington, we'd run into the wiseguys' wives and cousins on the street, in the grocery store—everywhere! They'd recognize me in an instant. Puh-leese!

Henry's Rules for Cooking on the Run:
HOW TO MAKE GOOD ITALIAN FOOD ANYWHERE

Rule 6: Not all stoves are the same. Especially the ovens. Some are hotter, some are tilted, some cook hotter at the back while the front remains almost raw. Burners tend to be more alike, but they're still not the same from stove to stove.

By the time we got off the plane, I was a nervous wreck. I expected someone would try and whack me the minute I was on the ground. The Kentucky head marshal, a guy named Al, met us with his crew at the gate. They were going to be in charge of us now. Al was a big, red-faced, tobacco-chewing guy. He reminded me of that fat sheriff in the Burt Reynolds movies. It was not exactly love at first sight between us.

The first thing out of my mouth to Marshal Al was, "No f___ing way are we gonna live in Lexington. Get us outta here now. It's too f___ing dangerous." He looked at me like I was crazy.

I told him about the penitentiary and the wiseguys there. Marshal Al dug his heels in. He was a stubborn SOB. And he'd lose a lot of face if he gave in to me. He said we were staying. I said no. We glared at each other. It was a standoff.

So I decided to call Ed McDonald, head of the Organized Crime Strike Force, and tell him what was going on. I made the call, and then we waited in stony silence. People were staring at us. We were supposed to be incognito, but we sure didn't look like the rest of the people in the Lexington airport. I felt like our cover was blown already.

A few minutes later, Al got beeped on his pager. He was being paged by the top marshal in Washington, D.C., who McDonald had called right after he talked to me. Al's face turned twelve shades of purple. He was fuming. He'd been told to move us; it wasn't safe. We had won.

If there's one thing marshals hate it's a change in plans. They have this tunnel vision, there's only one way to do things. The slightest variation and they flip out. And this was a major change.

Al had to get more marshals to help escort us. Some were called in on their day off. They had to arrange for a van for our luggage, they had to get cars for us all to travel in, and they had to decide where to take us and find a new safe house. It was a huge ordeal. Al was the most unhappy—none of the Feds were happy with us, but Al was the worst. He could see his new charge was going to be a headache.

He was right. I was a big headache. First off, they decided to move us to Independence, Kentucky, which is halfway across the state, and about a four-hour drive. Marshal Al lived in Lexington. Every time I went to New York, Al had to drive the four hours to pick me up, then four hours back to the airport in Lexington, and then do the reverse trip to get me home a few days later. It drove him crazy. And I hate to tell you this, but I loved every minute of it. I got a kick out of bugging the guy.

Marshal Al wasn't the only Fed I rubbed the wrong way. There've been quite a few. In those days, you could say I had an attitude. Don't get me wrong. The Feds were mostly decent people—it was their job that was lousy. Poor Marshal Al was probably trying to do his job. But he was also lazy—he didn't like to be bothered. He wanted to go coon hunting or something.

I never understood lazy. In the Mob, I always had lots of things going on, I *wanted* to do stuff. This guy wanted to do *nothing*. It was beyond me. He didn't like problems. And here I was, a very unruly problem who had just become his career.

So we went through another few weeks in hotels. This time we were in a new state, with new challenges of what to eat, and still no home to eat it in. I got the marshals to buy us some chickens. I'd seen a bunch of small farms—too small for cattle—on our drive across the state. Chickens don't need nearly as much room as cows. It was a good bet they raised a few cluckers in the area.

Serves 4–6.

Comfort Chicken and Rice Soup

There's nothing like hot soup when you need comfort, especially chicken soup. I don't know what's in it, but all those Jewish mothers are right: it'll heal what ails you. There's a chicken soup in every culture—with cilantro, lemon grass, jalapeños, dumplings, potatoes—you name it, there's a version. In Kentucky, I could find only the simplest ingredients, but that's all I wanted. That way, it still tastes like chicken instead of the chicken being a base for everything else.

One 4–5 pound chicken
12 cups water or 6 cups chicken broth and 6 cups water
2 cups diced onion (1 large or two small)
2 cups diced celery (about 4 large stalks)
2 cups peeled and diced carrots (about 5 regular)

1 packed cup chopped fresh parsley, large stems removed, or 2
   tablespoons dried
Salt and pepper to taste
1–1½ cups white rice (preferably Arborio)
4 sprigs fresh thyme or 1 teaspoon dried (optional)
Pinch saffron, crumbled (optional)

Rinse chicken in cool water. Remove gizzard, heart, neck, and liver from cavity and either set aside for other dishes or boil in a small pan of salted water as a "chef's appetizer"—something for the chef to nibble on as he/she cooks. Place chicken in a large pot and add water and broth (chicken should be covered—if not, add more water or broth). Bring to a boil and lower heat to simmer. Skim off foam and grease from the top of the mixture and discard. Add onion, celery, carrots, parsley, and salt and pepper. Simmer partially covered for 1½ hours, skimming off grease occasionally. Remove chicken from pot. When cool enough to handle, separate chicken meat from the bones and return meat to the pot. Add rice and optional thyme and/or saffron and cook until rice is tender but not falling apart (about 15 minutes). Check salt and pepper seasoning and serve.

If you're concerned about fat, take skin off chicken before cooking. But remember: the fat adds flavor too.

I recommend Arborio rice because it holds its shape better, but you can use almost any kind. Just know that instant rice will turn to mush pretty fast and you may need more broth.

Saffron is a spice the Sicilians probably picked up from the Arabs. It has a unique flavor, but it's expensive and can be hard to find. In the middle of the U.S., I usually left it out, with no harm to the dish.

If you're feeling lazy, you can leave the bones in the soup, but warn the eaters they're in there.

This soup freezes great! It can even taste better when it's been frozen. Add more broth when reheating it.

HENRY'S NOTES AND TIPS

Serves 4.

Chicken Cacciatore

What I love about this recipe is it's mostly "throw it in the oven and let it cook." Lots of people do it on top of the stove, but in the oven it'll cook while you do other stuff and be ready in an hour. You start by making Basic Tomato Sauce (see recipe on page 13) with a few additions, brown the chicken in the broiler, then throw it all together to bake in the oven. It makes a very tender chicken with a lot of flavor.

I like what I call a "wet sauce" with this, because then you can use the extra sauce to toss with whatever pasta you serve with it.

¼ cup olive oil
6–8 cloves of garlic (about 2 tablespoons)
2 large canned anchovies packed in oil, rinsed lightly
Two 28-ounce cans peeled plum tomatoes w/basil, drained, reserving juice
½ pound white mushroooms, trimmed and sliced (optional)
½ large green pepper, rinsed and cut in large dice (optional)
12 large basil leaves, torn in large pieces, or 1 tablespoon dried
¼ cup finely chopped Italian parsley or 2 teaspoons–1 tablespoon dried parsley
1 cup dry red wine
1 teaspoon each salt and black pepper
One 3–4 pound chicken, cut in serving pieces (you can buy a "Best of Fryer")
1 pound cooked and drained pasta of your choice (optional; see page 37 for how to cook)
2 tablespoons chopped fresh parsley leaves for garnish

HENRY'S NOTES AND TIPS

Make sure you skim the dish while it's baking.
The chicken should be so well done it's almost falling off the bone.
It won't dry out if it cooks a little longer—the sauce will keep it moist.
The anchovies really add a lot to this recipe—don't leave them out!

In a large skillet or medium-large wide pot, heat olive oil over medium-low heat. Mash garlic and anchovies until almost a paste. Add mixture to oil and cook briefly, stirring. Do not brown, or garlic will get bitter. Add the juice from the canned tomatoes and stir well. Raise heat to medium-high and add optional sliced mushrooms and diced green pepper. Cook, stirring, 1 minute. Crush tomatoes with your hands or chop well on a cutting board and add to the pan. Add basil, parsley, wine, and ½ teaspoon each salt and pepper. Cook over medium-high heat until sauce begins to bubble, stir well, then lower heat to a simmer while you broil the chicken.

Heat oven to broil.

Place chicken pieces in a roasting pan. (If breasts are large, cut in half.) Brush lightly with olive oil and season with a dash of salt and pepper on both sides. Broil chicken pieces until browned on one side; flip and brown on second side (about 2 minutes per side). Remove chicken from pan, and take all but 1 tablespoon oil out of the pan.

Lower oven heat to 350°F.

Skim tomato sauce and pour a small amount in the bottom of the roasting pan. Place chicken pieces on top and cover with remaining sauce. Place uncovered in oven and bake for 1 hour, skimming off any grease that accumulates every 15–20 minutes.

Place chicken pieces on a serving platter or in a large serving bowl. Toss optional pasta with 1–2 cups of sauce and top chicken with remaining sauce. Garnish with parsley if desired and serve.

INDEPENDENCE

What can you say about Kentucky? Not much. Outside of Lexington, which is kind of sophisticated, it's a spillover from the Appalachians. There're lots of small farms, and especially around Independence it's tobacco farming country. By New York standards, the people are backward, rednecks. We had nothing in common with them.

Our new home was a condo, about sixteen hundred square feet. In Omaha, we had a twenty-three hundred square foot house. Here we had a little yard. In Omaha, we had a huge backyard where we'd have barbecues. There weren't very many Jewish people in Kentucky. Karen had no friends. Omaha was starting to seem like heaven.

The food? I don't know which was worse, Nebraska or Kentucky. You would think with all the farms around that fresh ingredients would be easy to get, the people would eat well. Not true. Kentuckians eat what's called Southern food. I call it a shortcut to a heart attack.

Everything's fried or cooked into mush with tons of cheese and butter. They take a good healthy chicken, dip it in flour and deep-fry it. It's got about a zillion calories and will send your cholesterol through the roof. They deep-fry their vegetables. They fry cornmeal and make grits or hush puppies, which get eaten with some form of fatty pork and drenched in syrup or gravy. They have biscuits at every meal, made with lard. The biscuits are such a big deal they have chain stores named Biscuitville and Biscuit King. And don't forget the macaroni and cheese, floating in pools of butter.

Which is not to say Italian food doesn't have its share of heavy sauces, breading, and frying. But at least it's made with olive oil, which is a lot better for you than Wesson or butter. Plus I think the tomatoes, garlic, and lemon counteract the fat.

But hey, when in Rome . . . I loved eating all that lard at the beginning. I have to admit, there are some things they cook in the South that are delicious. They pan-fry local sunfish in cornmeal. Very tasty. I'm crazy about okra, fried and sautéed with tomatoes in gumbo. I also love black-eyed peas, collard greens, and yes, macaroni and cheese.

Serves 4.

Southern Fried Chicken with Gravy à la Henry

This is my version of Southern fried chicken, with a few Italian touches. Besides adding some garlic, I "double dip" the chicken, which keeps it moist and tender inside.

One 2-ounce piece of salt pork or 2 strips bacon, diced
1 cup flour
1 teaspoon each salt and black pepper

1 teaspoon garlic powder, onion powder, and cayenne pepper
(optional)
2 beaten eggs
1 cup canola oil
1 cup olive oil
3 large cloves of garlic, peeled
1 cup milk or buttermilk
1 frying chicken (3–4 pounds), cut in serving pieces

For gravy:

¼ cup flour
½ cup milk
½ cup half and half
½–1 cup canned chicken broth (if needed)
¼–½ teaspoon each salt and pepper (to taste)

Render bacon or salt pork in wide pot or skillet, 10 or 11 × 4 inches deep. Remove bacon or salt pork from fat and drain on paper towels, leaving bacon or pork fat in the pan.

Season flour with ½ teaspoon each salt and pepper and other optional spices (garlic and onion powder and cayenne pepper). Place in a plastic bag. Place beaten eggs in a bowl nearby.

Add oils to the pan and heat to medium heat. Add garlic cloves and cook until they turn light brown. Remove garlic from pan. Heat oil to about 350–375°F. If you don't have a thermometer, check oil heat by tossing a drop or two of water into the pan—when the oil spits on contact with water, it's ready.

Place milk in a large bowl. Add a few pieces of chicken and coat with milk. Remove chicken pieces to a colander and drain. Then add chicken to the bag with flour and shake to coat with flour. Remove one piece at a time, shaking off excess flour. Dip in egg and coat with flour, repeat egg/flour process, then slip chicken pieces into the hot oil.

Cook chicken in batches—don't crowd the pan. As soon as the chicken hits the pan, the temperature will drop, which is what you want. Lower the heat to medium-low and brown chicken on both sides, turning once, until cooked through. This will take 15–20 minutes per side, depending on the size of the pieces. (If they're bigger, it may take

Rule 7: Always check seasoning before you serve. Test it before your guests do. You'll be glad you did.

as much as 25 minutes per side.) If chicken starts to brown too fast, lower the heat.

Drain chicken on paper towels and place in a dish in the oven to keep warm (heat oven to warm setting or about 200°F). If you're doing a second batch, reheat oil, but don't let it smoke, or chicken will burn on the outside and not cook through.

For the gravy, remove all but about 3 tablespoons of oil from the pan and any blackened bits. Turn heat to medium-low. Stir in flour, whisking well. Cook 1 minute, stirring. Add a small amount of milk and stir well. Add remaining milk and the half and half, stirring to keep lumps from forming (if there seem to be lumps, keep stirring—most of the time they'll disappear). If gravy is too thick, add a little chicken broth. Season with salt and pepper to taste. Cook until heated through (do not boil).

Serves 4–6

as a side dish.

Black-Eyed Peas

The traditional way to cook black-eyed peas (and a lot of Southern vegetables) is with a chunk of salt pork or fatback. What could be wrong with that?

1 cup dried black-eyed peas
2 tablespoons olive oil
One 2-ounce chunk of salt pork or fatback

½ cup diced onion
1 large clove of garlic, minced
½ cup diced fresh tomato
¼ cup chopped fresh parsley or 1 tablespoon dried
¼ teaspoon crushed red pepper flakes (to taste)
¼–½ teaspoon each salt and black pepper (to taste)

Check peas and remove any that have turned a dark color or any pebbles you find. Rinse very well. Place in a medium-large pot and cover with water. Bring to a boil and lower heat to a simmer. Remove any foam that forms on top. Cover and cook 20 minutes. Check peas for doneness—if they can be pierced with a fork, they are ready. If not, cover and continue to cook a few minutes more and test again. The minute they are done, drain and rinse them well in cold water to stop the cooking (black-eyed peas will fall apart if overcooked). Set aside.

Heat oil in a medium-large pot over medium heat and add salt pork in one piece, onion and garlic. Cook, stirring, until onion is translucent (lower heat if garlic starts to brown). Add chopped tomato and parsley and cook 10 minutes, stirring occasionally. Season with ¼ teaspoon salt, black pepper, and crushed red pepper flakes.

Add black-eyed peas to the pot and stir well. Add a little water if mixture is dry and cook, covered, 5–10 minutes until heated through. Adjust seasoning and serve.

■■ *Serves 4.*

Southern Cooked Greens

You can use any of the usual Southern greens in this recipe: kale, mustard, collard, or turnip greens. My favorites are mustard and collards. You cook them very different lengths of time. Mustard greens have to be cooked at least forty-five minutes to get tender, collards will be done in twenty.

As usual, I've added garlic. You don't have to.

2 pounds greens of your choice
1 tablespoon olive oil
4 ounces salt pork, diced, or 1 large smoked turkey wing
4 large garlic cloves, minced (1 tablespoon) (optional)
2 quarts water
¼–½ teaspoon each salt and pepper (to taste)
A dash of Tabasco or other hot sauce (to taste)
White vinegar for serving

Soak and wash greens very well (see page 207 for how to clean greens). If you are using older greens, remove the leaves from the ribs and discard ribs. Tear greens in large pieces and set aside.

In a large pot, heat oil over medium heat. Add salt pork or turkey wing and cook, stirring, until beginning to brown. Add garlic if using and cook briefly (do not brown). Add ½ cup water, stirring to loosen any brown bits that have stuck to the bottom of the pot. Add remaining water and the greens, a bunch at a time, allowing them to cook down to make room for the remaining greens. Season with ¼ teaspoon salt and pepper and Tabasco or other hot sauce and stir well to combine. Cook uncovered over low heat for 20 minutes (or longer if cooking mustard greens), stirring occasionally and checking to make sure there is some liquid in the pot. Serve sprinkled with a bit of white vinegar if desired.

**HENRY'S
NOTES
AND TIPS**

If you use the smoked turkey wing, after fifteen minutes or so take it out and chop off the meat, adding both meat and bones back to the pot. Remove bones before serving.

Serves 4–6.

■■

Fried Okra

This is a great way to make okra, 'cause it gets rid of the sliminess but keeps the flavor. I ate these like popcorn in Kentucky.

½ pound okra
½ cup milk or buttermilk
½ cup flour
½ cup cornmeal
1 teaspoon each cayenne pepper, garlic powder, salt, and black pepper
1 tablespoon paprika
1 cup canola oil, peanut oil, or Crisco shortening

Wash okra pods and trim ends. Slice into ¼-inch rounds.

Place milk in a large bowl. Combine flour, cornmeal, and remaining seasonings and put in a plastic bag.

Put oil or Crisco in a large skillet to a depth of 1 inch. Heat oil until a drop of water makes oil spit (about 350–375°F).

Drop a handful of okra slices in the milk. Remove slices with a slotted spoon to strain off excess milk and add to bag with flour and cornmeal mixture. Shake to coat okra well. Put slices in a strainer and shake to remove excess flour and cornmeal. Slip slices into hot oil and fry until golden brown, about 2–3 minutes. Drain on paper towels. Place in 200°F oven on a cookie sheet to keep warm while cooking the rest of the okra.

FARM FOOD

Fact is, I was chowing down so much Southern food that pretty soon I had to loosen my belt a coupla notches. I was on my way to looking like Paulie.

Besides which, I got tired of it. I was dying for some vegetables that tasted like vegetables or a simple baked chicken. When I went past the local farms I could see the little plants growing, the chickens running around. It made my mouth water. I started thinking about sneaking into the gardens at midnight, like a wolf planning a raid on a hen house. I was sure I could get away with it.

But instead of returning to a life of crime, I tried a different approach. I checked out the nearby farms. One of the tobacco farmers didn't just grow tobacco. The guy had chickens. And a huge vegetable garden. In the spring, his garden was overflowing with asparagus, lettuce, green beans, spinach, broccoli, all kinds of squash, carrots, and beets. And of course tomatoes—the smell took me back to my mother's garden in Brooklyn. Fresh tomatoes on the vine smell like nothing else on earth.

I don't have to tell you I got very friendly with that farmer.

Serves 4–6.

Fresh (Uncooked) Garden Tomato and Basil Pasta

Our farmer neighbor was more than willing to talk about gardening. He'd go on and on about what kind of fertilizer grows the best tomatoes, how you keep the squash from taking over the asparagus patch. Of course he didn't know what to *do* with all his beautiful vegetables once he'd grown them except chop them up into salads or boil them until they were tasteless. When I got him to give me some tomatoes and basil and I made this dish for him, his eyes popped out of his head.

Make this pasta at the height of summer in the East or Midwest, or whenever you're lucky enough to have fresh garden tomatoes and basil around. There's nothing better than the taste of garden-grown tomatoes and real basil—believe me, I've been deprived of them too many times in the joint.

2–3 pounds fresh garden tomatoes (3–4 large), chopped
   (or grocery store on-the-vine tomatoes)
4–5 cloves of garlic, peeled and finely chopped
½–¾ cup (about 2 ounces) fresh basil leaves, coarsely chopped
¼ cup + 1–2 tablespoons olive oil
¼ cup fresh parsley, minced
1 tablespoon red wine vinegar
Salt and pepper to taste
1 pound capellini (or your choice of pasta)
½ cup freshly grated Parmesan or Romano cheese

Don't even think about making this sauce if you don't have either fresh garden tomatoes or the on-the-vine ones at the grocery store. Use only fresh basil. Same for the parsley—if you don't have fresh, leave it out. Don't substitute dried.

If raw garlic is hard on your stomach, sauté it one to two minutes in a tablespoon of olive oil, then add to tomato mixture.

Combine all ingredients except pasta, the 2 tablespoons of oil and cheese. Let sit at room temperature for a while—2–4 hours is best, but if 10 minutes is all you have, 10 minutes. Cook the pasta according to directions on page 37. Return to pot and toss well with 1–2 tablespoons olive oil. Add Parmesan cheese and toss again. For individual servings, place pasta on plates or in small bowls and top each with a few spoonfuls of tomato sauce. For family style, add sauce to the pot, toss to combine all, and serve in a large bowl.

Henry's Rules for Cooking on the Run:
HOW TO MAKE GOOD ITALIAN FOOD ANYWHERE

Rule 8: Not All Tomatoes Are Alike. Go for the ones that have a bright red color, are fairly soft, and give off a tomato smell when you sniff them. If they don't smell, they don't taste! If I'm going to be using them that day, I buy the ripest ones I can find. If I'm going to put them in a sauce, I even buy them overripe. Grab a vegetable grocer and ask him if he has any "seconds" they've pulled off the shelves—they're great for sauce.

Asparagus Vinaigrette

This is lovely as part of an antipasto, or as a summer vegetable salad. It's your choice what width asparagus spears you use. I think they're all good.

2 pounds thin, medium, or fat asparagus spears
1½ tablespoons good red wine vinegar or fresh lemon juice
⅛ teaspoon Dijon mustard (optional)
½ teaspoon finely minced shallot (optional)
4 tablespoons extra virgin olive oil
¼ teaspoon each salt and pepper (to taste)

Soak asparagus in a pan or sink of water for 5 minutes and rinse well to remove any grit. If you're using thin stalks, check for any "woody" ends and trim them off. For the medium or thicker stalks, hold each stalk at the base (stem end) and about in the middle with thumb and forefinger, and slowly bend the stalk until a piece of the stem end breaks off. (This is the easiest way to find where the woody section of the stalk ends and the more tender part begins.) Peel off any tough skin on the lower part of the spears with a vegetable peeler.

In a large skillet, bring an inch of water to a boil, add a tablespoon of salt and stir to dissolve. Lay the asparagus spears in the water and cover the pan. Cook, checking occasionally to make sure water doesn't boil dry, until the thickest part of the stems can be pierced with a knife. This will be only a few minutes for thin spears and about 10 minutes for thicker ones (but check early—you don't want them overcooked). Drain well and pat spears dry. Cool to room temperature.

Put vinegar or lemon juice and optional shallot and mustard in a

HENRY'S NOTES AND TIPS

Use less vinegar rather than more. There should be just a hint of it.

small bowl. Add oil, whisking to combine well. Check for balance of oil to vinegar and season with salt and pepper to taste. Place asparagus spears in a large bowl and toss with dressing. You can serve at room temperature or chill in the refrigerator (at least 20 minutes to half an hour) and serve cold.

■■■

Serves 4.

Roasted Asparagus

Roasted asparagus has a wonderfully nutty flavor. You can easily make this in the oven—you don't have to have a grill. Again, the width of the spears is up to you.

2 pounds thin, medium, or fat asparagus spears
2 tablespoons olive oil
1 small garlic clove, minced, or ¼ teaspoon garlic powder
¼–½ teaspoon salt and pepper (to taste)
1–2 tablespoons unsalted butter, melted

Preheat oven to 450°F or prepare and heat grill.

Soak asparagus in a pan or sink of water 5 minutes and rinse well to remove any grit. If you're using thin stalks, check for any "woody" ends and trim them off. For the medium or thicker stalks, hold each stalk at the base (stem end) and about in the middle with thumb and forefinger, and slowly bend the stalk until a piece of the stem end breaks off. (This is the easiest way to find where the woody section of the stalk ends and the more tender part begins.) Peel off any tough skin on the lower part of the spears with a vegetable peeler.

Combine olive oil, garlic or garlic powder, and salt and pepper to taste in a bowl and toss well with asparagus spears. Place in a grill basket or on a baking sheet lined with aluminum foil. Brush asparagus with melted butter and place on the grill or in the oven. Cook, turning once or twice and brushing with additional butter until the thickest part of the stems can be pierced with a knife. Thin spears will take about 5 minutes, the thickest ones 10–12 minutes. Serve immediately.

ASPARAGUS

When you're buying asparagus, don't be fooled by "young" (as in skinny) versus older. Unlike string beans, which get fatter as they get older, asparagus comes out of the ground as thick as they're gonna be. Some of the thinner ones are more "woody" and you need to trim off the bottom of the stalks, others are fine untrimmed. The fat ones are considered the "premier" spears, which is why they cost more.

The best way to figure out what part of the thick asparagus spears is usable, hold them with a hand at each end and bend them slightly. The stalk will naturally bend where the stem gets tough, and that's where you break them. It's usually about one-third of the way down the stem. You use the top part and discard the rest. Peel the ends if they seem a little tough.

ZUCCHINI

Except for Fried Zucchini (below), I find medium-size zucchini (four to six inches long) have the best flavor. The tiny ones are sometimes bitter and those over eight inches can be watery and bland.

Buy zucchinis that are firm and unblemished. If they feel "bendable" or have brown spots or bruises, you don't want them. Keep them in the refrigerator up to four days in a paper or plastic bag (I use paper bags—if they get damp they'll go bad faster).

A zucchini can be gritty and needs to be soaked and scrubbed well to clean. Soak 5 minutes covered with cold water in a pan or sink, scrub well with a soft brush (but don't break the skins) and rinse thoroughly.

Fried Zucchini

Zucchinis sliced into spears and fried are a delicious appetizer and a welcome addition to any antipasto.

3 medium-size zucchini, 4–6 inches long (1–1¼ pounds)
½ cup milk (regular or lowfat)
2 eggs, beaten
1 cup flour seasoned with ½ teaspoon each salt and black pepper and a dash of cayenne pepper, or 1 cup seasoned Italian bread crumbs
1 cup canola oil for frying

Clean zucchini per instructions above. Trim off ends and cut in wide wedges lengthwise (wide julienne) about 3–4 inches long. Drain well and pat dry.

Place milk in a bowl, the beaten eggs in a separate bowl next to it, and the seasoned flour or bread crumbs on a plate nearby.

Heat oil in a large skillet over medium-high heat to hot but not smoking. (Oil will sizzle on contact with drops of water when it's ready.)

Drop a number of zucchini spears in bowl of milk, remove a few, shaking to remove excess milk, dip in egg to coat, and then coat all sides with flour or bread crumbs, shaking off excess. Slip into heated oil.

Cook zucchini, browning on all sides until golden and remove to paper towels to drain, 3–4 minutes. Do not crowd; cook in batches if

You can make this dish with one or two larger zucchini if you want. The older zucchinis just have more water in them, which works well here. The high heat of the frying seals in the liquid, so you get crisp crust on the outside and moist zucchini on the inside.

I prefer flour to bread crumbs for deep frying. Some of the bread crumbs fall off and turn into burned bits in the oil, which means if you do a few batches, you'll have to replace the oil.

HENRY'S NOTES AND TIPS

necessary. Drain on paper towels and keep warm while you cook remaining zucchini. Sprinkle cooked spears with additional salt and pepper and serve immediately.

Serves 2–4.

■■

Braised Broccoli and Garlic

The combination of broccoli, garlic, and olive oil is one of the best. How nice that they've discovered broccoli is one of those vegetables that's so good for us we should almost bathe in it.

1 pound broccoli
2 tablespoons olive oil
4 large garlic cloves, minced
¼–½ teaspoon each salt and pepper (to taste)

Rinse broccoli well and trim florets from stems. Peel stems and slice into ½-inch pieces. Cut broccoli tops in 1-inch pieces. Rerinse pieces and drain well.

Heat olive oil in a large skillet over medium heat. Add garlic and cook, stirring, 1–2 minutes (do not brown). Lower heat and add broccoli and ¼ teaspoon each salt and pepper. Toss to coat broccoli with garlic and oil. Cover pan and cook 5 minutes. Stir mixture well and make sure it's not browning—turn heat even lower if it is. Re-cover and cook an additional 3 minutes, or until broccoli is still bright green but cooked through.

Serve immediately.

HENRY'S NOTES AND TIPS

You can use just the broccoli "crowns" and omit the stems if you want, but I find cooking the stems this way makes them just as good as the tops.

Sautéed Spinach or Greens

6 cups fresh spinach (½ pound) or other greens such as Swiss chard
2 tablespoons olive oil
1 large clove of garlic, peeled and cut in half
Salt and pepper to taste

Wash spinach well in several changes of water. Remove thick stems and tear large leaves in half.

Heat oil in large skillet over medium heat. Add garlic and cook until light brown. Remove garlic. Raise heat to high. Add spinach or other greens and a dash of salt and pepper. Toss for 2 minutes or until barely wilted. Remove from heat, adjust seasoning, and serve immediately.

Don't overcook. Remember the greens will continue cooking off heat.

If you're using young spinach, don't remove stems, just cook the whole thing! It's delicious and looks fabulous on the plate.

Add a second clove of garlic if you like. I like one—it makes the spinach stand out instead of the garlic.

HENRY'S

NOTES

AND TIPS

CLEANING GREENS

A lot of greens, like spinach and Swiss chard, hold dirt in their leaves. Soak them in a sink filled with water, remove and shake well, clean the sink and refill with clean water and soak the leaves a second time. Or you can rinse each leaf under running water. In either case, drain well and pat dry, or run through a salad spinner to remove excess water.

▪▪▪

Sautéed Carrots and Zucchini with Mint

Fresh mint is a wonderful flavoring for vegetables. You can make this recipe with any number of vegetables. This combination makes a very pretty dish.

1½ pounds small or medium zucchinis (about 4–6)
1 pound carrots (about 3 medium)
2 tablespoons olive oil
1 medium onion, sliced
½ teaspoon sugar
½ teaspoon each salt and black pepper
¾ cup chopped fresh mint leaves
¼ cup white wine
Juice of ½ lemon or 1 whole lime

Soak zucchinis in a sink or bowl of water for 5 minutes. Scrub lightly to remove any grit and rinse well. Peel carrots and trim ends. Slice carrots on diagonal in ¼-inch slices. Trim ends of zucchinis and slice on diagonal in ¼-inch slices. Set aside both vegetables.

Heat oil in a large skillet over medium heat. Add onion and cook, stirring, 3 minutes. Add carrots and cook, stirring, 5 minutes. Add zucchinis, sugar, salt and pepper, and mint. Cook, flipping once or twice to assure even browning, for 5 minutes. Add white wine to pan and stir to scrape up any bits sticking to pan. Add lemon or lime juice and toss with vegetables.

HENRY'S NOTES AND TIPS

The small amount of sugar brings out the natural sugars in the carrots and slightly caramelizes and browns the vegetables, giving them a nice nutty-sweet flavor. Just be careful not to burn them.

If you don't want to use wine, substitute a little canned chicken broth or water.

MINT

My mom always grew mint in her garden. In fact, left alone, it would start to take over the whole yard. We were constantly pulling it out to keep it under control. It's delicious with lamb, fish, and vegetables, and also adds zest cooked in a tomato sauce over a mild-flavored pasta like stuffed shells. It's also good for digestion.

Lucky 7 Minute Tomato Sauce

Makes 3 cups (enough for 4–6 people).

I don't guarantee that this'll be acid free, but it'll be ready in seven minutes. Using a very wide pan and high heat exposes all the ingredients to the heat much faster.

¼ cup olive oil
6–8 cloves of garlic, minced or thinly sliced (about 2 tablespoons)
One 28-ounce can crushed tomatoes
One 28-ounce can tomato purée
12 large basil leaves, torn in large pieces or 1 tablespoon dried
¼ cup finely chopped Italian parsley or 2 teaspoons–1 tablespoon dried parsley
½ teaspoon each salt and black pepper

Using a very large, wide skillet, heat olive oil over medium-high heat and add garlic, stirring constantly for 30 seconds. Add remaining ingredients and continue cooking, stirring constantly for 7 minutes.

Pasta with Chicken and Asparagus

Yes, there's a lot of garlic in this recipe, and yes, that's what makes the dish.

1½ pounds fresh asparagus
1½ pounds boneless chicken breasts
½ teaspoon salt
¼ teaspoon black pepper
¼ cup olive oil
2 large shallots, sliced, or ½ onion, diced (½ cup)
10–12 cloves of garlic, minced (3–3½ tablespoons)
⅓ cup white wine
12 ounces penne or similar pasta, cooked and drained (see page 37 for how to cook), reserving 1 cup pasta water
Freshly grated Parmesan cheese for serving

Soak asparagus in a pan or sink of water 5 minutes and rinse well to remove any grit. Hold each stalk at the base (stem end) and about in the middle with thumb and forefinger and slowly bend the stalk until a piece of the stem end breaks off. (This is the easiest way to find where the "woody" section of the stalk ends and the more tender part begins.) For the thicker stalks, peel the outer layer of skin (or if you're short of time, toss 'em). Cut asparagus into 2-inch pieces and reserve.

Remove most of the skin from chicken breasts, rinse thoroughly, and drain. Cut into about 1–1¼-inch pieces. Toss in a bowl with a dash of salt and pepper. Set aside.

Heat 2 tablespoons oil in a skillet over medium heat. Add shallots

HENRY'S NOTES AND TIPS

Try to time pasta and sauce so they're ready at the same time. If pasta is ready ahead of time, toss with a little olive oil and cover to keep warm.

or onions and cook, stirring, 3–4 minutes or until translucent. Add 1 tablespoon garlic and cook 1 minute. Add asparagus and cook, stirring, 5 minutes or until asparagus is al dente. Remove from pan.

Heat remaining oil in pan over medium-high heat. Add chicken and 1 tablespoon garlic and sauté, stirring constantly for 5 minutes or until chicken is no longer pink. Do not overcook. Add chicken to asparagus mixture. Add white wine to pan and stir, scraping up any bits that are stuck to pan. Cook briefly to reduce (1–2 minutes). Return chicken and asparagus to pan, adding pasta water if desired to create more of a sauce. Add remaining 1–1½ tablespoons garlic and heat through. Toss with penne and serve immediately with Parmesan on the side.

GENERAL RULES FOR PASTA WITH CHICKEN

My mother made very few sauces with chicken; we mostly baked whole chicken or pieces of it. That was before the days of the skinless boneless chicken breasts, which are a snap to cut up and throw in a sauce.

1. Cut-up chicken breasts are definitely the easiest piece of chicken to use in pasta. Just remember that chicken off the bone cooks in about 5 minutes (dark meat a little longer) and will get tough if overcooked. I usually sauté the boneless chicken pieces in a bit of garlic and seasonings and remove from the pan, adding them back in just to reheat at the end.
2. Chicken takes on the flavor of whatever is around it. The chicken provides the nuggets of meat, the sauce provides most of the flavor. Which means don't be afraid to add a lot of spices to a sauce with chicken. If you're using chicken pieces that have bone, you can cook them longer in a sauce and they'll stay more tender and take on more of the sauce flavor.
3. Remember that most Americans eat a lot of meat. Count on at least 6 ounces of boneless chicken per person (8–10 ounces with the bone).

Garlic Roasted Chicken with Rosemary

4–5 pound whole roasting chicken
8 garlic cloves, peeled and slivered
1 tablespoon fresh rosemary leaves (reserving stems if using) or 1½
    teaspoons dried
1 teaspoon each salt and pepper
2 tablespoons olive oil
½–1 cup canned chicken broth (as needed)

Preheat oven to 350°F.
Remove gizzard, heart, neck, and liver from chicken's cavity and either set aside for other dishes or boil in a small pan of salted water as a "chef's appetizer"—something for the chef to nibble on as he/she cooks. Rinse chicken in cool water inside and out, drain, and pat dry.
    Place chicken on a work surface or in a roasting pan. Mix slivered garlic and rosemary leaves in a small bowl. Divide mixture into about 8 equal portions and slide seven-eighths of the slivers and leaves under the skin of the chicken covering the breast (2 portions), back (1 portion), thighs (2 portions), and drumsticks (2 portions). Sprinkle the

HENRY'S NOTES AND TIPS

Use a roasting pan not much bigger than the bird—this helps keep the juices from burning. A 9 × 13-inch pan works fine for a 3–5-pound bird.
    It doesn't matter whether you use a rack or not.
    Cooking first at a higher temperature will sear the meat and help keep chicken juicy.
    Internal temperature of breast meat should be 160°–165°F when done.
    You can add potatoes and/or other vegetables like carrots, onions, and turnips. If you do, use a larger pan; roast longer; toss veggies in oil, garlic, and rosemary; and retoss when basting chicken.

cavity lightly with ¼ teaspoon each salt and pepper and the remaining garlic and rosemary leaves. If using fresh rosemary, add stems to the cavity.

Carefully rub chicken all over with olive oil and sprinkle with remaining salt and pepper. Place in roasting pan, breast side down, and bake uncovered for 1–1½ hours (check for doneness after 1 hour). Halfway through baking time, turn chicken breast side up. If pan is dry, add some chicken broth. Baste with pan juices every 15–20 minutes. If chicken starts to get too dark in color, cover pan with aluminum foil for the last part of baking time. The chicken is done when it is no longer pink (or only very, very slightly) when sliced—it should not be dark pink or red. After removing pan from the oven, allow chicken to rest on a platter at least 5 minutes before carving and serving. Meanwhile, skim pan juices of as much fat as possible and reheat, scraping up any bits from the bottom of the pan. Add more broth if desired and any juices that accumulate on the platter. Adjust seasonings (especially check salt level) and serve with the carved bird.

■■■

Serves 4.

How Much Time You Got Lemon-Basil Chicken

Handful fresh basil leaves (20–25), chopped coarse
Juice of 2 lemons or 4 tablespoons concentrated lemon juice
4 garlic cloves, peeled and minced
4 tablespoons olive oil
¼ teaspoon each salt and pepper
1 whole chicken (4–5 pounds), cut into serving pieces
1 teaspoon paprika
¼ cup fresh parsley leaves, chopped

Mix together basil, lemon juice, garlic, olive oil, and salt and pepper. If you have a whole chicken, save the neck, gizzard, heart, and back for making Chicken Stock (see page 21)—the liver you can use in

Sautéed Chicken Livers (see below). Toss remaining chicken pieces with basil mixture and place chicken and marinade in either a large sealable plastic bag or a large bowl (cover the bowl with a plate, plastic wrap, or foil) in the refrigerator. Marinate as long as you want (how much time you got?) up to 24 hours, or as short as 10 minutes. Mix up chicken and marinade occasionally.

Heat oven to 375°F. Put chicken and marinade in roasting pan. Cover with aluminum foil, cook 45 minutes, remove foil, and cook 15 minutes longer. Baste occasionally throughout. If you had a shorter marinating time, baste more often. Serve garnished with paprika and parsley.

Variation:

Wash and cut 3–4 large russet potatoes or 8–10 medium-size red potatoes into large bite-size pieces. Add to baking pan and toss with marinade. Bake with chicken until they can be pierced easily with a fork (they should cook in about the same time as the chicken—remove if they're done before).

Add a sliced onion to baking process.

Serves 6–8

as an appetizer,

3–4 as

a main course.

Sautéed Chicken Livers

This can be part of an antipasto or a main dish. For antipasto, serve it with baguette slices to spread mixture on, or for a main dish, serve with rice.

2 tablespoons olive oil
4–6 garlic cloves, minced (1½ tablespoons)
½ medium onion, sliced (½ cup)
1 pound chicken livers, cut in large pieces and seasoned lightly
    with salt and pepper
¼–½ cup chicken broth

¼–½ cup dry white wine
6 ounces fresh mushrooms, sliced
½ fresh green pepper, diced (optional)
1 large tomato, diced, or ½ cup canned tomato sauce
¼ cup chopped fresh parsley or 2 teaspoons dried
3 tablespoons red wine vinegar
½ teaspoon each salt and black pepper

Heat oil in skillet over medium heat. Add garlic and cook 2 minutes—do not brown. Add onion and cook an additional 2 minutes, stirring. Turn up heat and add chicken livers. Cook, stirring constantly to keep from sticking, until livers are barely pink, about 5 minutes. (If mixture starts to stick, add a couple of tablespoons of chicken broth or white wine and stir, scraping up any bits that are stuck to the pan.) Add mushrooms, green pepper (if using), tomato or tomato sauce, and parsley. Cook 3–5 minutes until vegetables are soft. Stir in vinegar, ¼ cup chicken broth and white wine and cook to reduce briefly 1–2 minutes, stirring gently. Add more broth and wine if more sauce is desired. Season with salt and pepper. Serve in small bowls with baguette slices or with rice.

THE RACE TRACK

People in Kentucky were crazy about horses. And I mean *crazy*. If you're not a farmer, the only other thing to do in Kentucky is have horses, or be in a business that has to do with horses. It was as weird as Omaha with the cows. I started thinking that, except in Brooklyn, all over America animals were more important than people.

I found out about the race track the first night we were in Independence. In those days how I'd learn about a town was to head to a local bar, have a few drinks, and talk to people. I met a girl there who had a job at the track—she was what's called a "hot walker," meaning she'd walk horses around when they finished a race to cool them down (if you put 'em in the stall right after they run they get sick). And I discovered she was a "hot walker" in more ways than one.

It turned out the race track was a stone's throw from our house. I couldn't believe it—I guess the Feds weren't thinking clear when they put us there. Here's the drill. Take a guy out of a life where he's been hooked up with numbers rackets, don't let him do anything like have a job because people might recognize him—basically try to bore him to death, then drop him next to a race track, tell him to behave, and see what happens. Puh-leese! I was hooked up with the racing crowd in a flash.

The hot walker intro'd me to the back stretch at the track, which was where the real horse people hung out. Not the owners, I'm talking about the trainers, the water boys, the vets, people who lived and breathed horses from dawn to midnight. But most important, it was the "world of the little people"—the jockeys. They were the kings of the back stretch. Everybody bowed to them. They got whatever they wanted—girls, drugs, hard-to-get tickets, clothes, you name it.

Despite their royal treatment, most of the jockeys didn't seem happy. They were bastards to anyone beneath them. They were under constant pressure to perform—one bad race, and a string of good ones were forgotten. They had to stay rail thin. If they gained even a quarter ounce, they'd be on drugs to get it off, or they'd do the throwing up thing. You'll never catch me wasting good food like that! But I learned a lot being around them, including respect for what they did. Think about it: you have a tiny guy who maybe weighs eighty-five pounds, but he can control a half-ton animal—that's worth something in my book.

Besides which my betting average got pretty good.

Racing attracts all kinds of folks. People came from all over the state and nearby Cincinnati, Ohio, which was only about forty miles away. There were the usual hopeless gamblers whose lives were going down the tubes from their habit. There were local cops, politicians schmoozing with fat cats, shop owners, hairdressers, husbands cheating on their wives. Everyone went to the races—I used to see my grocer there a few days a week.

The track was my kind of place. People get different when they get around gambling. It's like a minivacation. For a little while they don't have to be responsible adults. They hoot and holler, they drink too much, they eat junk food. Sometimes it almost felt like I was in New York again, minus the wiseguys, who rarely got stupid around gambling. To them, it was business.

They sold hot dogs at the races, but not like the ones in New York. At a track in New York or Jersey, they sell dogs with this great sauce of onions and tomatoes—the same as every street vendor in Manhattan sells off his cart. I got so hungry for them I made up my own version.

Makes 2 dogs.

Henry's New York Dogs with Onion Sauce

2 tablespoons canola oil
½ onion, sliced
2–3 garlic cloves, minced
1 large tomato, diced fine
½ teaspoon crushed red pepper
¼ teaspoon each salt and black pepper
2 hot dogs
2 hot dog buns or slices of bread
Mustard and green relish for garnish (optional)

To make the sauce:

Heat oil in a skillet over medium heat and add onion. Cook 2 minutes, stirring, turn down heat and add garlic. Cook one minute, stirring (do not brown garlic). Add tomato, red pepper and salt and pepper. Cook over low heat 5–10 minutes, stirring occasionally.

Boil hot dogs in a small saucepan 5–10 minutes. Drain. Or you can fry them in a skillet 5 minutes, till brown on all sides.

Toast buns or bread if desired. Place dogs on buns, top with sauce, optional mustard and relish, and eat.

Henry's Rules for Cooking on the Run:
HOW TO MAKE GOOD ITALIAN FOOD ANYWHERE

Rule 9: You Can't Always Get What You Want. But when you can't, you can substitute! Below is a list of some of the things I've used when I couldn't find the real Italian ingredients.

Prosciutto	Ham, salt pork (fatback), smoky bacon. To save, buy a big chunk of an end of bacon and freeze what you don't use.
Pancetta	Bacon.
Fennel	Anise seed for licorice-y flavor. Start with a small amount, crushed slightly, and add to taste.
Mozzarella cheese	Monterey Jack cheese.
Brined or cured black olives	In a pinch, canned American ones, but they're a bland cousin of cured. The smaller ones are a little better than the colossals.
Red peppers	Pimientos, which are roasted peppers. They usually come cut up small, so use them to get red pepper flavor, but not as real red peppers.
Escarole	*Faggeddaboudit*—there's no substitute.

Chapter Nine

Cincinnati

■■

THE QUEEN CITY TROLLEY

At the back stretch I hooked up with a guy who had a business helping race horses who'd hurt their legs. It was the weirdest process. He had this pond, and they'd put the horses in a huge sling that looked like a giant diaper. Then, using a crane, they'd lower them into the water, where they'd exercise the horses' legs without putting any weight on them. I guess it worked—he was making lots of money. But he was bored.

And I was bored. I was doing nothing but hanging at the race track, flying back and forth to New York. I had no schemes to work on, I had no job. So the horse exercise guy and I came up with an idea: we'd buy an old trolley car and turn it into a horse-drawn tourist bus and give tours between Union Terminal and downtown Cincinnati.

But like all new businesses, it cost a lot more than we thought. One Monday when we were building it, I could see we weren't going to be able to pay the construction workers on Friday. So I came up with a plan.

I'd noticed the workers, like most guys, would talk about three things: women, sports, and food—the food in this case being lunch. A lot of times lunch was at the top of the list. It's the one thing a working stiff's got to look forward to during the day. I decided I'd make lunches so good they'd come back the next week even without full pay, just for the food.

I knew my food would be good, but more important, I knew a secret about "guys" (you "dolls" might want to listen to this): never feed a man the same meal two days in a row. He needs variety with a capital V. It's genetic or something.

So I showered them with my best dishes, a different lunch every day. When we hit Friday and I confessed I was short some bucks, they were a little put off. But after discussing it, they decided to give me another week—as long as I made lunch.

Makes

two 8–9-inch

pizzas.

■■■

Henry's Pizza in a Flash

I didn't always have time to make pizza dough from scratch, but I chanced upon frozen bread dough at the grocery store. Like I'd learned from my mom, in a pinch you can substitute bread dough for pizza dough. You just treat it different than if you're making bread.

Dough:

1 pound frozen bread dough
¼ cup flour
2 tablespoons olive oil
4 large cloves of garlic, minced (1 tablespoon), or 2 teaspoons
    garlic powder
16 ounces tomato sauce
½ teaspoon crushed red pepper flakes
½ teaspoon dried oregano
2 tablespoons chopped fresh parsley or 1 teaspoon dried
¼–½ teaspoon each salt and black pepper (to taste)

Thaw bread dough. Place in a large oiled bowl and allow to rise 15 minutes. Divide in half and roll out with flour as you would other pizza dough (see Fat Larry's Pizza Dough on page 70).

To make the sauce:

Heat olive oil in a large skillet over medium heat and add garlic. Cook briefly, stirring (do not brown). Add remaining ingredients and cook 5 minutes to combine. Spread on prepared dough and top with desired toppings, ending with a drizzling of olive oil and a touch of crumbled dried oregano.

■■

Makes

1 large

sandwich.

Sausage, Provolone, and Roasted Pepper Sandwich

Sometimes when I went back to New York, I'd be able to get a "care" package of Italian foods—things like prosciutto and pancetta, salamis, cheeses. I gave up some precious provolone one week to make the workers lunch—they were happy that I did.

1 tablespoon olive oil
2 Italian mild or spicy sausages (or one of each)
¼–½ teaspoon each salt and pepper (to taste)
One 8–10" Italian sub roll
2 tablespoons Dijon mustard
4 thin slices provolone cheese
1 roasted red pepper (see recipe on page 23), cut lengthwise in ½–
   ¾" strips

Heat the olive oil in a medium or large skillet. Poke holes in the sausages with a fork and put in the pan. Sprinkle lightly with salt and pepper and cook on low to medium heat, turning occasionally, until

If the heat from the sausages doesn't melt the cheese as much as you want, you can run the opened sandwich under the broiler for thirty seconds before adding the red pepper strips.

HENRY'S NOTES AND TIPS

browned and cooked through, 15–20 minutes. Slice sausages in half lengthwise.

Slice roll almost in half lengthwise, but do not cut all the way through. Open up like a book and toast if desired. Spread 1 tablespoon mustard on each side. Place sausages on one side of the roll and top with provolone cheese slices and red pepper strips. Season lightly with salt and pepper, and close sandwiches. Cut in half if desired, and serve.

Makes 1 hero.

▪▪

Meatball Hero

This was one of the most popular sandwiches at the pizzeria. It's gooey and messy to eat and tastes terrific.

1–1½ cups Basic Tomato Sauce (see recipe on page 13)
3 meatballs (see Milly's Meatballs recipe on page 38)
One 8–10" Italian sub roll
¼–½ teaspoon black pepper (to taste)
¼–½ cup freshly grated, good quality Parmesan cheese

Place tomato sauce in a medium-size saucepan. Add meatballs and simmer, stirring occasionally, until meatballs are heated through, about 5–8 minutes.

HENRY'S NOTES AND TIPS

Some people add ¼–½ cup grated mozzarella cheese. I like mine with just the Parmesan. If you add mozzarella, add it when you add the Parmesan. You may need to run the sandwich under the broiler thirty seconds to melt the cheese.

If you find the hero awkward to eat, slice the meatballs in half before putting on the roll.

If the bread's a day old, toast it.

Slice roll almost in half lengthwise, but do not cut all the way through. Open up like a book and toast if desired.

Place meatballs on roll and top with about 1 cup of the tomato sauce, or more if desired. Sprinkle meatballs well with Parmesan, season with pepper, and close sandwiches. Cut hero in half if desired and serve immediately.

GOING BROKE

The trolley ended up being a bad dream. Even when we got it up and running, we couldn't turn a profit. We were going broke fast.

The more depressed and broke I got, the more I missed New York. And the more I missed New York, the more I missed the food. I missed fresh bluefish, lobster, the good Italian olives we'd munch on at card games like other people eat chips. I missed Fat Larry's steaming hot calzones Paulie and I'd burn our mouths on doing the rounds in his car.

And then I thought of my mom, and how she fed us all on a shoestring when we were broke, which was most of the time. Sicilian food is great if you're poor—it isn't called peasant food for nothing. My mom made simple, cheap pastas that were always delicious and inventive. My father used to tease her, "How many different pasta dishes have you made? one hundred? two hundred?" There's real satisfaction in coming up with a dish that costs pennies to make and tastes like a million bucks. And it's a truly Italian way to cook.

Serves 4–6.

Anywhere Pasta Amatriciana

As the name says, you can make this sauce almost anywhere on the planet. There's no garlic here because the star of this dish is the combo of smoky bacon and sweet onion. You don't really need the Parmesan— I like it best without.

1 pound dried pasta of your choice (linguine is good)
1 tablespoon olive oil
4–6 slices smoked bacon, diced or cut in ½ × 1-inch strips (about
    ½ cup diced)
1 large onion, peeled and diced (1 cup)
¼–½ teaspoon crushed hot red pepper flakes (to taste)
One 28-ounce can unseasoned tomato sauce
½ teaspoon black pepper
Freshly grated Parmesan cheese (optional)

Boil a large pot of salted water. Cook the pasta to al dente according to Cooking Pasta directions, page 37, reserving ½ cup of the pasta water. Meanwhile, heat the olive oil in a large skillet and add the bacon pieces. Sauté over medium heat, stirring, until crisp and brown. Remove to paper towels to drain. Pour off all but 2–3 tablespoons of oil in the pan. Add the onion and red pepper flakes and cook over low heat until onion is translucent, about 5–8 minutes (do not brown—add a tablespoon of water and scrape bottom of pan if onion starts to stick and darken). Slowly add the tomato sauce (careful, it may splatter), stirring to combine. Heat thoroughly, then lower heat and simmer 15 minutes, stirring occasionally, until slightly thickened. Season with pepper to taste. Toss pasta with sauce and sprinkle generously with reserved bacon. Serve with grated Parmesan if desired.

HENRY'S
NOTES
AND TIPS

You can use either canned or fresh tomatoes (a twenty-eight-ounce can or about two pounds fresh) instead of canned sauce if you have the time. If using canned, crush them in your hands before adding to onions. If using fresh, dice fine. They'll need five to ten minutes more cooking time to thicken.
    You can substitute diced pancetta or prosciutto for bacon. I like the bacon, and it costs a lot less.

Pasta Arrabiata

¼ cup olive oil
4 garlic cloves, minced (1 tablespoon)
One 28-ounce and one 14-ounce can peeled plum tomatoes with
   juice
¼ cup chopped fresh parsley
½–1 teaspoon crushed red pepper flakes
½–1 teaspoon salt (to taste)
1 pound penne or other pasta (rigatoni, ziti, etc.), cooked and
   drained, reserving ½ cup pasta water (see page 37 for how to
   cook)
½ cup freshly grated Romano cheese

Heat oil in a large skillet over medium heat. Add garlic and cook
3–4 minutes, stirring (do not brown). Stir in juice from tomatoes to
stop the garlic cooking and lower heat. Crush tomatoes or chop fine and
add, along with parsley and half of red pepper flakes. Simmer 20 minutes, stirring and skimming occasionally. Add salt and rest of red pepper
and cook another 10 minutes, until sauce is quite thick. Stir in up to ½
cup pasta water to reach desired consistency and cook a few minutes
more to combine flavors. Toss with pasta and serve sprinkled with
Romano cheese and more on the side.

This is a place I like to seed the tomatoes—it makes a smoother
sauce. To do this, cut tomatoes in half and scoop out the seeds into a
strainer over a bowl so you don't lose the juice. Push down on the seeds
to make sure you get all the juice you can.

**HENRY'S
NOTES
AND TIPS**

Serves 4.

Pasta with Peas and Bacon

4 tablespoons olive oil
2 tablespoons butter
¼ pound sliced bacon, or pancetta cut in ½–1" dice, or prosciutto
    cut in narrow strips
1 cup chopped onions or scallions
2 cloves of garlic, minced
½ cup chopped fresh parsley or 1 tablespoon dried
¼ cup chopped fresh basil or 2 teaspoons dried
½ cup white wine
½ cup chicken broth
1 pound pasta of your choice, cooked and drained, reserving 1 cup
    pasta water (see page 37 for how to cook)
One 10-ounce box frozen baby peas or 1½ cups fresh
1½ teaspoons lemon zest and/or 1 tablespoon lemon juice (optional)
¼–½ teaspoon black pepper
¼ cup grated Parmesan or Romano cheese

Heat 2 tablespoons olive oil and the butter in a skillet and sauté bacon or pancetta (if using prosciutto, add it later when you add the onion) over low heat until browned (about 5 minutes). Remove and

PANCETTA AND PROSCIUTTO

Although they are not the same (pancetta is really Italian bacon, prosciutto is an aged ham), they are often used interchangeably. Pancetta you treat like bacon—it needs to be cooked as long as bacon, prosciutto you can eat raw in an antipasto. Your choice—I love them both.

drain on paper towels. Drain excess fat from pan, leaving about 2 table-spoons. Add onion and prosciutto (if using) and cook 5 minutes. Stir in garlic and cook an additional 3 minutes until garlic gives off aroma but is not browned. Raise heat to medium. Add ¼ cup parsley, basil, and white wine. Reduce mixture by half. Add chicken broth and ½ cup (or more) of pasta water to create sauce. Cook 2 minutes. If using bacon or pancetta, return it to pan, add peas and lemon zest or juice and heat through. Season with pepper.

Toss hot pasta with pea mixture. Serve sprinkled with cheese and remaining parsley.

ITALIAN PEASANT DISHES

■■■ *Serves 4–6.*

Peas, Eggs, and Tomatoes

A friend calls this Italian *huevos rancheros*. It almost is, minus the jalapeño. In fact, a bit of cayenne or red pepper flakes might be a good addition. Forms of this recipe have been around for generations. Some Italians won't serve it; they think it's beneath them. I think it's yummy.

2 tablespoons olive oil
½ medium onion, minced (½ cup)
One 28-ounce can crushed tomatoes + ½ can water
¼ teaspoon sugar
2 cloves of garlic, minced (1 tablespoon)
One 16-ounce can peas with juice
¼ cup chopped fresh basil or 2 teaspoons dried
½ teaspoon salt (to taste)
¼ teaspoon black pepper
6 eggs

Heat olive oil in a pot large enough to hold all ingredients. Sauté onion in oil until soft. Add all other ingredients except eggs. Bring sauce to a full boil. Lower heat until mixture is simmering and cook 15–20 minutes, stirring occasionally. Crack each egg open one at a time and slip into sauce. Continue to simmer until eggs are cooked through, about 4–5 minutes.

Serve with large pieces of crusty Italian bread or over linguine (1 pound).

Serves 4

as a main course,

6 as a side dish.

■■■

String Beans, Potatoes, and Tomatoes

If you're broke, this can be your whole meal. It's also very tasty as a side dish with chicken or fish.

¼ cup olive oil
1 large onion, chopped (1½ cups)
6 baking potatoes, peeled and quartered
1 pound fresh string beans, trimmed and snapped
1 cup canned crushed tomatoes
2 cups water
1 garlic clove, minced
½ teaspoon salt
¼ teaspoon black pepper
½ cup chopped fresh parsley

Heat olive oil in a pot large enough to hold all ingredients. Add onion and simmer until soft, add potatoes and brown for about 5 minutes. Add all other ingredients and simmer about 30 minutes. Adjust seasoning. Serve in large bowls with crusty Italian bread.

GETTING OUT OF KENTUCKY

I was disappointed about the trolley. But to tell you the truth, I was kind of through with it as soon as it was up and running. The excitement for me was getting it together—building it, solving the problems, taking the first trip. Once it was finished, I wanted to move on. I was still the same kid from the cab stand, the one the wiseguys said had ants in his pants. Always after something new to do.

Now it was getting so I was after a new place to live. Kentucky was getting to be a real drag. Just to keep busy, I tried other projects, but everything else went sour too. I even got barred from the race track, through no fault of my own. I hit what they call a conella or trifecta—I won three races in a row! That's cause for celebration! But the race track officials saw it different—they decided I was cheating because of my connection with the back stretch and threw me out. For once, I'd been completely legit, and it didn't matter. So much for honesty.

So I couldn't go to the track which had kept me somewhat sane. Add to that, they were starting the basketball trials and I was back East ten days out of the month, and I wasn't flying direct. I was spending a hell of a lot of time in the air, and I wasn't getting any frequent flyer miles. I was just getting more and more frustrated.

So I started doing other things I knew would get us moved.

Common sense—when you're in the Witness Protection Program you're supposed to keep a low profile. Anything you do that gets you noticed is bad. Even doing something good can be bad. If you get written up in the local paper because you donated five grand to a church, it's as bad as being arrested for a DUI.

I'd already gotten attention from the trolley. When we started running it, the Cincinnati paper took a picture of me and the trolley and printed it (I was racing to get out of the frame). The marshals were already nervous from that. They kept saying, don't do anything, don't do anything.

Don't do anything? That's like being alive but not alive. I put one hundred thousand miles a year on a car in New York driving, doing things. It was all move! Work! Do! Now they wouldn't let me get a job, the trolley was a bust, I couldn't go to the track. I was bored out of my skull. The more bored I got, the more trouble I caused. It's a cinch, I ended up with a DUI.

The marshals were not pleased. People were noticing me. Yes, doing something good can get you noticed, but if you do something bad, people *really* notice. Hey, how many shows they got about criminals on TV, compared to how many they got about Mary Poppins? The Feds warned me if I got in any more trouble they might have to move us, I'd be too exposed. This was music to my ears.

SCOCCING MY SISTERS

One of the other rules of being in the Program is no contact with the family you left behind: your siblings, cousins, aunts, uncles. Phones are way too easy to tap and phone records, they're a snap. Paulie always had AT&T employees on the payroll. In the Mob, we could get anybody's phone record we wanted.

At first I was good about not calling anyone. The few times I did, I'd use a pay phone. It took rolls of quarters to call four hours away.

But as time went on I called more and more, and I got sloppy about it. Besides the fact that the quarters were a pain in the neck, after I got the DUI I really didn't care. I started calling them from home. A big no-no.

I was calling my sisters a lot—"scoccing" them, we called it (pronounced "scootching"). *Scocciare* is Italian for annoy, or nudge. *Tu me scocciare* basically means "You're bugging the shit out of me." And boy, was I bugging them! I'd interrupt them at dinner and want to have a nice long chat. I'd get drunk and call at 2 in the morning. There weren't a lot of answering machines in those days. If the phone rang, your choice was pick it up or let it ring, both of which are lousy choices at 2 a.m. Brother Henry was becoming a pain in the tush.

I started calling almost every day. Any excuse I could think of, I'd be on the horn to Stella, Marie, Lucille. Truth is, I missed them. When I first got in the Program, I took the rules very serious and knew I had to follow them to survive. But it was getting old. I couldn't imagine being cut off from my family the rest of my life. It broke my heart to think of it.

Even though they were annoyed I was calling so much, we had some great late night conversations (or at least I thought so). We'd reminisce about Brooklyn in the old days, our mom, we'd catch up on family news.

Or we'd talk food. Food talk made me feel right at home. We'd been cooking all our lives, but our recipes weren't written down. We learned from my mom the way most Italian families do—we cooked with her. Lucille and I would talk through stuffed veal like we were standing at a stove together. Or Marie would tell me about the great recipes my niece Bonni came up with.

Serves 4–6.

■■

Stuffed Veal

Veal breast is a bargain if you're buying veal. It's probably the cheapest cut and it tastes great.

You can stuff this however you like. It can be as simple as a little cheese and spices or even more complicated than this recipe. I mean, if you don't like spinach or if prosciutto's too rich for you, don't use them. If you want to add pine nuts, olives, capers, whatever—feel free. Improvise!

One ¾–2 pounds boned veal breast (about 4½ pounds with bone)
One 6-ounce package chopped frozen spinach or 12-ounces fresh
2 tablespoons olive oil
2 tablespoons unsalted butter
3–4 large cloves of garlic, peeled and halved
½ cup seasoned Italian bread crumbs
¼ cup freshly grated Parmesan or Romano cheese
½ tablespoon chopped fresh rosemary leaves or 1 teaspoon dried
¼ cup chopped fresh parsley leaves
¼–½ teaspoon each salt and pepper (to taste)
¼ pound thinly sliced prosciutto
½ cup dry white wine
½–1 cup canned chicken broth

Have a butcher remove the bones and gristle from the veal breast; or if you can't get it deboned, follow the same recipe and remove the bones just before serving (they'll slide out easily once they're cooked), or you can serve each person a bone with the meat attached to it, but taking out the bones makes for a nice presentation when you slice it.

Preheat oven to 350°F.

Defrost and drain chopped frozen spinach, squeezing dry to remove

HENRY'S **NOTES** **AND TIPS**	Use less salt than you think you need here because the prosciutto adds salt. To tie up a meat roll, make a loop crosswise about every two inches. If the roll still feels like it's not secure and might fall apart, add a couple more loops where it feels weak.

excess water. If using fresh, bring a large pot of water to a boil, adding a tablespoon of salt. Clean spinach well and remove stems. Drop them into the boiling water and cook until just limp (less than a minute). Drain and rinse in cold water to stop cooking. When cool enough to handle, squeeze as dry as possible and chop coarsely.

In a large skillet, heat 1 tablespoon each olive oil and butter over medium heat. Add halved garlic cloves and cook, stirring so they don't brown, 2 minutes. Add spinach and a dash of salt and pepper and toss together briefly. Remove mixture from pan and place in a bowl to cool.

In a large bowl, mix together bread crumbs, cheese, rosemary, and parsley. Add cooled spinach mixture and combine well. Season with ¼ teaspoon salt and pepper (to taste).

Lay veal breast on a flat surface, skin side down. Layer with prosciutto slices, leaving ½-inch edge uncovered on all sides. Cover prosciutto with spinach mixture, roll up breast, and tie well with string.

Clean skillet and reheat over medium to medium-high heat, adding remaining olive oil and butter. Add veal roll and brown well on all sides. Pour wine over veal and cook, turning, until wine almost all boils away. Season veal roll with ¼ teaspoon salt and pepper.

Place roll in a roasting pan that is not much larger than the roll and place in the oven. Pour ½ cup of chicken broth around it and put in the oven. Cook 1½–2 hours until the meat is pierced easily with a fork or knife, basting every 15–20 minutes and adding more broth or water if pan gets too dry. Remove from oven and let rest at least 5 minutes.

Slice veal vertically in ½-inch slices and place on a serving platter. Make sure you remove all pieces of string. Reheat the pan juices over medium heat on top of the stove, adding more broth if needed and scraping up any bits stuck to the pan. Adjust seasoning, drizzle juice over veal slices, and serve. Garnish with parsley if desired.

Bonni's Smoked Mozzarella with Tomato Appetizer

8 ounces round smoked mozzarella cheese
1 egg
1–1½ cups seasoned bread crumbs
½–1 cup canola oil

Tomato mixture:

6 plum tomatoes, seeds removed and roughly chopped
¼ cup red onion, peeled and diced
¼ cup chopped fresh basil leaves + additional for garnish
¼ cup extra virgin olive oil
¼ teaspoon each salt and pepper
Splash balsamic vinegar
1 teaspoon capers, drained (optional)

To prepare tomato mixture:

Mix all ingredients together and let marinate while preparing cheese.

To prepare the cheese:

Slice the mozzarella vertically in ¼-inch-thick slices. Stack slices and wrap in plastic wrap. Put in freezer for about 5 minutes (this will keep the inside creamy while frying and the cheese will not run).

Place egg in a bowl and beat until smooth. Place bread crumbs on a plate.

Heat ½ cup canola oil in a large skillet over medium-high heat until hot but not smoking. Dip each cheese slice in egg, then bread crumbs. Fry in hot oil until light brown on both sides, turning once. Drain on paper towels. Spoon 2–3 tablespoons tomato mixture on 6 individual plates and top with two slices of cheese per plate. Garnish with fresh basil leaves.

Serves 4–6.

Bonni's Favorite Pasta with Eggplant and Provolone

1 large or two small firm eggplant
1–2 tablespoons salt
¼ cup olive oil
1 medium onion, peeled and diced (¾ cup)
Two 28-ounce cans peeled plum tomatoes with their juice
3–4 cloves of garlic, minced (1 tablespoon)
¼ cup chopped fresh Italian parsley leaves or 2 teaspoons dried
¼ cup chopped fresh basil leaves or 2 teaspoons dried
1 teaspoon salt
½ teaspoon black pepper
4 ounces sharp provolone
Vegetable oil for deep frying (about 2 cups or more)
½ cup flour, seasoned with ¼ teaspoon salt and pepper
1 pound linguine or similar pasta

Peel eggplant and slice in half lengthwise, then in ¼-inch slices crosswise, and then into cubes. To cut the eggplant's bitterness, put cubes in a colander and sprinkle with salt, tossing so salt comes in contact with all the eggplant. Place a dish or bowl under the colander and a smaller dish or bowl on top for light pressure. Let eggplant sit 1–2 hours at room temperature. Discard whatever liquid drained from eggplant and pat cubes dry with paper towels.

Heat olive oil in a large skillet or 6- to 8-quart pot over medium heat. Add onion and cook until translucent, 5–8 minutes. Strain juice from tomatoes and add to pot. Crush tomatoes with your hands or chop on a chopping board and add. Add garlic, parsley, basil, and salt and pepper and simmer partially covered over medium-low heat. Cook for about 30 minutes, skimming off any oil or foam that rises to the top and stirring occasionally. Adjust seasoning. Keep sauce warm, or reheat when both eggplant and pasta are nearly ready. It needs to be very hot before serving.

Cut provolone into bite-size cubes, cover with a paper towel, and set aside.

When eggplant is ready, add oil to a large skillet to a depth of about 1 inch and heat over medium-high heat until oil is very hot but not smoking. The oil is ready for cooking when a small piece of eggplant thrown in it immediately sizzles.

While the oil is heating, place seasoned flour in a large sealable plastic bag. Add eggplant cubes and shake bag thoroughly to dust the cubes.

When oil is hot, add a batch of eggplant cubes (don't crowd them in the pan). Brown on one side, turn with a spatula and brown on second side. Remove and drain on paper towels. Repeat until all eggplant cubes are fried. Don't let oil smoke—remove from heat briefly to cool if necessary and/or turn down heat.

Cook linguine al dente and drain (see Cooking Pasta directions, page 37). Place in a large pasta bowl and cover with sauce. Top with eggplant and then provolone cubes. Toss pasta at the table. The provolone will melt into the dish.

Do not flour eggplant cubes ahead of time or the flour will get sticky and the eggplant won't get crisp.

HENRY'S NOTES AND TIPS

PULLED OUT

The marshals could tell something was up. Every time one of them came by the house, I'd be in the kitchen cooking with the phone in my hand. Who was I talking to so much? I was supposed to be incognito. I could see they were leaning toward moving us but were resisting the change. They didn't want to make the decision I wanted them to. So I dropped the news that I'd been calling my sisters from home—a lot.

They had no choice—they pulled us out of Kentucky. And I was glad to go.

Chapter Ten

Seattle and Washington State

▪▪

Next stop, the West Coast. About as far from New York as we could get.

We had to leave everything again. It seemed we were leaving pieces of ourselves all over the country.

Seattle. All I knew was it's a city on the Pacific and there's a bunch of aerospace companies there. That's it. I was just hoping it'd be better for us than Kentucky. Even though Karen was very outgoing, she'd only had one good friend in Kentucky, a transplanted New Yorker. The kids had always felt way different from the locals. I wanted a place to start over, where we'd fit in.

The plane touched down in Seattle and we did our usual "two marshal plan" disembark. Which means two Ohio marshals flew with us and when everyone else was off the plane, including the crew, they escorted us to our Seattle marshals and our new home.

Inside the terminal, I couldn't believe my eyes. This was a *city*? I thought we'd landed in Paul Bunyan land. Everyone was dressed in— you guessed it, flannel shirts and jeans. Down vests. Hiking boots. All these grown people with good jobs at Boeing trying to look like they didn't have a dime and lived in log cabins. Puh-leese!

So no surprise, we stuck out like a sore thumb. We thought we were going to a city, so we wore city threads—high heels, sport jackets. Not good for being inconspicuous. So we dumped our things at the hotel, and I made the Feds take us shopping.

Our first stop, a waste of time. We went to Pendleton's and outfitted ourselves. We bought Timberland hiking boots. But it was all new and stiff. Everybody else's clothes were worn in. We looked like aliens trying to look like humans. We were just like the undercover cops in Brooklyn who could never get it right—you'd spot them a mile off by their clothes. So we went to Goodwill and traded all our new stuff for used.

Our new head marshal, Marshal Bob, took us around to the stores. I could tell, this weren't gonna be no picnic. It was clear he didn't like me. Let me be even clearer: the guy hated my guts. He was one of those righteous, holier-than-thou types. A real stuffed shirt. Everything I stood for he hated—that I was in the Mob, that I had ratted on them, that I was like becoming a celebrity from all that, and that, no matter what I did, as long as the government needed me, they would protect me. On top of which, I'm sure he'd heard I was no day at the beach to deal with, and he was going to have to deal with me anyway. It must have been one of the worst days of his life when he heard they were moving me to Seattle.

Searching for clothes, we got to look around. Seattle wasn't like a real "city" city then. Except for one section, there weren't any skyscrapers, there was very little traffic. It felt peaceful and safe. In the stores, the clerks and customers were downright neighborly. They all knew each other, they knew whose kid was doing what. We passed a big college and a group of coffee shops nearby with students hanging out, playing guitars, working on their papers. There was a little place called Starbucks that sold gourmet coffee beans. No Internet hookups then. And in '82, Microsoft was just another company, nothing special.

The people in Seattle? Nothing like 'em. Like I said, how they dress you wouldn't write home about—I mean, these people could definitely do with a few fashion tips. But forget the frumpy clothes. They're wonderful folks—very friendly, funny, truly nice people.

I met a group of guys immediately. The first day I got there. The first night, in my new old clothes, I walked into a Mexican restaurant. I sat at the bar and bought a beer and this guy Len just started talkin' to me—like that, outta nowhere, he was so friendly! That, I'm not used to. He introduced me to Bob and his brother Rich. They were such great people I felt at home by the time I left that restaurant. It was a good sign—maybe our luck had turned.

The food? Well, the Mexican fare at the restaurant didn't look none too good. But I knew we were near water, a *lot* of water, and it was salt water. You could feel it everywhere—you could smell it in the air. My first whiff of ocean, my mouth started watering. Because where there's ocean, there's gonna be damn good seafood. I couldn't wait to start cooking.

I started hanging out with Len, Bob, Rich, and another guy, a lawyer named Jim. They grew up in the Northwest, they knew all about the seafood. In the Northwest there was shrimp season, there was salmon season. Hey, they taught me how to fish! We'd go river fishing, and catch crayfish (or crawfish). I laughed the first time I saw one—they're like tiny lobsters! Or we'd get steelhead trout when they were running. They knew a crazy Indian named Jim Clark who leased a fishing boat. He'd take us out a lot. I really got into it. We had barbecues every week-end to cook what we caught.

The seafood in Seattle was the best! Completely fresh. It has a lovely texture and taste. Have you ever eaten shrimp right out of the shrimp pot? I mean, right where you yank it up? You haul 'em up, and just pluck their heads off or leave 'em on, and they're ready to cook.

FROZEN SHRIMP

Almost all shrimp you buy these days, even at the fish market, has been frozen. It's so common they don't even bother to tell you any-more. But because of the new freezing techniques they've come up with, the shrimp still has wonderful flavor. Feel free to use them. If you're going to make a whole lot of shrimp, they can sell you a big block of it that's still frozen and you can defrost it just before you use it, but they usually won't sell it in smaller amounts.

Serves 6

as an appetizer,

3–4 as a

main course.

Scampi on the Barbie

This is a great "peel and eat" shrimp dish. Shrimp scampi is a classic Italian dish, it's on every restaurant menu. I ate it more times than I can count back in the Life. This is my West Coast version of scampi, where it's all about grilling 'em up in no time, and then sitting around talking while you peel and eat. It can be an appetizer or a whole meal if you add a salad and some bread. Keep in mind, if you have shrimp lovers, these'll fly off the plate—make plenty!

Shrimp and marinade:

½ cup extra virgin olive oil
4 cloves of garlic (1 tablespoon)
½ cup chopped onion
¼ teaspoon dried oregano
½ teaspoon each salt and pepper
2 pounds large shrimp, shells on

Dipping sauce:

½ cup olive oil
4 cloves chopped garlic (1 tablespoon)
¼ cup chopped fresh parsley
¼–½ cup lemon juice
½–1 teaspoon salt and pepper

To prepare marinade:

In a large bowl mix together olive oil, garlic, onion, oregano, and salt and pepper. Add shrimp and mix to coat. Marinate at room temperature 45 minutes, turning a few times.

Meanwhile, set up grill for cooking and make dipping sauce. In a medium bowl, mix together olive oil, garlic, parsley, lemon juice and salt and pepper to taste. Set aside.

Remove shrimp from marinade, shaking to remove excess. Discard marinade. Arrange shrimp next to each other lying flat in a grill basket and secure with top. Or you can put shrimp on skewers (keeping them flat) and place skewers directly on the grill. Grill shrimp until just pink—this will only take about two minutes on each side. Remove one shrimp and test for doneness. Serve shrimp with sauce. Peel, dip, and eat.

Len and his pals became like family. I loved these guys. They were the closest to my crew from New York I'd met, without the dark side. My girlfriend Linda back in New York used to say our crew was like a bunch of big kids. Len and Bob were like that—big kidders. They'd tease me, "Come on, we know you're a Company man." They really thought I was CIA!! "Come on, who're we gonna assassinate next? Tell us a secret." So I played along (I never told them the truth). I'd make up some outrageous lie. They'd even believe me.

The Indian guy Jim Clark got us all kinds of fish and shellfish from his boat trips. In Seattle, you can get any kind of seafood! It was amazing. We had salmon, halibut, tuna, crab legs as big as baseball bats! Or there's hard to find things like abalone, which is so good you barely want to do anything to it or you'll ruin the taste. Goeduck (you say it "gooey-duck") clams, they look like a horse's ga-dootz (or schlong), but they taste delicious! And halibut cheeks, so tender they melt in your mouth. We had all the oysters we wanted. We'd shuck them till our hands bled and eat 'em raw. Or if we were lazy we'd just toss 'em still in their shells on the grill and eat them hot with cocktail sauce.

Cornbread and Oyster Stuffing

At one point I met a nurse who lived way out in the country and had a side business raising pigs, turkeys, and cows. It was all natural stuff (today they'd call it organic). It had the best flavor. I used to buy half a side of beef at a time. And the turkeys, delicious! The breasts were huge! If you can get organic turkey where you live, do it—believe me, it's worth the extra bucks. That Thanksgiving I put together a real spread with one of those birds as the main event. And living in one of the seafood capitals of the world, I insisted we have my favorite stuffing, made with oysters and cornbread.

    4 tablespoons unsalted butter
    1 cup diced onion
    1 large stalk celery, diced (½ cup)
    4 large cloves of garlic, minced (1 tablespoon)
    ½ cup chopped fresh parsley leaves
    ½ teaspoon oregano
    1 teaspoon chopped fresh thyme leaves or ½ teaspoon dried
    24 shucked oysters + ½ cup of their liquor if needed
    1 recipe cornbread, crumbled (4–5 cups)
    ½ teaspoon salt and pepper (to taste)

Henry's Rules for Cooking on the Run:
HOW TO MAKE GOOD ITALIAN FOOD ANYWHERE

Rule 11: Do one experiment on holidays. If it works, you're a hero. If it doesn't, no one will notice. Needless to say, not everyone likes the same foods. That's okay—if there's a lot of dishes around, your one experiment won't really be noticed. And if they like it, you'll never hear the end of it.

Melt butter in a large skillet over medium-low heat. Add onion, cel-ery, and garlic and cook until onion is translucent, 5–10 minutes (do not brown mixture). Stir in parsley, oregano, and thyme and re-move from heat.

Chop oysters in large pieces. Toss cornbread in a large bowl with onion mixture and stir in oysters. If mixture seems at all dry add a little oyster liquor. Season with salt and pepper and mix well. Use to stuff bird or place in a buttered 9 × 12 inch baking dish and cover with aluminum foil. Bake in a 350°F oven for 30 minutes.

Enough stuffing for a 14-pound bird.

<hr>

Serves 4.

Pan-Fried Salmon

This is cooked on the stove, for when you don't want to grill. It's quick, easy, delicious.

1 tablespoon light olive oil
3 garlic cloves, minced (about 2 teaspoons)
2 pounds fresh salmon fillets
¼ teaspoon dried oregano or 1 sprig fresh
¼ teaspoon salt and pepper
2 teaspoons capers
3 tablespoons chopped fresh parsley
Juice of a medium lemon + ½ lemon cut in wedges

Heat oil over medium heat in large skillet. Add garlic and cook 2 minutes, stirring. Raise heat to high and add salmon, skin side down. The

If salmon fillets are thicker, lower heat and cook longer.

HENRY'S NOTES AND TIPS

fish should sizzle when it hits the pan. Cover pan and cook 2–3 minutes, until underside is browned. Flip fish and cover pan. Cook 2 minutes. Add remaining ingredients except 1 tablespoon parsley and lemon wedges. Cook 2 more minutes, scraping and stirring liquid in pan. The salmon should be done—it'll spring back slightly when tapped, or you can cut to check center. Serve garnished with remaining parsley and lemon wedges.

Serves 4.

Bowties with Grilled Salmon in Pink Sauce

Here's a great way to combine grilled salmon and pasta, adapted from my friend Eric from Boston.

½–¾ pound salmon fillet with skin
2 teaspoons olive oil
Juice of ½ lemon
1½ tablespoons chopped fresh dill or 2 teaspoons dried
¼–½ teaspoon salt and pepper (to taste)
2 ounces bacon, diced
4 large cloves of garlic, minced
2 large fresh beefsteak tomatoes
¼ cup chopped fresh basil leaves or 1 tablespoon dried
½ cup canned chicken broth
¼–½ cup heavy cream or half and half
¼ cup vodka
1 pound bowtie pasta, cooked and drained, reserving 1 cup pasta
    water (see page 37 for how to cook)
½ cup freshly grated Parmesan or Romano

Skin salmon, chop skin and reserve. Place salmon in a flat pan or a large bowl and coat on both sides with 1 teaspoon olive oil, juice of ½ lemon, dill (reserving a bit for later) and ¼ teaspoon salt and pepper. Set aside to marinate at room temperature for half an hour.

Heat 1 teaspoon olive oil in pan and add diced bacon, diced salmon

If you are using dried dill, don't add it at the end. Dried herbs need to be cooked to work in a sauce. Just serve it with the Parmesan or Romano topping.

skin and garlic over medium heat. Sauté until bacon is golden brown (do not brown garlic) and remove all to paper towels to drain. Remove all but 1 tablespoon oil grease. Turn off heat.

Heat grill or broiler. Rinse and halve tomatoes, brush lightly with olive oil and sprinkle with salt and pepper. Grill 2–3 minutes in broiler (until starting to blacken or fall apart). Remove tomatoes, chop, and add to pan with bacon grease.

Drain salmon from marinade and place on broiling pan. Grill 2 minutes per side, until just done. Set aside.

Reheat pan with tomatoes and add sautéed bacon, salmon skin, basil, and garlic mixture. Cook tomatoes until they are broken up. Add chicken broth and heavy cream or half & half and cook down 1 minute. Stir in vodka and cook until reduced by half.

Break up salmon into bite-size pieces and stir gently into sauce. Reheat and season with salt and pepper. Toss with bowtie pasta, add cheese, remaining dill and serve with additional cheese on the side if desired.

Serves 6.

Linguine with Shrimp

This dish is like Lobster Fra Diavolo made with shrimp instead of lobster. The flavor of fresh shrimp permeates the tomato sauce, making it irresistible to a seafood lover like me.

1½ pounds medium or jumbo shrimp, peeled and deveined, reserving shells
1 recipe Basic Tomato Sauce (see page 13) + ½ teaspoon red pepper flakes and ¼ teaspoon dried oregano
1 pound linguine or pasta of your choice, cooked and drained (see page 37)

Cook Basic Tomato Sauce according to directions on page 14, adding the red pepper flakes and oregano when you add parsley and basil. Simmer approximately 45 minutes, until fairly thick. Meanwhile, boil shrimp shells (and heads if you have them) in water to cover, 10–15 minutes. Strain well and add liquid to tomato sauce while it cooks. When sauce is done, add shrimp and simmer 1–2 minutes more, just until shrimp turn pink. Do not overcook the shrimp! They will shrivel up and have the texture of rubber. Adjust seasoning. Serve immediately over hot pasta with crusty bread to sop up the sauce.

SQUID

Len and my new Seattle "crew," we used to "jig" for squid. You use a special kind of hook called a jigger. It has a bunch of little hooks, and it's got a light on it, like the lights kids twirl at basketball games. You just jig it up and down, and the squid are attracted to the light. They have these big, long piers near Seattle, like in Edmonds, Washington. The piers go way out in the water, and they have huge lights on them. The squid swarm in. So when you drop your little light in the water and jig it, the squid grab 'em. It takes half an hour to get a whole pailful.

Serves 4.

Stuffed Calamari

You can buy cleaned squid lots of places these days, even in some grocery stores, or you can get a fishmonger to clean them for you. Buy them with the hoods in one piece for this dish (tell the fishmonger you're planning to stuff them).

These are great served with a pound of your favorite pasta tossed with some of the sauce or good bread, or both.

1 pound cleaned small or medium-size squid, hoods and tentacles separated

1–2 tablespoons olive oil

½ large onion, minced (½ cup)

2 large cloves garlic, minced (1 tablespoon)

2 cups seasoned Italian bread crumbs

¼ cup chopped fresh parsley leaves or 1 tablespoon dried

1 tablespoon capers, drained

1 cup grated Parmesan or Romano cheese (or a mix of the two)

1 large egg, beaten

¼ cup olive oil

¼–½ teaspoon salt and pepper (to taste)

2½–3 cups Basic Tomato Sauce (see page 13) or jarred equivalent of marinara sauce

Preheat oven to 300°F.

Heat oil in a large skillet over medium heat. Chop tentacles in pieces small enough to be stuffed into squid hoods and add to pan, along with onion. Cook, stirring, until onion is translucent, about 5 minutes. Stir in garlic and cook an additional 2 minutes. Cool mixture to room temperature. Add bread crumbs, parsley, capers, cheese, beaten egg and ¼ cup olive oil and mix well. Season with salt and pepper to taste.

Stuff squid hoods about ¾ full (don't overstuff—they shrink when cooking and will split if overstuffed). Close ends with toothpicks. Place in a baking dish that can hold them all in one layer and cover with tomato sauce. Cover dish with aluminum foil and bake 45–60 minutes, until calamari are tender but not rubbery (check after 45 minutes). Serve immediately.

I add more sauce than needed to this, and then toss with one pound cooked and drained pasta to serve with it.

HENRY'S NOTES AND TIPS

■■■

Squid Salad

This is basically the Octopus Salad from my mom's recipe on page 51 using squid instead, which doesn't have to cook anywhere near as long.

1 pound squid, cleaned (have your fishmonger do this)
2–4 tablespoons extra virgin olive oil
1 large stalk celery, trimmed and diced or sliced thin (¾ cup)
¼ cup diced red onion
1 tablespoon drained capers
1 tablespoon black kalamata olives, sliced
¼ cup chopped fresh parsley leaves
3 tablespoons lemon juice (to taste)
½–1 teaspoon salt and pepper (to taste)

Bring a large pot of water to a boil, then add 1 tablespoon salt and the squid. Boil for about 3 minutes, drain, and rinse in cold water to stop cooking. Drain and cool. Slice in ¼-inch rings, and cut any large tentacles in half.

Combine the remaining ingredients in a large bowl with the squid. Chill thoroughly and serve cool.

HENRY'S NOTES AND TIPS	Add some crushed red pepper flakes if you like it hot.

THE RANCH AND OLD C.P.

I loved it in Seattle. Everything was great. Except I still had no job.

I guess I'm just one of those people who likes to be busy. Tons of guys would give an eye to be doing what I was—nothing. Early retirement? To me, it's a death sentence. I want to be doing deals when I drop.

Besides, I was broke.

The government gave us an allowance of like fifteen hundred dollars a month to live on. Puh-leese! I could spend that in a weekend partying. Karen was finishing up getting her cosmetology license, hoping to open a beauty shop and make some good money. She was always learning new skills. She already knew how to be a dental technician, groom dogs, and had a nursing degree.

But while she was learning how to make old women look good, she lucked into a nursing job that paid us big-time. She hooked up with a gay nurse named Bill who was taking care of a very wealthy guy. I mean, this guy he was taking care of was loaded! She and Bill started giving the rich guy twenty-four-hour care. Karen was averaging two thousand dollars a week—in 1982, that wasn't chicken scratch. So we decided it was time to invest in a real home. I talked to my real estate friend Len and he helped us find a ranch to buy.

The ranch was a beautiful piece of property in Redmond. Redmond, the "bicycle capital of the world"—like I'd ever ride a bicycle. But I loved the place. The house was big—there were at least five bedrooms. We had a nice barn for the horses we bought. We had pear trees. The place looked out over a polo field, and then acres and acres of fields, cut in half by a river. And next to that was Microsoft. I wish we had it today; I'm sure it's worth millions.

For a while I was okay with being a house husband. Setting up the ranch was my new project. And of course I was doing the cooking.

This guy Karen took care of, what a character! C.P. Middleton. He was like ninety-five years old and sharp as a tack. He'd been "in textiles." A real blueblood. He was the oldest living Harvard graduate. Every year, he'd go back and march in the alumni parade. He was a little frail, but he was in great shape for a guy his age. He didn't really need twenty-four-hour care. He just got it 'cause he could afford it.

C.P. lived in an upscale nursing home, a real fancy place. But he didn't like it—there was nothing to do there. One day to entertain him, Karen brought him out to the ranch, and he was crazy about it. He wanted to stay. So we fixed up one of the bedrooms for him, and he would be there three, four days at a time. Karen got paid around the clock for that and really raked in the dough.

This old geezer, I really liked him, but we couldn't have been more opposite. The guy had real class. You could see he'd lived all his life with a silver spoon in his mouth. He had the best table manners I've ever seen. And here he was ninety-five, spending like twenty-thousand a month just staying alive. At his age, he still had enough left to do that. All the money I'd had, and I'd had a lot—gone. Through my hands like water. I really respected old C.P. for how he handled his money.

But he was also like people I used to rob with the Arico gang back in the Life. Back then, we'd hit real rich folk, Upper East Siders. We'd tie them up and steal their jewelry. (If we'd known anything, we woulda taken the Picassos on the wall too—stupid!) Who would have thought one day I'd be talking and laughing with a guy like them!

I started cooking for him at the ranch. He loved my food, but he needed blander stuff—one of the drags about getting to his age is you can't eat what you want anymore. So I'd make him a mild pasta like stuffed shells with just a little sauce, a baked chicken without garlic. He never ate at the table with us, so as not to invade our family time, or maybe we were too rowdy for him. Karen would set up a table by the window and he'd look out over the polo field. I would have been lonely like that, but he seemed very happy. That way, he had a family atmosphere in the next room, and he had his privacy.

Serves 6.

Stuffed Shells with Tomato Mint Sauce

A guy I know from Chicago says his mom always put mint in tomato sauce. It sounded like it was worth a try, especially since mint would be soothing to old C.P.

16 large shells (jumbo)

For the sauce:

2 tablespoons olive oil
4 large garlic cloves, minced
One 28-ounce can crushed tomatoes

One 28-ounce can plain tomato sauce
¼ cup chopped fresh mint leaves or 2 teaspoons dried (or more to taste)
¼ cup finely chopped Italian parsley or 2 teaspoons dried
¼–½ teaspoon salt and pepper (to taste)

For the filling:

15-ounce container ricotta cheese (about 2 cups)
8 ounces shredded mozzarella cheese (about 2 cups)
1 cup freshly grated Parmesan or Romano cheese (or a mix of the two)
1 large egg, beaten
¼ cup chopped fresh Italian parsley or 1 tablespoon dried + additional for garnish
¼ teaspoon each salt and pepper
¼ cup freshly grated Parmesan or Romano cheese for topping (optional)

Cook the shells until barely al dente, rinse, and drain well. Toss with olive oil to keep moist.

For the sauce:

In a large skillet or medium-large wide pot, heat olive oil over medium-low heat. Add garlic to oil and cook briefly, stirring (do not brown). Add the crushed tomatoes and tomato sauce and stir well. Add mint and parsley, and season with half the salt and pepper. Cook over medium-high heat until sauce begins to bubble. Stir well, then lower heat to a simmer. Cook ½ hour while you stuff the shells, skimming every 15 minutes. Taste for seasoning and add additional mint if desired.
Preheat oven to 350°F.

For the filling:

Combine cheeses in a large bowl and add beaten egg, parsley, and salt and pepper. Mix thoroughly.

If you find the shells are sticking to each other after cooking, toss with a teaspoon of olive oil. They'll be a little slippery when you go to stuff them, but at least they'll separate without breaking.

Make sure you don't overcook the shells or they'll fall apart when you go to stuff them.

Spread a small amount of tomato sauce over the bottom of a baking dish large enough to hold the shells in a single layer. Fill shells with the ricotta mixture and place in baking dish. Top with the remaining sauce and sprinkle with optional Parmesan or Romano cheese. Bake about 20 minutes until heated through or until cheese has melted and has a slight crust.

Serves 4.

C.P.'s Roast Chicken

This is so simple you won't believe how good it is. The leftovers make great sandwiches too.

One 4–5 pound roasting chicken
2 fresh lemons, halved
½ medium onion
1–2 tablespoons canola oil
1 teaspoon salt
½ teaspoon black pepper

Preheat the oven to 350°F. Rinse the chicken and parts. Remove extra fat. Drain the chicken well. Either save the gizzard, heart, neck, and liver for stock or chicken livers, or boil them in water seasoned with salt and pepper for a "chef's appetizer"—something to munch on while making dinner. Put 1½ lemons and the onion in chicken cavity and close both ends of the chicken with skewers or toothpicks. Rub the breast side of the chicken with half the canola oil and season with half the salt and pepper. Place on a rack in a roasting pan, or right in the pan if you don't have a rack, breast side down. Rub the other side of chicken with remaining oil, season with rest of salt and pepper. Roast in oven 30 minutes, turn chicken breast side up and roast an additional 30 minutes, basting occasionally. Raise the heat to 375°F and continue roasting for about 20 minutes more. Let chicken rest 5–10 minutes before cutting into pieces.

Serves 2.

Linguine with Zucchini

Zucchinis are full of water, so I like to dry them a few minutes in the oven before adding to a pasta dish—they hold up better.

3–4 medium-size zucchinis, 4–6 inches each (1¼ pounds)
¼ cup olive oil
¼–½ teaspoon each salt and pepper (to taste)
½ brown onion or 2–3 shallots, diced
4 garlic cloves, minced (1 tablespoon)
1 small tomato, seeded and chopped (about 2 tablespoons)
¼ cup chopped fresh parsley leaves
¼–½ cup chopped or slivered fresh basil leaves
½ cup whole-milk or part-skim ricotta cheese
½ pound cooked and drained linguine or *linguine fini* (thin linguine) or other long pasta of your choice, reserving 1 cup of pasta water (see page 37 for how to cook)
½ cup freshly grated Parmesan or Romano cheese

Preheat oven to 200°F.

Soak and clean zucchinis well, trim their ends, and pat dry (see page 204 for details on how to clean zucchini). Cut them lengthwise in thin strips (julienne) 3–4 inches long. Toss with 1 tablespoon olive oil and place on a baking sheet lined with aluminum foil. Sprinkle with a little salt and pepper and place in the oven for 5 minutes, or until they look a little "dried out." Remove from oven and cool.

Heat 3 tablespoons oil in a skillet over medium heat. Add onions or shallots and cook, stirring 3–4 minutes, until translucent. Add garlic and cook for one minute, stirring. Add chopped tomato, parsley, and basil and cook, stirring 2–3 minutes, or until tomato starts to break down. Add zucchini and toss to reheat, 2–3 minutes.

In a medium-size bowl, combine ricotta with a few tablespoons reserved pasta water and stir until water is evenly dispersed. The mixture should resemble a thick sauce—add more water if necessary to reach this consistency. Add ricotta to zucchini mixture and lower heat. Stir gently to mix cheese with vegetables until cheese is heated through. Season with salt and pepper to taste and toss with cooked linguine. Serve immediately, topped with Parmesan or Romano if desired.

Serves 2

generously.

Chicken Marsala with Mushrooms

There are two basic kinds of Marsala wine: dry and sweet. Make sure you get the sweet kind for this dish.

¼ cup flour
½ teaspoon each salt and pepper
2 skinless boneless chicken breasts (1–1½ pounds)
2 tablespoons olive oil
2 tablespoons butter
½ cup sweet Marsala wine
½ pound mushrooms, cleaned and sliced
1 tablespoon capers

3 tablespoons chopped fresh parsley
½ cup canned chicken broth (optional)

Mix flour with salt and pepper and place on a plate. Set aside. If chicken breasts are very large, cut in serving pieces. Pound as thin as possible (about ⅛-inch thick).

In a large skillet, heat oil and butter until hot but not smoking. Dredge chicken breasts one at a time in the seasoned flour on both sides, shake to remove excess flour and slip into the hot oil. Cook 2 minutes on each side and remove to a plate. Do in batches if necessary—don't crowd the chicken while it cooks.

If there are any bits that are too browned in the remaining oil, remove from pan. Add a tablespoon of the Marsala to deglaze pan and scrape up remaining bits. Add mushroom slices and sauté briefly, stirring. Stir in capers and parsley and cook 1–2 minutes, stirring constantly. If you want more sauce, add up to ½ cup chicken broth and reduce to thicken sauce.

Return chicken breasts to pan with sauce and cook to reheat. Serve immediately.

■■■ *Serves 3–4.*

Brussels Sprouts with Pancetta

While I was being a house husband, I started a vegetable garden. I planted a lot of things we had back in Brooklyn: tomatoes, zucchinis, fresh basil, mint. I also planted Brussels sprouts. If you've never seen a Brussels sprout plant, they're very funny looking. They have a thick pale green stalk and the sprouts grow all up and down the stalk. My plants got so tall I couldn't reach the top, it was like Jack and the Beanstalk! I gave them to the whole town and we still had too many.

This is my favorite way to make Brussels sprouts. You peel off all the outer layers and just eat the very tender inside. The inner layers are much sweeter than the rest of the sprout.

1 pound Brussels sprouts (about 30)
2 tablespoons olive oil
2 large garlic cloves, peeled and left whole
2 ounces pancetta, diced
¼–½ teaspoon each salt and pepper (to taste)

Trim the bottom of each sprout and peel off all the outer layers until only a light green nugget of sprout remains. (You may have to retrim the bottom a second time, as the leaves anchor on the bottom of the stem and can be hard to pull off.) Rinse sprouts in cold water and drain well. Cut sprouts in quarters lengthwise.

In a large skillet, heat the olive oil over medium heat and add the garlic cloves. Cook 5 minutes and remove garlic. Add the diced pancetta and cook, stirring, about 2 minutes. Add sprouts and cook, stirring, until sprouts can be pierced with a fork, 3–5 minutes. Season with salt and pepper to taste and serve.

MARSHAL BOB

Like I said, there was no love lost between me and Marshal Bob. But it was still his job to "watch over me" and it pissed him off to no end. As far as he could tell, I was living the life of Riley on the government's dime, and he couldn't do anything about it. I could see the smoke come from under his collar whenever he had to deal with me. And I tormented this guy, I really did. 'Cause I knew what an uptight, straight-laced dope he was. I didn't even have to do much. The slightest thing would bug him. I'd just lift my pinky and then sit back and watch him steam.

It was his job to transport me to and from the airport for the New York trips. When he showed up to get me, I'd make him wait outside in the car. Even if I was ready, I'd make him wait. I'd make him wait until we barely had time to make the flight. It used to drive him nuts.

Or he had to bring me money. We got a stipend from the government every month, and they paid us in cash so nobody could trace it to me, so I'd be safe. Later on when *Wiseguy* came out, I'd get royalty checks that the government would launder and again pay me in cash. Sometimes I'd get thirty thousand dollars, sixty thousand dollars at once! They'd give it to me all in hundreds. Marshal Bob had to drive out to the house with my money. He's making what, sixty grand a year? Here he is handing me his salary four times over (and I'm not paying any taxes on it either). When he gave it to me, I'd make him count it in front of me, "One . . . two . . ."

And when he finished, I'd make him count it again. "One . . . two . . ."

Serves 2

generously.

Pasta Carbonara

A lot of times when Marshal Bob came to take me to the airport, I'd make sure he caught the aromas of whatever dinner I'd been cooking and eating while he sat in his car with a cold cup of coffee. This was one of my quick pastas that made him drool. And no, I never offered him a single bite.

1 tablespoon olive oil
1 tablespoon unsalted butter
6 ounces pancetta or bacon, diced or cut in thin strips 1" long
1 large clove of garlic, minced
½ pound cooked pasta of your choice (I like spaghetti or thin
   spaghetti; see page 37 for how to cook)
3 large eggs, beaten
1 cup Parmesan or Romano cheese, or a mixture of the two, plus
   additional for serving
¼ cup chopped fresh parsley leaves
½–1 teaspoon black pepper (to taste)

Heat olive oil and butter in a large skillet over medium heat. Add pancetta or bacon and cook, stirring, until lightly browned. Add garlic and cook 1–2 minutes (don't let garlic brown). Remove from heat.

Cook and drain pasta and return to pot to keep warm.

In a large bowl, combine eggs, cheeses, and parsley, mixing well. Turn pan with pancetta mixture to medium-low heat, add egg mixture

The traditional way to cook carbonara sauce is to toss the heated pasta and bacon with the uncooked eggs and cheese right in the serving bowl, but these days it's safer to precook the eggs slightly. They should just start to cook before you add the pasta, not turn into scrambled eggs.

This is not a lowfat meal, but if you want you can drain off some of the bacon grease.

and cook 15–20 seconds, stirring and tossing. Add pasta to the skillet and toss thoroughly. Season with black pepper and retoss. Place in a serving bowl and serve immediately with more grated cheese on the side.

STRAWBERRIES

Maybe sixteen miles from Redmond, where our ranch was, there's a town called Duvall. Tiny. You wink and you're through it. It has one street, one little street.

Me and my pals used to go to Duvall just to get out of Redmond. Or we'd go fishing, and on the way back we'd stop at the bar in Duvall—there was only one.

The bar was right on a river, and attached to it was this big restaurant that had been closed down. The restaurant was in a sad state; it had been neglected for a long time. I needed something to do—I was getting more than a little house bound, and when I saw the restaurant, it was like it was meant to be. I talked to the owner of the place and convinced him to do a deal like I did at Roger's Place: I'd fix up the restaurant and run it. He'd get the bar money, and I'd get the restaurant take.

We named the place Strawberries, because it was right next to the strawberry capital of the state. We used strawberries as the theme—it was all red and white, there were strawberries on the curtains and the tablecloths.

I was excited to be back in the restaurant business and wanted to experiment with the food. Karen was so glad I had some kind of employment, she helped me set up the place and even waitressed for a while.

I had traditional American fare on the menu, things like burgers and sandwiches for those that wanted them. I added Sicilian pizza, sausage and pepper heros. And of course I added some seafood dishes. I pulled recipes from back in New York—things like shrimp with peppers, linguine with clam sauce. I made an eggplant appetizer that even people who claimed they didn't like eggplant would devour.

■■

Makes appetizers for 4–6 people.

Eggplant "Sandwiches"

I get a lot of requests to make this dish. It can be an appetizer, a side dish, or a vegetarian meal with a little pasta and salad.

1 tablespoon salt
1 tablespoon lemon juice
1 eggplant, about 1–1½ pounds, peeled and cut into ½" thick slices
2 eggs, beaten, seasoned with ⅛ teaspoon salt and pepper
½ cup flour seasoned with ¼ teaspoon salt and pepper
1 cup ricotta cheese
2 tablespoons chopped fresh Italian parsley or 1 teaspoon dried
2 tablespoons grated fresh Parmesan cheese
½–1 cup olive oil
Black pepper
1 cup Basic Tomato Sauce (see page 13), roughly puréed in a
     blender
2 ounces mozzarella cheese, grated
Fresh basil leaves for garnish

To cut the eggplant's bitterness, add salt and lemon juice to a large bowl of water. Place the slices in the bowl and weight with a plate or small pan to keep them submerged. Let sit for an hour. Drain off the liquid and dry slightly but not completely with paper towels—that way, the flour will stick great, and the slices will cook up crunchy as a cucumber. Meanwhile, prepare the rest of the ingredients. See page 27 for other ways to prepare eggplant.

Beat the eggs in a shallow bowl. Set aside.

Make sure there is plenty of oil in the pan—add more and reheat if necessary, or cook in a nonstick pan if you want to use less oil. Make sure the oil is very hot so the eggplant won't absorb a lot of it—an eggplant is like a sponge!

You can add things to the ricotta, depending on what you have around. Like chop up a couple of black olives and toss them in. They'll just add more flavor.

Peel the eggplant or not depending on what you like, or how much time you got.

Spear with toothpicks if sandwich layers slide a bit.

In a pinch, you can substitute canned or jarred tomato sauce for the Basic Tomato Sauce. Heat in a saucepan and season to taste with salt, pepper, garlic powder, dried basil, and parsley.

Place seasoned flour on a plate.

Mix the ricotta in a medium bowl with parsley, Parmesan, and ½ teaspoon black pepper.

Heat 3–4 tablespoons of the oil in a large sauté pan until very hot. Oil should ripple but not be smoking.

Dredge both sides of the eggplant slices first in the flour and then the egg. Slip the slices into the hot oil and sauté quickly until golden on both sides. Do this in batches if slices won't all fit in the pan. Drain well on paper towels.

Preheat the broiler or set oven to broil. Place one eggplant slice on a foil-lined baking sheet. Spread 2–3 tablespoons ricotta on it and top with a second eggplant slice. Cover just the top of the "sandwich" with some of the tomato sauce and a large pinch of grated mozzarella. Repeat with remaining eggplant slices. Broil 2 minutes or until cheese is melted. Garnish each sandwich with a basil leaf and serve. (They can also be cut in halves or quarters before serving.)

Variation:

If you want to make the dish a little lighter, skip dipping the eggplant slices in the flour and egg and instead simply season them with salt and pepper before frying. I often do this if I'm going to have another breaded or fried dish in a meal.

Fusilli with Mixed Seafood

This recipe was inspired by having no time. I was racing my shopping cart down the frozen food aisle and spied something called "Seafood Medley": a combo of quick-frozen shrimp, scallops, squid, mussels, and clams—a wonderful assortment. And cheap! I grabbed a bag and hurried home to throw dinner together.

Note that I've added oregano and the optional onion to the sauce. I like a little of both with seafood, but only a little. I never buy what they call "Italian Seasoning" because it's *loaded* with oregano, far more than I ever use.

Tomato Sauce:

5–6 garlic cloves, peeled and minced
¼ cup olive oil
1 small onion or ½ large, peeled and diced (about ½ cup)
One 28-ounce can + one 14-ounce can whole tomatoes
10 large basil leaves, torn into large pieces or ¾ tablespoon
    dried basil
¼ cup Italian parsley, chopped fine
½–1 teaspoon dried oregano
¼–½ teaspoon each salt and pepper (to taste)

Seafood:

1 pound fresh or frozen mixed seafood (i.e., a combination
    of peeled and deveined shrimp, cleaned and cut squid,
    scallops, scrubbed mussels, and clams with or without their
    shells)
1 pound fusilli pasta, cooked and drained (see page 37 for how
    to cook)

To make the sauce:

Sauté garlic in olive oil over medium heat in a large skillet. Add the onion and cook until translucent, about 5 minutes (do not brown). Coarsely chop tomatoes and add them and their juice to the sauce. Stir in basil, parsley, ½ teaspoon oregano, ¼ teaspoon salt and black pepper and stir well. Cook, skimming off fat every 10–15 minutes for half an hour.

If using frozen seafood, defrost and drain well. Add all seafood to tomato sauce and cook just until seafood is cooked through, 3–5 minutes. Adjust seasonings, toss with fusilli, and serve immediately.

GENERAL RULES FOR PASTA WITH SEAFOOD

1. The biggest rule to remember when making pasta with seafood is: don't overcook the seafood. Overcooked seafood or fish either becomes rubbery and tasteless or falls apart. To avoid this, I make the sauce separately, adding the seafood only in the last few minutes.
2. I always add a little oregano when I'm cooking with seafood.
3. To sweeten a seafood sauce, add a little grated carrot or a tablespoon of tomato paste.

Serves 4–6.

Seafood Risotto

When I made this risotto for Strawberries, I used fresh seafood. But this version gives you the option of frozen, which is easier to get and cheaper.

For the seafood:

1 tablespoon olive oil
1 pound mixed frozen seafood (shrimp, scallops, and squid rings),
    defrosted and drained, or the equivalent of fresh
¼ teaspoon each salt and pepper
¼ cup dry white wine

For the risotto:

2 tablespoons butter
1½ tablespoons olive oil
1 medium onion, diced (¾ cup)
4 garlic cloves, minced (1 tablespoon)
1 cup Arborio rice
1 cup diced fresh or canned tomatoes
1 cup dry white wine
4 cups canned or fresh chicken broth, heated to a simmer
¼ cup chopped fresh parsley or 1 tablespoon dried
¼ teaspoon salt
1 teaspoon black pepper
½ cup freshly grated Parmesan cheese

To make the seafood:

Heat oil in a small sauté pan over medium heat. Add seafood, salt
and pepper, and wine. Cook 2–3 minutes, until seafood is barely done.
Set aside.

To make risotto:

Heat butter and oil in a large skillet or nonstick pan over medium
heat. Add onion and cook 4 minutes, stirring. Add garlic and cook 1
minute. Add rice and cook, stirring constantly, 3–5 minutes, until rice
is "gravelly." Stir in tomatoes and cook, stirring, 2–3 minutes until tomato liquid is absorbed. Add wine and cook, stirring, until liquid is absorbed. Add two cups of broth and cook 5–8 minutes, until liquid is
gone. Stir thoroughly, add 1 cup of broth and cook, stirring occasion-

Risotto has to be eaten as soon as it's done, or it becomes like glue. So have everything else set up before you get to the final stages of cooking.

ally, until broth is absorbed. At this point, rice should be close to done. Add last cup of broth and cook until half the liquid is absorbed. Stir in seafood and salt and pepper. Cook, stirring, until almost all liquid is absorbed and the rice has a creamy consistency. Stir in Parmesan cheese, check seasoning, and serve immediately.

Serves 4–6.

■■

Angel Hair with Scallops and Peas in Cream

Being from Southern Italy, I'm not a big butter or cream guy. But a bargain is a bargain. The town of Carnation was just down the road, so dairy products were dirt cheap. I started trying a few things. Now I know why people cook with the stuff.

1 cup green peas, fresh or frozen
1 pound dried angel hair pasta
4 cloves of garlic, sliced very thin
¼ cup chopped onion or shallots

When sauce is thickening, keep stirring off the bottom of the pan and watch for scorching. If it starts to scorch, immediately pour into another pan, leaving anything browned behind. Taste to be sure it doesn't taste burned before continuing.

On a diet, cut the amount of butter in half and use regular or lowfat milk instead of half and half. The sauce won't be as thick, but neither will your waistline.

2 tablespoons olive oil
1 pound sea scallops, cut in thirds or quartered (bite-size)
2 tablespoons butter
¼ cup dry white wine
Juice of ½ a lemon (about 1 tablespoon)
1 egg yolk
1 cup half and half
¼ cup fresh grated Parmesan or Romano cheese
½ teaspoon crushed hot red pepper flakes
¼ cup chopped fresh basil
Salt and pepper to taste
¼ cup chopped fresh parsley
1½ lemons cut in wedges

In a small saucepan boil peas in lightly salted water until tender (about 5 minutes). Drain and set aside.

Cook angel hair in pot of boiling salted water until al dente, 3–5 minutes. Drain and set aside.

Sauté garlic and onions or shallots in olive oil in frying pan over medium low heat until translucent (2–3 minutes). Add scallop slices, season lightly with salt and pepper, and sauté 2 minutes, until scallops are white and opaque (do not overcook!). Remove scallops from pan and set aside (don't worry if some of the onions and garlic get removed with the scallops).

Add butter, white wine, and lemon juice to the frying pan. Cook, stirring occasionally, until liquid is reduced by about half. Beat egg yolk in a bowl with 2 tablespoons half and half. Add rest of the half and half to pan, bring to a boil, and reduce heat to low. Add yolk mixture a little at a time, stirring. Cook until slightly thickened, stirring constantly. Stir in grated cheese and red pepper flakes, then reserved scallops, peas, basil, and salt and pepper to taste. Cook one minute to reheat scallops and peas.

Pour sauce over angel hair and toss gently, coating pasta. Sprinkle with parsley and serve garnished with lemon wedges.

Rule 12: Add a tablespoon of butter. If your dish is "missing something," try adding a tablespoon of butter at the very end. No, it's not very Sicilian, but if it works, it works.

Serves 6–8.

Penne with Ricotta and Tomatoes

Roasted red peppers really kicks up the taste of this dish.

6–8 cloves of garlic, minced or thinly sliced (about 2 tablespoons; see Garlic note below)
¼ cup olive oil
One 28-ounce can peeled plum tomatoes with basil, drained, reserving juice
One 28-ounce can chopped tomatoes
12 large basil leaves, torn in large pieces, or 1 tablespoon dried
¼ cup finely chopped Italian parsley or 2 teaspoons–1 tablespoon dried parsley
2 roasted red peppers (see page 23) or 2 good quality jarred roasted red peppers, diced, or a 6 ounce jar pimientos, drained
½–1 teaspoon each salt and black pepper (to taste)
1½ pounds penne, cooked to barely al dente and drained
1½ cups whole-milk or part-skim ricotta cheese
¾ cup freshly grated Parmesan or Romano cheese

Preheat oven to 350°F.
In a large skillet or medium-large wide pot, cook garlic briefly in olive oil over medium-low heat (do not brown). Add the juice from the canned whole tomatoes to stop the garlic cooking. Crush drained toma-

toes with your hands or chop well on a cutting board and add to the pan. Add crushed tomatoes, basil, parsley, roasted peppers, and ½ teaspoon each salt and pepper to sauce. Bring to a boil, stir once thoroughly, then reduce heat to a low simmer. Cook 15 minutes, skimming off acid from tomatoes.

In a large bowl, combine cooked pasta with partially cooked sauce. Add ricotta and Parmesan or Romano cheeses and stir gently to combine. Check for seasoning. Place mixture in a large casserole and place in the preheated oven. Bake 30–45 minutes, skimming off any oil that flows to the top every 10 minutes or so.

Serves 6.

Panna Cotta with Fruit Sauce

A _panna cotta_ is different depending on where you're from in Italy. I like mine firmer, and after trying a number of recipes, I found that you have to adjust the amount of liquid versus gelatin in most recipes to make it as firm as I like. It doesn't affect the flavor if you add more gelatin, just how it reacts when when you top it with fresh fruit or a sauce.

This is lovely to serve from individual baking custard cups or ramekins, but if you don't have them, put in an 8-inch baking dish and spoon out onto dessert plates or into cups from there.

1½ rounded tablespoons powdered gelatin (1¼ packets)
¼ cup water
4 cups heavy cream + ¼ cup lowfat milk
½ cup sugar
1 vanilla bean, split, or 1 large teaspoon vanilla extract
Vegetable oil to coat custard cups or a medium-size baking dish
Fresh fruit or fruit sauce as accompaniment

Place gelatin in ¼ cup water and let sit until dissolved (do not stir). Lightly oil 6 custard cups or ramekins and set aside.

Heat cream, milk, and sugar in a medium-size saucepan until warm over low heat. Add gelatin mixture and cook, stirring, until gelatin is dissolved into the milk. Add vanilla bean or vanilla extract and heat briefly, stirring. Strain mixture through a fine sieve into a bowl or directly into oiled cups or ramekins. If straining into a bowl, transfer into ramekins or cups. Place ramekins or cups in refrigerator and chill overnight, until firm. Unmold by dipping bottom of ramekins briefly in warm water and reversing onto a plate. Serve drizzled with fresh fruit sauce or sprinkled with fresh berries, or both.

Fruit sauce:

One 12-ounce package frozen fruit, such as raspberries or
    strawberries, thawed and drained
4 tablespoons sugar (to taste)

Place fruit in a blender or the bowl of a food processor. Pulse or blend briefly to break up fruit. Combine in a bowl with sugar to taste, stirring to blend well. Run mixture through a fine strainer to remove seeds.

Serves 4.

Macerated Strawberries

1 pint fresh strawberries
2 tablespoons sweet vermouth or other sweet liqueur (such as
    Cointreau) or good quality balsamic vinegar
1 tablespoon sugar, or to taste

Rinse, dry, and hull strawberries and cut in half if large. Toss with your choice of liqueur or balsamic vinegar and sugar just before serving.

HENRY'S NOTES AND TIPS	If the strawberries are very ripe and sweet, you may not need any sugar at all. The only way is to test them. Add the liqueur or balsamic vinegar first and check the flavor before adding sugar.

NICK

I actually met Nick Pileggi in 1981. My attorney had been pushing me to hook up with a writer to get my Mob story down on paper. So I met with three different writers, and it was no contest—Nick was the guy for me.

It was a risky business, for both of us. There was always the chance the wiseguys would try to use Nick to find me, or that he'd become a target himself. The government was afraid they'd kidnap him and force him to reveal my whereabouts. So they tried like hell to keep our contact to a minimum.

But we were on the phone almost every day. I'd call him collect at his office or at home. We're talking thousands and thousands in telephone bills. As a result, we also became good friends. He knew me, he knew the whole family. When one of our horses foaled after we moved to Redmond, we named the colt Nicky P.

At one point, Nick said he needed to see me face-to-face. He needed pictures, and no matter how much yakking you do on the phone, it's not the same as talking in person. The government forbade it, but he came to Redmond a few times anyway.

One time when Nick came west to work we went up to Vancouver so we could really concentrate. There were a bunch of good Italian restaurants in Vancouver, and I was dying to try one—but no way. It was too dangerous. Back in New York, we'd never even gone out in public together, let alone to an Italian joint—it would have been suicide! So in Canada, we didn't dare risk it. Instead we ate sushi or Chinese. Which is how I learned that Nick loves Chinese food—he always voted for Chinese.

But I also knew he loved Italian food. Even though I couldn't go to Italian places in New York, Nick was free to. We'd talk about what he ate at Rao's, Don Pepe's, the spicy sauce at Vincent's Clam Bar.

A while after I moved to Seattle, I called Nick from Nevada. "Congratulate me," I said, "I just got married!" Now, Nick knew Karen. He knew her well. He knew I'd been married to her for many years, and still was. So he asked if, considering I'd committed almost every other major crime, I'd decided I might as well add bigamy to the list. At which point I explained to him it wasn't bigamy—I married my new wife using my Witness Protection Program name. Nobody said I couldn't, did they?

Chapter Eleven

California

<hr />

KELLY

I first met Kelly on St. Patrick's Day, 1985. I knew her ex-husband and he had tried to keep her away from me. Even though he was her ex, he was still very protective, and he knew I'd be attracted to her. But I don't think he knew what would happen between us.

And neither did we. We knew each other a year before anything romantic developed. But the minute it did, there was no turning back. It was very simple—we fell in love.

Falling in love with Kelly changed my life. It wasn't easy or pretty. You don't leave your wife and kids after 25 years and boom, start a new life. But at first my relationship with Kelly was so beautiful to me, nothing else mattered.

NORTHERN CALIFORNIA

Early on Kelly and I ran away to Northern California. It was just a romantic whim. We thought we were going away for the weekend, but it turned out to be much longer. While we were gone, Karen thought I was face down in a ditch somewhere, and the Feds were frantically searching for me. Meanwhile, we were off enjoying our newfound love.

CASTROVILLE

Our plan was to go to Monterey, which we'd heard was a beautiful town on the ocean with lots of sea lions, which Kelly was excited about seeing (she's a big animal lover).

But on the way to Monterey, we turned off Route 101 onto Route 156, and where 156 meets Route 1, the Pacific Coast Highway, there's a town called Castroville. Population like seven thousand. It just cracked me up, this place.

Across the main street in Castroville is a huge banner: "Welcome to Castroville—The Artichoke Capital of the World." They really mean it.

The place is nothing but artichokes. Look left or right, there's miles and miles of artichokes growing in neat rows. There's a place called the Artichoke Inn. If you go to a restaurant, they have artichokes in every form: marinated, stuffed, grilled, deep-fried, plain, ground into pesto, on hamburgers, in a stuffing, as the whole stuffing. You can't get away from them.

Not that you'd want to. Not at first. I love artichokes. The baby ones are especially good. If you catch 'em young, you don't have to strip off so many leaves to get to the part you can eat, and they're full of flavor.

We ate ourselves silly. After a couple of days, I could honestly say I'd had my fill of artichokes for a while. I was almost sprouting leaves.

■■

Serves 4–6

as an appetizer.

Artichoke Purée

12 ounces artichoke hearts, jarred or canned in water or frozen
2 large cloves of garlic, coarsley chopped
½–1 tablespoon extra virgin olive oil
½–1 tablespoon mayonnaise
½–1 tablespoon prepared horseradish (to taste)
1 teaspoon prepared mustard
¼ cup fresh parsley leaves (loosely packed)
¼–½ teaspoon each salt and pepper (to taste)
Crackers or toasted baguette slices

Drain artichoke hearts well and place in bowl of a food processor. Add chopped garlic, ½ tablespoon each of olive oil, mayonnaise, and horseradish, plus the mustard, parsley leaves, and ¼ teaspoon each of salt and pepper. Process until fairly smooth (1–2 minutes). If mixture is too thick, add more olive oil and/or mayonnaise. Taste and adjust seasonings. Serve with crackers or toasted baguette slices.

Serves 3–4

as an appetizer.

French-Fried Artichoke Hearts

This is my version of the fabulous battered and fried artichokes I had in Northern California. I don't know if this is how they make them, but these taste great. Eat them as soon as they're done—they should be hot and juicy inside for them to be at their best.

1 cup flour
1 cup regular or light beer
½ teaspoon each salt and pepper + kosher salt for garnish
2 pounds fresh baby artichokes, or 1 pound frozen, canned or jarred
    artichoke hearts (not marinated)
Juice of 1 lemon, divided (about 2 tablespoons)
    + an additional lemon cut in wedges for serving
1–2 cups canola oil for deep frying
Dipping sauce (optional)

For dipping sauce:

1 cup mayonnaise
Juice of ¼–½ lemon (½–1 tablespoon, to taste)
Dash salt and pepper (to taste)
Pinch of dried sage

Place the flour, beer, and salt and pepper in the bowl of a food processor. Mix until well blended. Or whisk ingredients together in a large bowl until well combined and smooth. Let sit for 15–20 minutes while you prepare artichokes.

Rinse, peel and trim baby artichokes until all sections are edible (peel off the outer layers of leaves until you reach paler green tender-looking leaves, and chop off stem and very top of each 'choke). Drop into a large bowl of water to cover with the juice of half a lemon squeezed into it to prevent discoloration. Drain and dry well before using.

To make the dipping sauce:

Combine mayonnaise, ¼ cup of lemon juice, ⅛ teaspoon each salt and black pepper and the sage in a medium-size bowl and blend well. Taste for seasoning and add more lemon juice, salt, and pepper if desired. Set aside.

Preheat oven to warm setting.

In a deep skillet or medium wide pot, heat 1–2 cups of oil to a depth of 1 inch. Oil is ready to use when it registers 350–375°F on a candy thermometer. If you don't have a thermometer, check oil heat by tossing a drop or two of water into the pan—when the oil spits on contact with water, it's ready.

Drop prepared artichokes into batter, shake to remove excess and slip into the hot oil. Cook the artichokes in batches (don't crowd them), turning, until all sides are light golden brown. Remove from oil as they are done and drain well on paper towels. Place cooked artichokes in the oven to keep warm and continue frying the rest. Serve with dipping sauce on the side.

Baked Baby Artichokes with Olives

3 pounds baby artichokes
Juice of a lemon
2 lemons, sliced
¼ cup olive oil
2 large garlic cloves, minced
1 cup sliced black kalamata olives
½ teaspoon dried thyme, marjoram, and sage, crumbled
1 teaspoon each salt and pepper

Peel or break off the outer leaves of the artichokes until you reach the pale green leaves. Chop off the tops. Cut off stems to bottom of 'chokes. Add each 'choke as it is done to a bowl of water with juice of a lemon added (to keep them from discoloring). When all are done, drain 'chokes well and pat dry. Return to bowl. Add sliced lemons, olive oil, garlic, olives, spices, and salt and pepper and toss well to combine.

Heat oven to 350°F. Place mixture in a medium-size roasting pan or casserole and cover with a lid or aluminum foil. Bake 20 minutes. Remove cover and stir well, but don't break 'chokes. Re-cover and bake an additional 20–30 minutes, until 'chokes are tender.

Henry's Marinated Artichoke Hearts

I often make a simple marinade for artichoke hearts rather than buy commercially marinated ones for two reasons: I like a lot less vinegar in the marinade, and two, it's cheaper.

12–14 ounces artichoke hearts, canned or jarred in water
3 large garlic cloves, minced (1 tablespoon)
½–1 cup extra virgin olive oil

1–2 teaspoons red or white wine vinegar
¼–½ teaspoon each salt and pepper (to taste)

Drain artichoke hearts very well and pat as dry as possible with paper towels. Place in a bowl and add garlic, ½ cup olive oil, 1 teaspoon vinegar, and ¼ teaspoon each salt and pepper. Toss gently so hearts don't break apart. Taste oil and adjust seasoning.

Put artichokes in a glass jar or plastic container and pour in olive oil mixture. Olive oil should almost cover the hearts—add more if necessary. Cover container and refrigerate, turning upside down once or twice every few days to mix up ingredients. Hearts will keep refrigerated for 2–3 weeks.

RUSSIAN RIVER VALLEY

After the weekend, we started home by a different route. Someone had told me the Russian River Valley was very nice—undeveloped, except there were some wineries that had tastings and stuff. We decided to check it out.

The Russian River Valley is beautiful. Even today because of the wineries, it hasn't gotten real built up. It's curvy roads that go through gentle valleys, vineyards all over the place, small towns.

Kelly and I loved it there. We spent the first couple of nights in a cheap hotel. We had very little cash—we'd go to the wineries during the day and eat their pretzels and peanuts, or munch on samples at grocery stores. And the only stove we had was a microwave in the hotel room.

I don't like microwaves; they're not my kind of cooking. But hey, if there's nothing else . . . Problem was, I didn't know how to use one. What can you cook in those things? I tried pasta—faggedaboudit! The water boiled over and the pasta all stuck together in a clump. I thought maybe risotto would work, but there was no way to stir it the whole time—besides which I didn't want to. So I tried cooking the rice a little, stirring it, cooking it a little more, etc. until it was done. The trick was to imagine cooking it on a regular stove and then transferring the steps to a nuker. Turned out, I stirred it a lot less than you do regular risotto and it was fine. I was ready to call the Italian Chamber of Commerce with my discovery.

■■

Microwave Risotto with Mushrooms

If you can't find Arborio rice, you can use any kind of rice except instant. Don't rinse it so you get a creamy texture.

Microwave at full power (100%) unless stated otherwise.

3 tablespoons olive oil
1 tablespoon butter
1 large clove of garlic, minced (optional)
¼ white or brown onion, minced
1 cup Arborio or other rice, unrinsed
Two 14-ounce cans low-sodium chicken broth (3–4 cups)
8 ounces fresh button mushrooms, cleaned, trimmed, and sliced
¼ cup fresh chopped parsley leaves or 1 tablespoon dried
½–1 teaspoon each salt and pepper (to taste)
½ cup freshly grated Parmesan or Romano cheese (optional)

Put olive oil and butter in a glass or ceramic dish that fits in your microwave. Heat until butter melts, about 1 minute. Stir in chicken broth.

Add minced garlic and onion to liquid and stir to coat. Microwave 2–3 minutes, or until onion starts to get translucent. Stir. Add rice and stir well to coat. Microwave 3–5 minutes to start rice heating and breaking down a bit. Stir briefly.

Add 1 cup of chicken broth, stir, and microwave for 4 minutes. Stir mixture and add 2 cups remaining broth, mushrooms, parsley, and ½ teaspoon each salt and pepper. Cook mixture 8–10 minutes, checking

HENRY'S NOTES AND TIPS

If you want more mushroom flavor, soak four or five dried mushrooms (porcinis are the best) in a quarter cup hot water for five minutes. Strain mushrooms and liquid over a bowl, reserving mushroom liquid. Chop mushrooms and add when you add other mushrooms. Replace part of the chicken broth with the strained mushroom liquid.

after 8 to make sure there's still liquid. Add more broth if necessary. Cook 5–8 more minutes, stir, and check rice for doneness. The mixture should be creamy and a little "soupy." If not, add a little more broth and microwave 2 minutes. Stir in optional cheese, adjust seasonings, and serve immediately.

RUSSIAN RIVER HONEYMOON

Finally we couldn't afford to stay at a hotel anymore, but we weren't ready to go back to Seattle—we were having too good a time. We lucked into a guy who had a house right on the Russian River that had been messed up in the last big rainfall—he said it was unlivable. We were crazy to stay and asked if we could crash there.

That flooded-out house, it was a mess. One wall was gone, half the

---

Henry's Rules for Cooking on the Run:
HOW TO MAKE GOOD ITALIAN FOOD ANYWHERE

Rule 13: Cook either very fast or very slowly. This is truly Italian—you can either cook dinner in half an hour, like when you're playing up the tastes of a few fresh ingredients, or simmer sauce all day when you want a mellow blend of deep rich flavors.

Rule 14: On a budget, use a little of the good stuff. When I couldn't afford olive oil, I have cut it with others—even corn oil if it was the only thing around. Nowadays you can usually get canola for cheap, which has a cleaner taste and is better for you than corn oil. The point is to have at least a taste of olive oil. Sometimes I even prefer to cut it—olive oil can overwhelm a dish with a delicate flavor. The same is true for Parmesan cheese. If you can't afford a big hunk of good Parmigiano-Reggiano (who can?—it's insulting how much they charge!), buy a small piece and use just a little. You'll need less if you use the real thing, and you can always mix it with the cheaper stuff.

downstairs was a wreck and you couldn't even walk through it. The only bathroom that worked was upstairs. But it was like the honeymoon suite at a swanky hotel to us.

We found a sleeping bag to cover the wall that was gone. Kelly decorated it with a bunch of pictures. We found a mattress on the side of the road. We bought Russian River "wedding rings." We made do with whatever food we could afford to buy and cook, and we were very, very happy.

Serves 2

as a main dish

or 4

as a side.

Vegetables and Smoked Gouda

Kelly's favorite dish I cook for her is mostly vegetables. But what really makes it tasty is a cheese I discovered in Northern California: smoked gouda. Smoked gouda ain't cheap, but you don't need a lot, a small piece flavors the whole pan. When you don't have the bucks, make this dish and you'll eat like kings.

¼ cup olive oil
1 medium onion, sliced (1 cup)
3 large cloves of garlic, minced
One 28-ounce can plum tomatoes with juice
6 fresh basil leaves, torn in large pieces, or 1 teaspoon dried
¼ cup chopped fresh Italian parsley or 2 teaspoons dried
2 small zucchinis, scrubbed and sliced ½" thick
4 ounces fresh mushrooms, ends trimmed and halved
½ pound green beans (1 cup), ends trimmed and snapped in half
¼ teaspoon each salt and pepper
½ cup grated smoked gouda cheese
⅛ cup grated fresh Parmesan or Romano cheese

Preheat broiler if planning to use at end. In a medium-size saucepan or a casserole that can go on top of the stove as well, heat olive oil over medium heat. Add onion and cook 2–3 minutes, stirring, until translu-

Add any other vegetables you have around to this dish: leftover pieces of red or green peppers, thawed frozen peas, broccoli, cauliflower. Keep in mind that things like broccoli and cauliflower take longer to cook, peas only a few minutes.

cent. Add garlic and cook 1 minute, without browning. Drain tomatoes, crush and add along with ¼ cup of their juice, the basil and the parsley. Cook 10 minutes, skimming off any oil that rises to the top and stirring occasionally. Add zucchini, mushrooms, green beans, and salt and pepper. Cook 5 minutes, or until green beans and zucchini are just tender. Add more of the tomato juice if none left in pan. Sprinkle smoked gouda over the top and allow it to melt. The cheese will seep down into the dish. Sprinkle with Parmesan or Romano, and run under broiler to brown top if you want. Serve with warm bread.

SOUTHERN CALIFORNIA

Back in Seattle, a lot of things happened. I'm not gonna give you all the details—that's a whole book in itself.

Truth is, my life was a mess, what with the triangle of me, Karen, and Kelly. And I got involved with drugs in a way that landed me in jail again, accused of something I didn't do. Eventually I got sent to a sober house in Southern California.

Moving to SoCal changed everything. My marriage to Karen was over. It was hard, but the distance made it easier. Kelly came down and joined me, and we started our new life together.

LOS ANGELES

What a change. Los Angeles, the City of Angels. By the time Kelly and I got there, I felt as though I'd been saved by an angel. Considering my past life, I was amazed I had any angels left.

LA was way different from anywhere I'd ever lived. It felt like Omaha 'cause it's all spread out. But it's not like Omaha at all. In Omaha you can drive for miles and never see another person, just cows and sky. In LA you can drive forever and you're never out of the city—there's always more buildings, more shops, more people, on and on and on.

So we were in a city, but it didn't feel like a city. There's only a couple of areas of LA with skyscrapers. Mostly it's one and two-story buildings. There were tons of little bungalow houses with manicured lawns, and what they call "pod malls," or minimalls, that have restaurants, mom-and-pop stores, 7-Elevens, fast food places. And copy shops! There's a copy shop every coupla blocks. I couldn't figure it, how many copies do they need? Of what?

And Los Angelenos were a whole new breed of folks. The first day there, I saw an eighty-year-old woman in a turquoise jogging outfit. She was walking her Siamese cat on a leash, and the cat looked none too happy about it. At first I thought she was a nut. But she wasn't. I soon realized that a turquoise jogging outfit, something my mother or any woman in Kentucky or Seattle wouldn't have been caught dead in, was the norm. And cats on leashes? Well, I guess they need their exercise too.

Everybody in LA is into exercise. They're all trying to be younger than they are. It's the culture of youth or death—you're young and your skin is stretched tight and you look like you're twenty until you drop. Then people realize you were really ninety-five, though nobody could figure out what age you were. Everyone looks younger than their age, except the Hispanics who ride the bus to work to clean or baby-sit for the youthful aging population. They look miserable and fifty when they're really only thirty.

Kelly'd left her family in Washington, I'd left Karen and the kids and my Seattle pals. All we had was each other. We were more isolated than we'd ever been.

Of course I looked to food to make us feel at home. And I soon discovered one of the best things about Southern California: the sun! Almost any day of the year you can get a tan! It's like a joke to have a weatherman in Southern California. Every day, it's the same thing: beautiful weather, no clouds in the sky—perfect! You get so you love it when it rains just for the change.

All that sun means things are growing all the time—you can get fresh fruits and vegetables all year round! Peaches, apples, tomatoes, basil—and there's so much of it, it's incredibly cheap! There are still growing seasons. Though you can get them almost any time of year, things like artichokes and strawberries are fresher and cheaper during certain months.

And LA has tons of ethnic groups and neighborhoods. There's Ethiopian, Indian, Vietnamese, Japanese, Sri Lankan, Chinese, Russian, Welsh, Irish, German, and every kind of Hispanic you can think of. There's people from El Salvador, Cuba, Mexico, Argentina—you name it, they've got a neighborhood.

And there's Italian. I started checking out the grocery stores in neighborhoods where I'd seen some Italians. Did they have *rapini* (broccoli rabe)? Yes. Escarole? Yup. Prosciutto? Yes, but it was way overpriced for a tiny amount wrapped in plastic. How 'bout endive? Again yes, but expensive.

I asked, was there an Italian deli anywhere? I was told there was one on the west side of LA. I couldn't wait to get there.

So I drove to Sorrento's in Culver City.

When you're in the Mob, you learn to keep your eyes and ears open all the time. You have to pay attention or you get "caught from behind." If you look at pictures of how Italian Mob guys act in New York, you'll see what I mean—they're always looking around, checking things out. They're awake to anything different—a new person walking in the neighborhood, an unfamiliar car driving by.

So I'd learned to always check out places everywhere I went. When I go into a new place, my sensors are up. Is this place friend or foe, where's the bullshit, what's really going on?

Walking into Sorrento's, it was definitely friend. And it was Italian to the bone. It wasn't just Italian, it felt like I was back in New York. It wasn't big, but it was stacked high like skyscrapers—they use every square inch of space. I started cruising the narrow aisles. You can barely move in there! Up on the shelves there was the brand of canned scungilli my mother used, there were plum tomatoes from all over Italy, Arborio rice, a zillion kinds of olive oils and olives.

I made my way over to the deli counter—and I was in heaven!

They had *chevalott*! That's the circle sausage that Paulie is cooking on the grill in a scene in *GoodFellas*. I hadn't had it for years. I bought a coupla pounds.

I took the *chevalott* home and grilled it on our little Weber grill (which is another LA thing—get a grill, even a small one, you can grill stuff on Christmas Day, the weather's so good!). That's all you need to

Henry's Rules for Cooking on the Run:
HOW TO MAKE GOOD ITALIAN FOOD ANYWHERE

Rule 15: Your grocer is your friend. Remember not all grocers are alike. They like different foods, and will stock partly what they like and partly what they know they can sell. If one store doesn't carry what you want, maybe the place down the block does. Even the big chains had different stuff depending on the neighborhood. I had to try three different stores in the same chain before I found ground veal.

GENERAL RULES FOR PASTA WITH FRESH VEGETABLES

1. Fresh vegetables are like fresh seafood—you don't want to cook them too long or they lose their texture and flavor. Certain vegetables you can cook a bit longer, but none of them should be added to the pasta until the very end. Exceptions to this are vegetables you're using as a flavor base, things like any onions and sometimes red peppers or mushrooms in slow-cooked sauces. These are supposed to fall apart, giving their flavor to the sauce.
2. When using leafy veggies like spinach, add them just before serving or they'll turn to mush.
3. You may need to precook crucifers like broccoli and cauliflower depending on the sauce. Rinse well in cold water to stop their cooking process.

do with *chevalott*—throw it on the grill and make a simple pasta and salad, open a bottle of red wine, and you'll be very happy.

Later I discovered other Italian delis—there's a great one in Santa Monica called Bay Cities. It's much bigger and very popular. But Sorrento's was always my favorite.

I also discovered that some of the bigger supermarkets stocked all kinds of things. There were wonderful vegetables: the freshest greens, zucchinis, broccoli were normal. And some places had really good artichokes. I didn't know until I lived there that California provides a lot of the rest of the U.S. with fresh vegetables. And I was getting the benefit of being very close to all that fresh produce.

Serves 4.

Shell Pasta with Italian Broccoli (Cavatelli con Broccoli Rabe) à la Aunt Elivera

Broccoli rabe is very popular in Italy. It's a slightly bitter version of broccoli, with more flavor. Nowadays I know you can get it in LA, and I'm sure you can in other parts of the U.S. It's also called *rapini*. It looks like broccoli that got too long and didn't have enough buds.

1¼ pounds broccoli rabe (*rapini*)
½ cup olive oil
1 cup finely diced onion
2–4 fresh plum tomatoes, chopped (to taste—see Henry's Notes and Tips)
1 pound cavatelli (medium-size shells) or other medium-size pasta
1–2 tablespoons pine nuts (to taste—see Henry's Notes and Tips)
½ teaspoon each salt and pepper
½ cup freshly grated Parmesan or other hard cheese

Wash broccoli rabe well, trim ends, and chop in 1-inch pieces (tear leaves in medium-size pieces).

Heat olive oil over medium-high heat in a large skillet, add onions and sauté until softened, about 5–8 minutes. Add broccoli rabe and tomatoes and sauté, stirring constantly, until soft, being careful not to burn.

Cook pasta in salted water until al dente and drain, reserving 1 cup

You don't have to trim broccoli rabe stems as much as you do American broccoli—it's not as tough.

If you find the broccoli rabe too bitter, add more tomatoes and pine nuts to suit your taste. Most of my "American" friends like it with more tomatoes and pine nuts, the "Italians" like the original version.

of water (see page 37). If you want more liquid in the sauce, add part of the reserved pasta water to rabe mixture. Add rabe mixture and pine nuts to pasta and toss. Season with salt and pepper. Serve with a little cheese grated on top and additional cheese on the side.

Serves 4–6.

Fusilli with Cauliflower

Pasta and cauliflower may seem like a strange combo, but it can be very tasty and comforting. The Sicilians have been putting them together for years. They even add potatoes sometimes.

If you can't afford saffron (though they're growing it here now and American saffron is a lot cheaper), substitute turmeric. I call it the poor man's saffron.

1 whole head of cauliflower weighing about 1 pound
¼ cup olive oil
4 cloves of garlic, minced (1 tablespoon)
¼ teaspoon salt
½ teaspoon saffron threads softened in ¼ cup hot water or
    ½ teaspoon ground turmeric
¼–½ teaspoon dry mustard
1–3 tablespoons lemon juice
1 cup canned low-sodium chicken broth
1½ tablespoons currants
1 tablespoon pine nuts
¼–½ teaspoon each salt and pepper (to taste)

½ pound fusilli or other curly pasta, cooked and drained, reserving
   1 cup pasta water (see page 37 for how to cook)
½ cup freshly grated Parmesan or Romano cheese

Rinse cauliflower, trim bottom of stem, and remove any small green
leaves at the base of the head. Bring a large pot of salted water to a boil
and add whole head of cauliflower to pot. Boil until it can just be pierced
with a fork, 5–7 minutes. Remove head and drain in a colander. Cut
individual cauliflower florets from the thick stalk. Discard stem (or keep
for use in soup or stock). Cut any larger florets into bite-size pieces. Pat
florets as dry as possible with paper towels and set aside.

Heat olive oil over medium heat in a large skillet. On a cutting
board, combine garlic and salt and mash together to make a paste.
Scrape mixture off board into oil and cook, stirring well, 1 minute (do
not brown garlic). Add saffron and its soaking water or ground turmeric
to the skillet, plus mustard, 1 tablespoon lemon juice, chicken broth,
currants, and pine nuts. Lower heat to a simmer and cook 8–10 minutes,
stirring occasionally. Add cauliflower florets and coat well with sauce.
Season with salt and pepper to taste and cook until cauliflower is heated
through, about 5 minutes. Adjust seasonings and add more lemon juice
if desired.

Add cooked and drained pasta to the pan and toss well. Add some
of the reserved pasta water if you want more liquid. Serve topped with
grated cheese if desired and a few grindings of black pepper.

Cooking the whole head is the easiest way I know to cook cauliflower or broccoli. But you can cut the cauliflower top in large florets and
boil them three to five minutes. Be sure not to overcook them.

HENRY'S NOTES AND TIPS

Escarole and White Bean Soup

You won't believe how quick and tasty this soup is. Served with a few pieces of warm bread, it's a delicious light meal.

2 tablespoons regular olive oil
½ medium onion, chopped
3 medium garlic cloves, minced (about 1 tablespoon)
1 large stalk celery, sliced thin
¼ cup fresh Italian parsley, chopped fine
¼ cup fresh basil, chopped fine
4 cups chicken broth
One 15-ounce can small white beans with their juice
1 head escarole with outer leaves discarded, washed, and cut in
    large pieces
⅛–¼ teaspoon salt
½ teaspoon black pepper
¼ cup grated fresh Parmesan cheese

Heat olive oil in large pot. Cook onion over medium heat 2 minutes, until soft. Add garlic and celery, cook 2 minutes, stirring a few times. Stir in parsley, basil, chicken broth, and beans with their juice. Bring to a boil and lower heat to simmer. Cook 2 minutes. Add chopped escarole and salt and pepper. Cook until escarole is tender, approximately 4 minutes. Serve with grated cheese on the side.

HENRY'S NOTES AND TIPS

The beans and chicken broth already have salt in them. Depending on your taste, you may not need to add any extra. The pepper, you need.

Braised Endive

Belgian endive is still an expensive vegetable. My mom made it only for special occasions—everyone knew how much it cost, so we would savor every bite.

3–4 heads of Belgian endive
1 tablespoon olive oil
1 large clove of garlic, peeled and halved
¼ cup canned chicken broth
¼–½ teaspoon salt and pepper (to taste)
A dash of balsamic vinegar (optional)

Cut off ends of endive and separate the leaves, the way you would a head of lettuce. Rinse leaves well in a sinkful of cold water, drain thoroughly, and pat dry.

Heat olive oil in a large skillet with a cover over medium heat. Add the garlic halves and cook, stirring, 1–2 minutes (do not brown garlic). Remove garlic. Add endive and cook, stirring and turning, 3–5 minutes (they should start to brown). Add chicken broth, ¼ teaspoon salt and pepper and stir to loosen any bits stuck to the bottom of the pan. Cover and cook 15 minutes, checking occasionally to be sure there's liquid in the pan. Adjust seasonings. Serve drizzled with balsamic vinegar if desired.

Look for endives that are more white than green. The whiter ones are less bitter.
Inexpensive balsamic vinegar is fine here.

HENRY'S

NOTES

AND TIPS

Pasta with Pesto

If you're in an area where fresh basil is plentiful, this is a cheap dish to make. And you can easily grow your own basil, even on a balcony. Put the plant in the sun and it'll grow like crazy.

You can either use all basil or a mix of basil and fresh parsley. Both are delicious.

4 cups fresh basil leaves (packed) or 3 cups basil and 1 cup fresh
    parsley leaves
3 large garlic cloves
½ cup extra virgin olive oil
¼ cup pine nuts, lightly toasted
⅓–½ cup freshly grated Parmesan or Romano cheese
¼–½ teaspoon each salt and pepper (to taste)
1 pound cooked pasta of your choice (see page 37 for how to cook
    pasta), reserving ½ cup pasta water

Rinse and pat dry basil or basil and parsley. Put in bowl of food processor. Add garlic cloves and a few tablespoons of olive oil. Process briefly until chunky. Scrape down mixture, add remaining olive oil, pine nuts, cheeses, and ¼ teaspoon each salt and black pepper. Process until smooth. If mixture is very thick, add ¼–½ cup pasta water and reprocess. Taste and adjust seasonings, toss with warm pasta and serve.

HENRY'S NOTES AND TIPS

This is a time I like to use a mortar and pestle to grind the ingredients together. (Do this in front of a girl, you'll impress the heck out of her.) It's more work, but it makes a nice smooth sauce and the flavors are very fresh. Start with the garlic and a pinch of salt and grind fine, then add the pine nuts (chopped), then the leaves, then the cheese, grinding fairly smooth with each addition. Season with salt and pepper to taste.

Broiled Fresh Peach Tart

Make this at the height of summer when fresh peaches are cheap and plentiful. You can buy the peaches a little underripe a day ahead and ripen them at room temperature. But watch them carefully—they can go bad very quickly. When they are perfectly ripe, refrigerate them and use within a day.

½ cup graham cracker crumbs (about 4 crackers)
½ cup amaretto cookie crumbs (about one cup small cookies)
1–1½ tablespoons white sugar (to taste)
4 tablespoons unsalted butter, melted
4 large ripe peaches (about 2 pounds)
1 tablespoon softened unsalted butter
2 tablespoons brown sugar
1–2 tablespoons sweet vermouth, Cointreau, Grand Marnier,
    amaretto, or other liqueur of your choice

Preheat oven to 350°F.

In the bowl of a food processor, combine graham crackers broken in large pieces, amaretto cookies broken in half, and 1 tablespoon white sugar. Process to fine crumbs. Place in a medium bowl and add melted butter. Stir to mix well. Cover the bottom and sides of a 9-inch tart or cake pan with crumbs. (Pile the crumbs in the middle of the pan, cover your hand with plastic wrap, and spread crumbs evenly over the bottom and sides, pressing gently to make them stick.)

Rinse peaches lightly. Boil a medium-large pot of water and drop

You can use any kind of peach you want, or substitute nectarines (though I don't think they have as good a flavor). Some people prefer the white peaches; I'm perfectly happy with the usual yellow ones.

HENRY'S NOTES AND TIPS

peaches into water for half a minute or less and rinse immediately with cold water. The peels should come off easily. Cut peaches in half, removing pit and any bits of it clinging to peach. Arrange peach halves cut side up on crust. Put a dot of softened butter in each half, sprinkle with brown sugar, and your choice of liqueur.

Bake peaches 15 minutes. Raise heat to broil and cook 3–5 minutes more, just until edges of peaches begin to brown (be careful not to burn). Serve warm, with heavy cream or a bit of vanilla ice cream if desired.

WOODLAND HILLS

We lived in tons of places in Southern California. Being near a big city meant there was a better chance of someone spotting me, so the Feds were a lot more cautious and would relocate us at the drop of a hat. We lived in Pasadena, Woodland Hills, Alta Dena, Palmdale, Venice, Santa Monica, Valencia—all over the place. We never knew from month to month where we'd be.

Early on, Kelly and I house-sat in Woodland Hills. The house was unbelievable, with lots of rooms, a Jacuzzi in the master bathroom, and all those Los Angeles luxuries you read about in magazines. We felt like real Hollywood types, relaxing in the Jacuzzi, eating in the sun.

Woodland Hills was way out of town—it's in what they call "the Valley"—so it was a haul to get to the Italian delis for ingredients. Most of the time, I'd work with what I could get locally. It's still the best rule: use what you can get close by that's fresh and cheap.

There were a lot of "white folks" neighborhoods in the Valley. Out there, the food was changing like crazy, like it was in LA too. People were tired of the California food stereotypes—salads with everything but the kitchen sink (as long as there's avocado), giant steaks as in Lawry's Steak House, and low-rent Mexican and Chinese food. They finally noticed that their other ethnic neighbors had very tasty stuff. So now they wanted Vietnamese and Thai food, they wanted Moroccan cuisine, and there were sushi bars springing up everywhere. Wolfgang Puck was changing the face of pizza by topping it with ham and goat cheese, smoked salmon and caviar. At home, people served hummus as an appetizer like it was a new invention (it's only a few thousand years old) and started making their own pesto.

Which was great news for me. It meant I didn't have to drive for hours to find arugula—they had it at the regular grocery store. They always had fresh basil and Italian parsley, and they also stocked fresh fennel, dried saffron, and pine nuts (which they'd always had but called *pignolis*, the Hispanic name). They started selling different kinds of mushrooms: portabellas, creminis, even dried porcinis though they were still expensive.

Serves 4.

Fettuccine with Mixed Greens

Unless you're making long, slow-cooked Southern greens, you only need to give leafy greens the slightest bit of heat. In fact, you could almost toss them raw with a pasta and they'd cook enough to be perfect by the time they're on the table.

    4 cups fresh greens: arugula or a mix of arugula and mixed greens,
        like spinach, beet greens, and Swiss chard
    2 tablespoons olive oil
    2 ounces pancetta or bacon, diced
    2 medium or one large red onion, peeled and cut in large dice
        (1" pieces)
    5–6 cloves garlic, minced (1½ tablespoons)
    1 large beefsteak tomato, chopped
    ½ cup chopped fresh Italian parsley leaves
    ¼ cup chopped fresh basil
    ½–1 teaspoon salt (to taste)
    ½ teaspoon black pepper
    1 pound dried fettuccine
    ¼ cup pine nuts
    Juice of one medium lemon (optional)
    ½–1 cup freshly grated Parmesan or Romano cheese

For this dish, use greens that cook very quickly like the ones listed above. Things like mustard, collards, and kale won't work here.

Wash arugula and/or other greens well and remove any large stems or ribs (see page 207 for how to wash greens). Drain or pat dry and chop very coarsely or tear in medium-large pieces. Set aside.

Heat oil in a large pot over medium heat. Add diced pancetta or bacon and cook briefly. Add onion and cook 5 minutes, stirring. Add garlic and cook an additional 2–3 minutes (do not brown garlic). Add chopped tomato, parsley, basil, and half the salt and pepper. Lower heat and cook 3–5 minutes, stirring occasionally, until tomato starts to break down. Remove from heat.

Meanwhile, cook and drain pasta, reserving 1 cup pasta water (see page 37 for how to cook). Return sauce to low heat and stir in pine nuts. Add greens a handful at a time until all the greens are incorporated, cooking very briefly. Toss sauce with pasta and mix well. Sprinkle with lemon juice if desired and a bit of Parmesan or Romano. Serve with remaining Parmesan or Romano on the side.

Serves 4.

Pasta with Mixed Mushrooms

2 tablespoons dried porcini mushrooms (⅛ ounce)
6 ounces fresh white mushrooms
6 ounces fresh portabella mushrooms
¼ cup regular olive oil
¼ cup chopped shallots or onion
1 tablespoon garlic, minced
½ cup chopped fresh parsley or 1½ tablespoons dried
½ cup chicken broth
¼ cup Marsala, Madeira or dry sherry
½ teaspoon each salt and pepper

1 pound long pasta of your choice (capellini, spaghetti, linguine, etc.), cooked and drained (see page 37 for how to cook), saving 1 cup pasta water
2 tablespoons extra virgin olive oil

Soak porcinis in a medium bowl in ½ cup hot water for 20 minutes. Strain soaking liquid through a fine sieve or one lined with cheesecloth and reserve. Rinse porcinis well, removing any sand or grit, and roughly chop.

Quickly rinse or wipe clean white and portabella mushrooms. Remove stems and slice in ⅛–¼-inch-thick slices.

Heat ¼ cup olive oil in a large skillet over medium heat. Add shallots or onion and cook 2 minutes. Add white mushrooms, portabellas, and garlic and cook until mushrooms give off their liquid, 5–8 minutes. Stir in ¼ cup fresh parsley (or all of the dried), the porcinis, the soaking liquid, and chicken broth. When adding soaking liquid, leave behind any sediment at bottom of container. Raise heat to high and reduce liquid by about half. Add wine or sherry. Reduce briefly. Lower heat to medium. Season with salt and pepper. Toss with pasta, add remaining fresh parsley and extra virgin olive oil and retoss.

Serves 2.

Arugula and Parmesan Salad

My favorite way to use arugula is in a salad. Serve this with a lightly sauced pasta and you have a meal.

2 cups fresh young arugula
1½ tablespoons extra virgin olive oil
⅛–¼ teaspoon each salt and freshly ground pepper (to taste)
4 large white mushrooms, trimmed and sliced thin
One 1-ounce piece of fresh, good-quality Parmesan cheese, cut in very thin slices with a vegetable peeler
¼ cup thinly sliced fennel bulb
¼ cup thinly sliced red onion (optional)
1–1½ tablespoons fresh lemon juice (to taste)

Remove any tough stems from arugula leaves, rinse well and pat dry (or use a salad spinner). Place in a large bowl and toss with olive oil and a dash of salt and pepper. Place leaves on one large or two individual plates.

Top arugula with sliced mushrooms, Parmesan, fennel bulb, and red onion (if using). Drizzle lemon juice over all and sprinkle with salt and a grating of fresh black pepper. Serve immediately.

■■■

Makes about

3 cups of sauce

(enough for

4–6 people).

Pasta with Fresh Tomatoes
Fileta de Pomodoro

As I said, you can get fresh fruits and vegetables all over the LA area. Even as far away as Palmdale I could get tons of fresh tomatoes for pennies. Go to a farmer's market and buy what they call "seconds," or the stuff they can't sell as "perfect" tomatoes—they're a steal! They're so ripe you have to use them that day. But I've always been a bargain hunter. How could I resist? My mom would make fresh tomato sauce from whatever was abundant in the garden in the summer, but I'd always made sauce from canned tomatoes. It was cheaper in LA to make sauce with fresh! This is a quick sauce, less than half an hour, and tastes great.

3 pounds fresh tomatoes, rinsed
¼ cup olive oil
6–8 cloves of garlic, minced or thinly sliced (about 2 tablespoons)
12 large basil leaves, torn in large pieces, or 1 tablespoon dried
¼ cup finely chopped parsley leaves or 2 teaspoons–1 tablespoon dried
½ teaspoon each salt and pepper

HENRY'S

NOTES

AND TIPS

If you're lazy, cook the tomatoes without skinning them. The skins will mostly dissolve in the sauce.

Boil a large pot of water and drop the tomatoes in it. Cook for about 30 seconds and remove immediately to a large bowl or pan of cold water. Remove green tops and skin the tomatoes. Chop coarsely on a cutting board and reserve, making sure to keep the juice.

In a large skillet or medium-large wide pot, cook garlic briefly in olive oil over medium-low heat. Do not brown, or it will get bitter. Add the chopped tomatoes and their juice. Add basil, parsley, and half the salt and pepper to sauce. Bring to a boil, stir once thoroughly, then reduce heat to a low simmer. As the acid from the tomatoes flows to the top, skim it off every 10 minutes. Sauce is ready in 20–30 minutes. Serve over cooked, drained pasta, topped with Parmesan or Romano cheese if desired.

Variation:

I love fresh tomato sauce with pancetta or prosciutto added. Dice 4 ounces of either and add when you cook the garlic at the very beginning.

■■■   *Serves 2–4.*

Dessert Platter of Cheeses, Grapes, and Walnuts

This is a very European-style dessert and a wonderful, no-work ending to a meal. It makes you want to sit around relaxing, talking, nibbling, enjoying life.

I've had this with both Italian and French cheeses. Good Italian choices for this dish are mild cheeses like Bel Paese or fontina, Taleggio (which is like an Italian brie), Stracchino (a lovely creamy cheese), or Gorgonzola (Italian blue cheese). Soft French cheeses like Morbier are also delicious, as would be Brie or an English Stilton.

HENRY'S NOTES AND TIPS

½ pound Italian or French cheeses (see recommendations below)
½ cup walnut halves
1–2 cups green or red grapes, rinsed and removed from their stems

Arrange cheeses on a large, decorative plate. Scatter with walnuts and grapes. Serve with individual plates and small knives for each person.

Chapter Twelve

Hooray for Hollywood

■■■

In 1990, the movie *GoodFellas* came out. Directed by Martin Scorsese, it was based on Nick Pileggi's book, *Wiseguy*, and starred Ray Liotta, Robert DeNiro, and Joe Pesci. My life in the Mob had made me famous.

Kelly and I celebrated. We were flush. We rented a house in Valencia and went to Ventura to buy lots of antiques to furnish it. While we were there, we lunched on a great fish chowder at a place right on the pier. It made me want a real full-blown Cioppino, which I used to serve at The Suite. When you have the bucks, do it up with all the trimmings—Dungeness crabs, lobster claws and tails, shrimp, squid, clams and mussels, good quality fish. It's worth the time and money. Or you can make my version of the Ventura chowder, which is much faster and cheaper than real cioppino.

■■■

Serves 6–8.

Cioppino

This is the whole shebang cioppino. You can also make it with about half the types of seafood listed and it'll still be delicious.

1 pound medium-size shrimp, peeled and deveined, reserving shells
¼ cup olive oil
1 large onion, diced (1 cup)
4 large garlic cloves, minced (1 tablespoon)
Two 28-ounce cans peeled plum tomatoes
¼ cup chopped fresh basil or 1 teaspoon dried
1 tablespoon chopped fresh oregano leaves or ½ teaspoon dried
½ cup chopped fresh parsley leaves or 1 tablespoon dried
½–1 teaspoon salt and pepper (to taste)
1½ cups dry red wine
1 dozen littleneck or cherrystone clams, soaked if necessary and
    scrubbed well
1 pound mussels, scrubbed and debearded
2 large lobster claws, cleaned and cracked (ask your fishmonger to
    do this)
1 lobster tail, cut in half lengthwise (ask your fishmonger to do
    this)
1 Dungeness crab, cleaned and cracked (ask your fishmonger to do
    this)
½ pound squid rings
1 pound firm fresh fish such as halibut, or ling cod, cut in chunks
One 8-ounce bottle clam juice (if needed)

Place shrimp shells in a medium-size pot and add water to cover.
Bring to a boil, lower heat to a simmer and cook, covered, ½ hour.
Strain liquid through a fine sieve and reserve.

In a large pot, heat olive oil over medium heat. Add onion and
cook, stirring, until onion is translucent (about 5 minutes). Add garlic
and cook briefly, stirring. Add the juice from the canned tomatoes to
stop the garlic cooking. Crush tomatoes with your hands or chop well
on a cutting board and add to the pot. Add basil, oregano, parsley, and
half the salt and pepper to sauce. Bring to a boil, stir once thoroughly,
then reduce heat to a low simmer. Cook 5 minutes.

Stir in red wine. Add clams and mussels and cook 2–3 minutes. Add
lobster claws and tail, crab, squid, shrimp, and fish. Cook, covered, 3
minutes. Stir in reserved shrimp broth and add part of bottled clam
juice if you want more liquid. Cook, covered, 2–3 minutes more, or

until clams and mussels have opened and fish is just cooked through. (Remove and discard any clams or mussels that don't open.) Serve immediately with crusty bread to sop up the broth.

Serves 4.

Henry's Quick Fish Soup

This is a simple warming soup that's great when you don't have a lot of time, or the bucks for real Cioppino. Served with a green salad and chunks of bread, it's a lovely light meal.

1–2 tablespoons olive oil
1 large onion, diced (¾–1 cup)
1 large stalk celery, trimmed and diced (½ cup)
1 large carrot, peeled and sliced thin (½ cup)
1 tablespoon chopped fresh garlic (3–4 cloves)
One 28-ounce can peeled plum tomatoes + juice, tomatoes
    coarsely chopped
5–6 cups canned or fresh chicken broth or a combination of
    vegetable broth and chicken broth
1 bottle clam juice (8 ounces)
¼ cup chopped fresh parsley leaves
2 teaspoons chopped fresh oregano leaves or 1 teaspoon dried
½ teaspoon anise or fennel seeds, crushed
1 cup white wine
1½ pounds fresh white fish fillets (i.e., cod, red snapper, or
    halibut), cut in large bite-size pieces
½–1 teaspoon salt and pepper (to taste)

In a large pot, heat the olive oil over medium heat. Add the chopped onion, celery, and carrot and cook, stirring, until onion is translucent, about 5 minutes. Add garlic and cook, stirring, 1 minute. Add chopped tomatoes and their juice, broth and clam juice, parsley, oregano, and anise or fennel and bring to a boil, stirring occasionally.

If you can get fish bones, boil them in water to cover for fifteen to twenty minutes and strain to make a mild fish stock, in which case you'll need about half the chicken broth and can omit the clam juice if you want.

Make sure you check the fish fillets for any bones. Don't be afraid to poke them with your fingers to check for the bones, they're gonna be cut in pieces anyway.

Add white wine and cook over high heat, stirring, 2 minutes. Lower heat and simmer 10 minutes. Add fish and cook, stirring occasionally, 5 minutes, until fish is cooked through. Season with salt and pepper, cook an additional minute and serve.

Variations:

You can add three or four small red potatoes, scrubbed and cut in large dice (no need to peel them) to make the soup more substantial. Add potatoes when you add the tomatoes and broth. You may have to cook the soup a little longer before adding the fish for the potatoes to be cooked through—spear one with a fork to test it.

GARY AND SITE VISITS

I was still working with the FBI. There'd been a short lull, but soon after I moved to LA, they contacted me to help nail down a wiseguy in Philly who I knew a lot about from working with Paul Mazzei. The Feds sent an agent named Gary to meet with me; and when I was able to help, they started sending him out with more questions. So Gary became my link to the Feds. If they wanted to reach me, they'd call him, and he'd call me.

Gary grew up in the Bronx. Hey, we were almost *paisan*. He told me when he first came to LA in the early 1980s, you couldn't get *anything* Italian—no provolone, no fresh Italian parsley, no *nothing*, just bad spaghetti and meatballs. Los Angeles was Reagan country then—like a real Western town which just happened to have the movie and TV industry attached to it. He hated it.

So when the Feds would call up and want to set up what they called a "site meeting," Gary and I would go together. They'd fly us out so I could talk to a whole group of agents either in general about organized crime or help them with specific cases—whatever they needed me for. It'd be me and Gary in this roomful of Feds, answering question after question. It got to be a regular thing.

After our first meeting at a particular site, we'd have short meetings for a couple of days, and the agents would relax, doing whatever they could in the towns where we met. Truth is, they'd choose some place they wanted to party. We'd meet in Montana or Wyoming where they'd go skiing, or in Arizona or Texas so they could play golf. I'd already tried skiing in the Army—no way. And golf? I'd never have the patience for that crazy game. I started making sure I had a kitchen where they put me up so at least I could cook.

Gary and I discovered that the rest of the country was just like LA in the '80s. It was like going back in time. The great "West" hadn't changed foodwise. So as usual, I cooked with whatever I could get fresh locally. In Montana or Wyoming, I could get lovely young lamb. In Arizona and Texas, it was back to the beef route. I'd make pan-fried steaks or Steak Pizzaiola for Gary and me and any agents who weren't out on the driving range 'til midnight under the lights. Below are a few recipes for lamb.

Serves 2.

Lamb Chops with Garlic and Mint

6 large garlic cloves, minced (1½ tablespoons)
½ cup olive oil
1 teaspoon salt
½ teaspoon black pepper
½ cup chopped fresh mint leaves
1 pound lamb loin chops
½–1 cup mint jelly

Combine garlic, olive oil, salt, pepper, and mint leaves in a medium-size bowl. Place lamb chops in a shallow bowl and add garlic mixture, coating chops well on all sides. Marinate, refrigerated, 1–4 hours (how much time you got?).

Heat grill or broiler. Remove chops from marinade, brushing off excess, and cook to desired doneness, turning once (about 5–7 minutes on the first side and 5 minutes on the second for medium rare). Serve chops with mint jelly on the side.

Serves 2.

■■

Pan-Grilled Lamb Chops with Olives and Lemons

2 tablespoons olive oil
¼–½ teaspoon salt and pepper (to taste)
1 pound lamb loin chops
3–4 large cloves of garlic, sliced thin
10 black kalamata or other olives, pitted and sliced
¼ cup chopped fresh parsley leaves or 1 tablespoon dried
½ cup dry white wine
1 tablespoon grated lemon zest
3–6 tablespoons lemon juice (to taste)

Heat olive oil in a large skillet over medium-high heat. Lightly salt and pepper chops on both sides, and add to pan. Brown quickly on both sides and reduce heat to medium. Add sliced garlic, olives, and half the parsley and cover pan. Cook, covered, 3–5 minutes per side (to desired doneness). Remove chops from pan and keep warm.

Add white wine to skillet and stir liquid quickly, scraping up any bits that have stuck to the bottom of the pan. Add lemon zest and juice to taste and continue cooking and stirring, about 1 minute. Stir in remaining parsley and adjust seasonings. Return chops to pan and heat through, turning once. Serve immediately, topping with pan sauce.

Pasta with Lamb Ragù

2–3 tablespoons olive oil
2 ounces bacon or pancetta, chopped
4 large garlic cloves, minced
1 large onion, diced (¾–1 cup)
1 large carrot, peeled and diced (½ cup)
½ cup chopped fresh basil leaves
1 teaspoon chopped fresh rosemary leaves or ½ teaspoon dried
¼–½ teaspoon dried red pepper flakes
2–2½ pounds lamb shoulder, cut in bite-size cubes (½–¾ inches each)
½–1 teaspoon salt and black pepper (to taste)
½ cup dry white wine
One 28-ounce can peeled plum tomatoes with their juice
2–3 cups beef broth (low-sodium if you can find it)
1 pound rigatoni or other medium-large pasta, cooked and drained (see page 37 for how to cook)
½–1 cup freshly grated Parmesan or Romano cheese

In a medium wide pot, heat 2 tablespoons olive oil over medium heat. Add chopped bacon or pancetta and cook briefly, stirring. Add chopped garlic, onion, carrot, basil, rosemary, and red pepper flakes and cook, stirring, until onion is translucent, about 5 minutes.

Lightly season lamb with salt and pepper and add to pan. Brown well on all sides, about 10 minutes total. Add wine and boil until liquid

HENRY'S NOTES AND TIPS

You can also cook the sauce up through adding the beef broth; cover, and place in a 325°F oven for half an hour to finish cooking.

Be generous with the lamb. Americans usually like a lot of meat in their sauce.

You can make the sauce a day ahead, refrigerate, and reheat before making pasta.

has evaporated, about 5 minutes. Add juice from canned tomatoes and stir well. Crush tomatoes with your hands or chop coarsely on a cutting board and add to sauce, along with 2 cups beef broth. Cover pot and lower heat to a simmer. Cook, stirring occasionally, 15–20 minutes, adding more beef broth or water if needed. While sauce is simmering, cook and drain rigatoni and return to the pot, tossing with 1 tablespoon olive oil if desired to keep noodles separated. Serve noodles topped with sauce and cheese if desired.

LAMB

If you want less of a "lamby" taste, go for spring lamb, which is younger and has a more delicate flavor. When it's older lamb it's called mutton and has a lot of lamb flavor.

When buying chops, I like the loin chops best. But if you can't afford them, the shoulder chops are the least expensive and are also very tasty. They can be a little tough, so use a recipe with a marinade and be careful not to overcook them (which will make them tougher).

PETER

About a year after *GoodFellas* came out, I had a meeting with a producer from "60 Minutes," who introduced me to Peter Doyle, a screenwriter living in LA. The producer thought maybe we could collaborate on some writing projects. We met for drinks at Trader Vic's, sipping on those rum-based things that come with chunks of pineapple with little umbrellas stuck in them.

I wasn't sure about this guy. Peter and I came from very different lives. He was top of his class in high school and graduated summa from Yale. He used big words, and he would say fifty of them to my five.

But he got the five words I said. Despite the hoity-toity background, we got along great. Maybe it's because we're both half-Irish, maybe it's just chance. At any rate, we've collaborated on a bunch of projects, including a screenplay, "33 Liberty Street."

One of the first times we went out for a real meal together, we went to a very fancy-schmancy place. I was still flush from *GoodFellas*, and I wanted to see what LA "gourmet" food was all about. I can't remember what I had—it was a chef's special, something very high class, probably with caviar, one of my favorites. Peter ordered meatloaf. I couldn't believe it! Here we are in a top joint, and the guy gets meatloaf! I almost left from embarrassment.

Peter defended himself later. The restaurant was known for its meatloaf. But the real reason he ordered it is 'cause he's a big red-meat fan. When I used to go to his house and cook dinner, he always wanted red meat: Fugazy Cutlets, meatballs, steaks—or better yet, two out of three! And nothing green. Well, maybe a little salad, a sprig of parsley for garnish. So one night I made him my version of meatloaf, the Sicilian one with a mix of beef and pork, stuffed with eggs, prosciutto, and cheese. He devoured it.

■■■

Serves 4.

Sicilian Meatloaf

This is a distant cousin of American meatloaf. Very distant. My mother used to like to make it 'cause it looks so nice when you slice it. I've seen it with a green sauce of parsley, capers, and olive oil served on the side, but I like it topped with tomato sauce, 'cause that's the way my mom made it and it reminds me of her.

You don't need to add salt to this because the prosciutto and provolone have enough already. If you leave out the prosciutto/salami part of the filling, add a dash of salt, but no more.

The cooked meatloaf gives off enough pan juices to make a light sauce for one-half to one pound cooked pasta on the side.

You don't have to soak the bread crumbs beforehand—they will get soft while they bake.

HENRY'S NOTES AND TIPS

½ tablespoon olive oil

½ pound ground beef

½ pound ground pork

3–4 tablespoons dried seasoned Italian bread crumbs

½ large onion, finely diced (about ½ cup)

1 egg, slightly beaten

1 tablespoon chopped fresh Italian parsley or 1 teaspoon dried

3 tablespoons freshly grated Romano or Parmesan cheese (1 ounce)

⅛ teaspoon marjoram

½ teaspoon Worcestershire sauce

¼ teaspoon black pepper

8–10 ounces canned tomato sauce, divided

1 hard boiled egg, cooled, peeled and cut in half lengthwise

1½ ounces sliced prosciutto, salami or ham (optional)

2 ounces sliced provolone, cut in 1½" strips

Preheat oven to 350°F. Lightly coat a loaf pan about 8½ × 4 × 2½ inches with olive oil.

In a large bowl, combine all ingredients except 4–6 ounces of the tomato sauce (add 4 ounces), the hard boiled egg, prosciutto, and provolone and mix well (easy to do with your hands). The mixture should hold together but not be hard. Adjust the consistency if needed by adding either bread crumbs or tomato sauce. Divide mixture in half.

Put one half of meatloaf mixture into the prepared pan, shaping to fit into the corners and flattening slightly. Cover with a layer of prosciutto, salami, or ham (if using) and place the egg halves cut side up in a horizontal row down the middle of the pan. Cover the egg halves with strips of provolone and add more cheese strips to cover almost to the edges of the meatloaf. Top with the remaining half of meatloaf mixture and seal meatloaf halves together, covering the filling.

Bake 30 minutes. Spread desired amount of remaining tomato sauce on top and return to oven for 15 minutes more, cooking until tomato sauce has started to darken and thicken slightly. Remove from oven and let rest on counter at least 10 minutes (or it'll fall apart when you slice it). Slice vertically and, using a spatula, move slices to a large platter. Drizzle with some of the pan juices and serve with warm crusty bread for sopping up the sauce.

POVERTY ROW

I've never been good at holding onto money. I live high when I have it and work like hell to get more when it's gone. So no surprise, we went through all the money from *Wiseguy* and *GoodFellas* and at one point were scraping the bottom of the barrel.

And we had another mouth to feed. Kelly and I were blessed with a son a few years after we moved to LA. Which made it all the more important that we spend our pennies carefully.

I hated giving up my luxuries in the food department. I loved going to the butcher and buying the best steaks he had without even caring about the price. I loved using all fresh seafood for Cioppino and eating lobsters and caviar whenever I wanted. But those days had to be over, at least for a while.

Living on a skinny budget, you can be miserable about it, or you can find a way to enjoy it. My way to enjoy it was to go back to my wiseguy self. I wanted to "get away with it"—find a way to take inexpensive cuts of meat and make them taste like filet mignon. Sometimes all it takes is a little ingenuity. I wanted people to think I'd paid nine dollars a pound for something that cost much less. I loved pulling the wool over their eyes.

London Broil

Serves 4–6,

or fewer with

leftovers.

London broil is a cheap cut of meat and you can get it all over the U.S. Sometimes you can get a real bargain if you buy a few more pounds, which just means there'll be more leftovers for sandwiches the next day. Don't skip the marinade! Without it, the meat's tough and tasteless. Come to think of it, I knew some tough and tasteless goombahs in Brooklyn coulda used a little marinating.

One 3-pound cut of London broil
Salt and pepper to taste
1 teaspoon dried oregano
2 cloves of garlic, chopped
4–6 tablespoons red wine vinegar (¼ cup)
⅛ cup soy sauce

Marinate meat in salt and pepper, oregano, garlic, vinegar, and soy sauce for 10 minutes to 4 hours (how much time you got?).

Preheat broiler or heat oven to broil setting. Drain meat from marinade and broil or cook in oven 7–10 minutes on each side for medium-rare to medium. Remove from oven and allow to rest 5 minutes before slicing across the grain as thin as possible. Place slices on plates and drizzle with pan juices. Delicious served all-American style with baked potatoes and a green salad. Refrigerate leftovers wrapped in plastic.

Makes 2

sandwiches.

London Broil Sandwich

I made these longing for the fabulous steak sandwiches I used to have in Brooklyn.

2 rolls (preferably Italian) or English muffins, halved
2 tablespoons any brand garlic-cheese dip: Rondelé, Boursin, or
    homemade (see recipe below)
1 pound leftover London broil, sliced
1 teaspoon–1 tablespoon prepared horseradish (to taste)
Sliced red onion (optional)
Sliced tomato (optional)
Lettuce leaves (optional)
Salt and pepper to taste

Toast rolls or English muffins. Spread 1 tablespoon of garlic-cheese dip on both sides. Top with approximately ½ pound of meat. Add horse radish and optional sliced onion, tomato, and lettuce leaves. Season with salt and pepper, put together, and serve.

For homemade garlic-cheese dip:

½ pound cream cheese
2 cloves of chopped garlic
1 teaspoon chopped fresh or dried parsley and/or chives
2 tablespoons mayonnaise
Salt and pepper to taste

Combine all ingredients in a bowl and mix well. Makes ½ cup.

Serves 2.

▪▪▪

Henry's Quick Fish and Sauce

Red snapper is one of the least expensive fish you can buy. If the flavor's a little "fishy" for you, soak it in milk for half an hour and drain it before cooking. You can buy a milder fish, but it'll probably cost more.

For the fish:

¼ cup olive oil
½ cup flour
1 teaspoon paprika
1 teaspoon garlic powder
1⅛ teaspoons salt
½ teaspoon black pepper + additional ⅛ teaspoon
1 egg + 1 tablespoon water
2 red snapper fillets or other white fish of your choice
   (about 1 pound)

It's a crime to overcook fish! It's done as soon as it seems firm. It'll spring back at you when you pat it with a spatula or back of a spoon.

The fastest way I've found to make this dish is to start the onions cooking, chop the tomatoes and parsley, and then add them to sauce. While tomatoes are simmering, set up flour and egg and get the fish cooking. Then go back to the sauce and add in lemon juice, etc. Flip fish. By the time the fish is cooked on the second side, the sauce will be cool enough to add mayonnaise, and you'll be sitting at the table.

For the sauce:

1 tablespoon olive oil
1 medium yellow onion, diced fine (½–¾ cup)
½ pound fresh tomato, diced fine
¼ cup chopped fresh parsley or 1 tablespoon dried
Juice of ½ lemon (about 1½ tablespoons)
¼ teaspoon each salt and pepper
¼ cup mayonnaise
Lemon wedges (optional)

To make the sauce:

Heat oil over medium heat in a small saucepan. Add onion and cook 2 minutes, stirring. Add tomato and parsley and bring to a boil, then lower heat and simmer 5 minutes, stirring occasionally. Remove

Henry's Rules for Cooking on the Run:
HOW TO MAKE GOOD ITALIAN FOOD ANYWHERE

Rule 16: Don't follow all the rules. In the Mob, we never did. You follow the rules, you get a nice wreath on your casket and that's it. Italians have been known for centuries for their creativity, and their cooking reflects it.

from heat and add lemon juice and salt and pepper. Cool to room temperature and mix in mayonnaise.

To make fish:

Heat oil in a skillet over medium-high heat. Mix together flour, paprika, garlic powder, 1 teaspoon salt, and ½ teaspoon pepper and put on a plate. Put egg and water in a shallow bowl, season with ⅛ teaspoon each salt and pepper and beat well. Flour both sides of fish and then dip both sides in egg. Sauté until light to golden brown on both sides, turning once. Do not overcook! Depending on their thickness, the fillets will be done in 3–6 minutes. Serve with sauce and lemon wedges if desired.

Epilogue

The Present and the Past

▪▪▪

It finally got too hot for us to stay in Los Angeles. The Feds had moved us everywhere they could think of in the area, and they were still hearing bad rumors that we could be in danger. So they moved us to . . .

Whaddya think, I'm nuts? I'm not going to tell you, I'm not even going to give you a hint. But you can be sure of one place I'm not!

SUNDAY DINNER IN BROOKLYN

After all the moving around I've done, I still miss Brooklyn. I guess I always will. But what I miss now is different from what I used to miss.

It used to be I longed for the excitement of the Mob and the schemes, the danger, not knowing where I'd be or what crazy thing I'd be doing that day.

Now I miss the traditions, and mostly I miss the traditions of my family—the family I couldn't wait to get away from when I was a teenager.

There was an order to my life at home in Brooklyn. Even later in the Mob there were rules—just some of their rules were different. In both, you did things a certain way. Certain people were in charge, other people were the children or the soldiers. There was a set of rules we followed that comforted us.

Nowadays lots of kids grow up without those rules and traditions.

Especially when it comes to meals and family time. We always sat down to dinner as a family. Today I see all these kids with nose rings and tattoos, eating McDonald's for dinner with their pals. Where are their parents? The kids don't know what a good thing they're missing. You need the rules, even if it's just to have something to rebel against!

The center of tradition in our family, and many families then, was Sunday dinner. Sunday was its own special day that had its own set of rules. Even in the Mob, Sunday was sacred. It was a day to go to church and spend time with your family. You'd go to church in the morning, then come home and cook the dinner, and everyone—and I mean everyone: cousins, aunts, uncles, grandparents, nieces, nephews, friends— would gather. We'd start eating at around 2 p.m. The rest of the afternoon and evening were spent eating and socializing, rekindling our relationships. We'd even watch "The Ed Sullivan Show" as a group. This wasn't just on holidays or birthdays—it happened once a week, every week, without fail! It was a lovely tradition.

A big part of the tradition was the food and cooking. Cooking has its own rules. They're flexible, but they're rules. You simmer the sauce, you don't scorch it; you peel the garlic and chop it fine; you rinse the greens; you salt the eggplant. You set the table and lay out the food in a way that pleases you and your company. The food adds to the talk, the talk adds to the food.

■■■ *Serves 4–6.*

Garlic Mashed Potatoes

Potatoes almost beg you to add stuff to them. And adding garlic— what an Italian thing to do! I don't know why it wasn't popular years ago.

I've tried many ways to mash potatoes. I can tell you, a food processor or one of those handheld blenders doesn't work. They ruin the texture of the potato. A good old-fashioned masher is best, and you can work out a few aggressions using it.	**HENRY'S NOTES AND TIPS**

These are great with any meat or poultry dish, but I especially like them with pork and my version of Southern Fried Chicken (see recipe on page 194).

2–3 pounds russet potatoes
4–6 large cloves of garlic, peeled
1 tablespoon salt
3 tablespoons butter
½–¾ cup milk or half and half
¼–½ teaspoon each salt and pepper (to taste)

Peel potatoes and cut in large pieces. Place in a fairly large pot with the garlic cloves. Add water to cover and the tablespoon of salt. Bring to a boil and cook, covered, over medium heat 15–25 minutes until potatoes can be pierced with a fork. Drain potatoes and garlic and return to the pot. Mash with a potato masher or fork until potatoes and garlic are slightly broken up. Add butter and a small amount of milk or half and half and mash well until garlic and potatoes are well broken up. Add some of the remaining liquid, ¼ teaspoon each salt and pepper, and continue to mash. Add more liquid to reach desired consistency, check for seasoning, and serve.

Serves 4–6.

Roast Pork Loin with Sage and Rosemary

This is a great Sunday dish, especially in winter. You can get either a pork loin with bone or one without. With-bone loin has more flavor, but the boneless is easier to carve. It's great with Garlic Mashed Potatoes (see previous recipe).

2 tablespoons olive oil
2 tablespoons Dijon mustard
6–8 garlic cloves, minced (2 tablespoons)
2 tablespoons chopped fresh sage leaves or 2 teaspoons dried

2 tablespoons chopped fresh rosemary leaves or 2 teaspoons dried
½–1 teaspoon each salt and pepper (to taste)
One 3–4 pound pork loin roast with bone or 2½–3 pounds
   boneless
1–2 cups chicken broth
½ cup white wine
2–4 tablespoons flour

Combine olive oil, mustard, garlic, sage, rosemary, and ¼–½ teaspoon salt and pepper (to taste) in a bowl and mix well. Make slits ¼ to ½-inch deep and placed 1 to 2 inches apart all over pork loin. Stuff slits with garlic/herb mixture. Rub the remaining garlic/herb mixture over the outside of the loin. Put loin in a large plastic bag or a bowl covered with plastic and allow to marinate in refrigerator 1–2 hours.

Preheat oven to 425°F. Place pork loin in a roasting pan about 9 × 13 inches or 10 × 14 inches, depending on size of the loin. Roast uncovered in middle of the oven for 30 minutes. Baste loin with any juices in the pan. If there is little juice, add 1 cup chicken broth, stir to scrape up any bits on bottom of the pan, and baste loin with broth. Lower heat to 350°F and continue cooking, basting every 20–30 minutes, for about 45 minutes more. Pork is done when a meat thermometer registers 145–150°F or when interior of meat is no longer pink (don't overcook it or it'll be dry). Remove from oven and allow to rest 10 minutes.

While meat is resting, place the roasting pan on top of the stove. Remove any excess grease, leaving about 1–2 tablespoons in the pan. Heat over medium heat (it'll probably be on two burners). Add white wine and scrape up any bits sticking to bottom of pan with a large spoon or spatula. Reduce liquid for 2–3 minutes. Add 1 cup chicken broth and whisk in 2 tablespoons flour. Cook, stirring constantly, until sauce thickens. Add more flour if necessary to reach desired consistency. Check for seasoning.

Carve pork loin into slices and serve with pan gravy.

▪▪

Roast Leg of Lamb with Carrots and Potatoes

Roast lamb is traditional at Easter, but we'd sometimes have it on Sundays. For this recipe I usually use regular lamb (or mutton), not the spring lamb.

One 3–4 pound leg of lamb
3–4 large cloves of garlic, cut in slivers + 2 cloves, minced
3–4 tablespoons olive oil
1 tablespoon fresh minced thyme leaves or 1½ teaspoons dried, crumbled
1–1½ teaspoons each salt and pepper (to taste)
1 large onion, cut in large pieces (about 2")
2–3 large carrots, peeled and cut in large chunks, or ½–1 pound baby carrots
2–3 pounds red-skinned potatoes, scrubbed, trimmed, and cut in large pieces
1–1½ cups chicken broth
1–1½ cups mint jelly for serving (optional)

Preheat oven to 450°F.

Trim as much fat from lamb as possible without disturbing the skin. (If you're using spring lamb, there may be no fat to trim off.) With a paring knife, make vertical slits all over the roast and fill with slivers of gar-

---

HENRY'S NOTES AND TIPS

The usual rule for how many potatoes to cook is half a pound of potatoes per person. I usually allow at least that much—it's better to have too much than too little.

Substitute roasted potatoes with Garlic Mashed Potatoes (see recipe on page 313) if you want.

---

lic. Rub lamb with 2 tablespoons olive oil, then with thyme leaves and ½–1 teaspoon each salt and pepper. Place in a roasting pan.

Toss onion, carrots, and potatoes with 1–2 tablespoons remaining olive oil, the minced garlic, and ½ teaspoon each salt and pepper. (If using baby carrots, do not add here—see later instructions.) Scatter vegetables around lamb in roasting pan and add ½ cup chicken broth. Place pan in oven and cook 30 minutes, turning once when browned.

Lower heat to 350°F and continue to cook, basting occasionally and carefully stirring vegetables. Add more broth or water if pan gets dry.

If using baby carrots, peel and trim green ends. Add to roasting pan after 45 minutes and stir gently to combine with other vegetables. Check every 10 minutes or so for doneness, removing when barely tender (they will continue to cook out of the oven).

After about 1 hour, check other vegetables and remove if they are tender. Keep warm. Also check lamb with a meat thermometer at its thickest part. Cook about 20–30 minutes longer if needed, to desired doneness—the roast is medium-rare when the thermometer reads 130°F. Remove from oven, place on a carving board or work surface, and allow to rest 5 minutes before carving.

When pan juices are slightly cooled, skim them of any excess fat that accumulates on top. Add more broth or water if desired and reheat, scraping up any browned bits that are stuck to the pan. Adjust seasonings.

Arrange carved lamb on a serving platter and surround with vegetables. Serve with pan juices and mint jelly if desired.

Henry's Rules for Cooking on the Run:
HOW TO MAKE GOOD ITALIAN FOOD ANYWHERE

Rule 17: Keep your eyes open and your head down. In a big city, staring at the tall buildings will get you rolled as an out-of-towner. So the rule is pay attention—on the street, in the kitchen, in your life. If you don't pay attention in the kitchen, a lot of bad things can happen. And if you do, delicious won't be far behind.

Fast Recipe List

∎∎

Here are the recipes that you can make "on the run." Any one of these will take you less than an hour to make from start to finish.

Recipe By Type or Ingredient

DESERTS

SANDWICHES AND EGGS

FISH

MEAT

BREAD AND PIZZA

Index

∎∎∎

Hill, Henry
    army life of, 84–85,
        93–96, 100
    arrest of, 119–20, 147, 229
    as restaurant cook,
        100–102
    at racetrack, 215–17, 229
    at ranch, 248 50
    childhood of, 9–10
    drugs and, 147, 151
    father of, 9, 10, 51, 55,
        84, 223
    fixing games, 141, 144–45
    grandfather of, 10
    in Boston, 141
    in Kentucky, 193–94
    in Omaha see Omaha
    in Pittsburgh, 139
    in prison, 119–20, 128–30
    in Redmond, 249–50,
        258, 269
    in Russian River Valley,
        275, 277–78
    in Seattle see Seattle
    in Virginia, 93
    Karen see Hill, Karen
    Kelly see Kelly (second
        wife)
    mother of see Hill, Mother
    pizzeria, employee of,
        56–58
    pizzeria, ownership of,
        105–6
    Peggy and, 95–96, 100,
        102–3
    Queen City Trolley and,
        219–20, 223
    sisters of, 12, 43, 230–31
    Suite, The and, 106–7,
        117–18
    teenage years, 77, 78–79

    testimony of, 178
    tornado and, 181–82
    Wiseguy, 269
    Witness Protection
        Program see Witness
        Protection Program
Hill, Joe, 43, 141
Hill, Karen, 105, 178, 258
    C.P. Middleton and,
        249–50
    Henry and, 103, 120,
        269, 270, 279, 280
    in Kentucky, 193
    in Omaha, 180, 181
    in Seattle, 237–38
    Witness Protection
        Program, 155, 160,
        183–84
Hill, Michael, 147, 149–50
Hill, Mother, 8, 10, 25
    holiday cooking, 41–42,
        80, 88
    influence of, 11–12, 209,
        223, 294, 305
    special dishes, 51, 52
Holiday Stuffed Artichokes,
    45–47
Honeycomb Tripe with
    Parmesan Cheese, 52–53
Hoover, J. Edgar, 9
Horseradish, 186–87
Horses, 215–16, 219
Hot dogs, 217
How Much Time You Got
    Lemon-Basil Chicken,
    213–14

I
Independence, 189, 193–94
Insomnia Frittata for Four,
    Henry's, 178–79

IRS, 120
Italian "quartet," 158

J
Joe's Corned Beef and
    Cabbage, 143–44
Joe's Stone Crab, 145

K
Kelly (second wife), 270–71,
    275, 277–78, 279–80,
    290, 297, 307
Kennedy Airport, 105–6, 119,
    147
Kentucky, 188–90, 193–94,
    215–16, 228–29, 236,
    237, 280
Kickback Antipasti Hero,
    Henry's, 77–78
Kuhn, Rick, 141

L
LaGasse, Emeril, 13
Lamb
    cooking tips, 304
    Chops with Garlic and
        Mint, 301–2
    Pan-Grilled Lamb Chops
        with Olives and
        Lemons, 302
    Pasta with Lamb Ragù,
        303–4
    Roast Leg of Lamb with
        Carrots and Potatoes,
        316–17
    selection and
        preparation, 304
Lamb Chops with Garlic and
    Mint, 301–2

Rosemary
    Garlic Roasted Chicken
        with Rosemary,
        212–13
    Roast Pork Loin with
        Sage and Rosemary,
        314–15
Rose's Bakery, 78
Ruggierio, Andy (Fat Andy),
    128
Russian River Valley, 275,
    277–78

S
Saffron, 132–33, 191
Saffron Risotto, 132–33
Sage
    Veal Chops with White
        Wine and Sage,
        115
    Roast Pork Loin with
        Sage and Rosemary,
        314–15
St. Patrick's Day, 270
Salmon
    Pan-Fried Salmon,
        243–44
    Bowties with Grilled
        Salmon in Pink
        Sauce, 244–45
Salmon, Pan-Fried, 243–44
Salt cod, 42–43
San Gennaro festival, 79
Sardines, 137–38
Sausage
    Baked Polenta with
        Sausage and Tomato
        Sauce, 172–73
    Calzone, 66–68
    cooking tips, 34, 134

Oven Penitentiary Sauce
    with Sausage,
    133–34
Sausage and Pepper Hero,
    79–80
Sausage, Provolone, and
    Roasted Pepper
    Sandwich, 221–22
Sunday Gravy (Meat
    Sauce), 33–34
Sausage and Pepper Hero,
    79–80
Sausage, Provolone, and
    Roasted Pepper Sand-
    wich, 221–22
Scallops, 264–65
Scampi on the Barbie,
    240–41
Scorsese, Martin, 297
Seafood Risotto, 262–64
Seafood Salad, 127–28
Seattle, 237–39, 241, 246,
    279, 280
Sfingi, 82–83
Shell Pasta with Italian
    Broccoli à la Aunt
    Elivera, 283–84
Shells with Tomato Mint
    Sauce, Stuffed, 250–52
Shrimp
    cooking tips, 127, 239
    Linguine with Shrimp,
        245–46
    Scampi on the Barbie,
        240–41
    Seafood Salad, 127–28
    Shrimp-Stuffed
        Mushrooms,
        124–25
    Shrimp with Roasted
        Peppers, 125–26

Shrimp-Stuffed Mushrooms,
    124–25
Shrimp with Roasted Peppers,
    125–26
Sicilian Easter Bread with
    Colored Eggs, 88–89
Sicilian Meatloaf, 305–6
Snails, 54
Sorrento's, 281–82
South Carolina, 93, 94, 103
Southern Cooked Greens,
    197–98
Southern Fried Chicken with
    Gravy à la Henry,
    194–96
Spinach
    cooking tips, 207
    Sautéed Spinach or
        Greens, 207
    selection and prepara-
        tion, 207
    Stuffed Veal, 231–32
Spinach or Greens, Sautéed,
    207
Squid
    Salad, 248
    Stuffed Calamari, 246–47
Squid Salad, 248
Steak Oreganato, 162–63
Steak, Pan-Fried, 187–88
Steak Pizzaiola, 164–65
Stone Crabs with Mustard
    Sauce, 145–46
Strawberries, 258, 268
    Macerated, 268
Strawberries (restaurant),
    258–59, 262
String beans, 228
String Beans, Potatoes, and
    Tomatoes, 228
Striped bass, 68–70